AGENCIES IN FOR

Also by Goran Hyden

BEYOND UJAMAA IN TANZANIA

GOVERNANCE AND POLITICS IN AFRICA (*co-editor*)

NO SHORTCUTS TO PROGRESS

Also by Rwekaza Mukandala

LIBERALIZATION AND POLITICS (*co-editor*)

STATE-OWNED ENTERPRISE IN AFRICA (*co-editor*)

Agencies in Foreign Aid

Comparing China, Sweden and the United States in Tanzania

Edited by

Goran Hyden
Professor of Political Science
University of Florida

and

Rwekaza Mukandala
Professor and Dean
Faculty of Arts and Social Sciences
University of Dar es Salaam

First published in Great Britain 1999 by
MACMILLAN PRESS LTD
Houndmills, Basingstoke, Hampshire RG21 6XS and London
Companies and representatives throughout the world

A catalogue record for this book is available from the British Library.

ISBN 978-1-349-14984-1 ISBN 978-1-349-14982-7 (eBook)
DOI 10.1007/978-1-349-14982-7

First published in the United States of America 1999 by
ST. MARTIN'S PRESS, INC.,
Scholarly and Reference Division,
175 Fifth Avenue, New York, N.Y. 10010

ISBN 978-0-312-22098-3

Library of Congress Cataloging-in-Publication Data
Agencies in foreign aid : comparing China, Sweden and the United States in Tanzania / edited by Goran Hyden and Rwekaza S. Mukandala.
p. cm.
Includes bibliographical references and index.
ISBN 978-0-312-22098-3 (cloth)
1. Economic assistance, Chinese—Tanzania. 2. Economic assistance, Swedish—Tanzania. 3. Economic assistance, American--Tanzania. I. Hydén, Göran, 1938- . II. Mukandala, Rwekaza Sympho.
HC885.A54 1999
338.91'09678—dc21 98-54941
CIP

Softcover reprint of the hardcover 1st edition 1999

10 9 8 7 6 5 4 3 2 1
08 07 06 05 04 03 02 01 00 99

Contents

List of Tables and Figures

Tables

Figures

Notes on the Contributors

Ai Ping is a Senior Research Fellow and Council Member of the Chinese Association for International Understanding (CAFIU), Beijing, China.

Ole Elgström holds the rank of Docent in the Swedish academic system (the equivalence of Senior Lecturer in the British or Associate Professor in the American systems) and teaches in the Department of Political Science at the University of Lund, Sweden.

Goran Hyden is Professor of Political Science at the University of Florida, Gainesville, Florida, USA.

Kenneth Mease is Coordinator of the Survey Research Program at the Bureau of Economic and Business Research, University of Florida, Gainesville, Florida, USA.

Rwekaza Mukandala is Dean of the Faculty of Arts and Social Sciences and Professor of Political Science and Public Administration, University of Dar es Salaam, Dar es Salaam, Tanzania.

Stephen L. Snook is Country Director, International Foundation for Electoral Systems (IFES) based in Accra, Ghana.

List of Abbreviations

AFER	Administration of Foreign Economic Relations
AM	Assisting Ministry
ATAP	Agricultural Transport Assistance Program
AU	Assisting Unit
CAFIU	Chinese Association for International Understanding
CAPs	Country Assistance Programs
CCCPC	Central Committee of the Communist Party of China
CFER	Commission for Foreign Economic Relations
CIA	Central Intelligence Agency
COMPLANT	China Complete Export Corporation
CPC	Communist Party of China
CU	Contracting Unit
DAC	Development Assistance Committee
DAP	Development Assistance Program
DCO	Development Cooperation Office
DFA	Development Fund for Africa
DU	Design Unit
ECA	Economic Cooperation Administration
ERP	Economic Recovery Programme
ESAF	Enhanced Structural Adjustment Facility
FAA	Foreign Assistance Act
GAO	Government Accounting Office
GCS	General Contractual System
GDP	Gross Domestic Product
GNP	Gross National Product
IBRD	International Bank for Reconstruction and Development
IDA	International Development Association
IETCO	International Economic and Technical Cooperation Corporation
IMF	International Monetary Fund
LDCs	Less Developed Countries
MAC	Means of Administration and Coercion
MFER	Ministry of Foreign Economic Relations
MFT	Ministry of Foreign Trade
MOAD	Ministry of Assisting Deliverer
MOFERT	Ministry of Foreign Economic Relations and Trade
MOFTEC	Ministry of Foreign Trade and Economic Cooperation

MOGD	Ministry of General Deliverer
MSF	Mbarali State Farm
NAFCO	National Agricultural and Food Corporation
NDC	National Development Corporation
NGOs	Non-Governmental Organizations
NIEO	New International Economic Order
NPC	National People's Congress
ODA	Official Development Assistance
OECD	Organization for Economic Co-operation and Development
OGL	Open General License
PRC	People's Republic of China
PU	Preparatory Unit
RG	Regional Government
RUM	Responsibility of the Undertaking Ministry
SAP	Structural Adjustment Programme
SAREC	Swedish Agency for Research Cooperation with Developing Countries
SASDA	Secretariat for Analysis of Swedish Development Assistance
Sida	Swedish International Development Cooperation Agency
SPC	State Planning Commission
TAZARA	Tanzania–Zambia Railway
TPDF	Tanzania People's Defence Force
UFI	Ubongo Farm Implements
UM	Undertaking Ministry
UN	United Nations
URT	United Republic of Tanzania
USAID	United States Agency for International Development

Introduction

RATIONALE

Foreign aid has come to play a very critical role in the economy of many developing countries. Even though it is necessary to take official statistics on the national economy of these countries with caution, current figures indicate that the official development assistance (ODA) constitutes more than 25 per cent of the gross domestic product (GDP) in some countries (Riddell 1995:41), and between 10 and 25 per cent in many others. These figures indicate a high level of aid dependency and how important is the role that external resources, provided in the form of official government aid, play in the economy of developing countries, especially in sub-Saharan Africa.

Against this background, it is surprising how little scholarly attention has been paid to the role of foreign aid agencies in the context of efforts to assist low-income countries accelerate their development. To be sure, foreign aid is not a novel subject to academics, but it has largely been treated, especially in US circles, as an instrument of foreign policy. Scholars have analysed the rationale provided for foreign aid and treated it in the light of broader foreign policy objectives. Another set of studies has primarily focused on the impact of foreign aid: that is, aid effectiveness. Many such studies have been evaluations of individual projects or programmes, often commissioned by the aid agencies themselves or by the relevant auditing agencies interested in knowing how public funds have been used. The problem with many of these studies is that they are not easily available for public use and that they are case studies without attempts to make comparisons. There are exceptions to this trend: for example, Lele (1990) examined World Bank assistance for agricultural development in Africa in a comparative perspective. Similarly, Esman and Uphoff (1984) analysed official aid reports with a view to tracing the role of local organizations in rural development. Kottak (1991) carried out a similar review of assistance extended to settlement projects, drawing on a significant number of case studies.

All the same, a gap exists in the literature on foreign aid in that virtually all studies to date have focused on either the macro level (foreign aid as an instrument of policy) or the micro level (the impact of foreign aid). Little significant attention has been paid to the meso level, more specifically the role played by the aid agencies themselves. There are several reasons why this gap has been allowed to exist. One is that development has for a long time been conceived largely in economic terms. Economists have dominated the agenda and set the tone for studies in this field. As a result, it is no surprise that the principal interest has been in terms of efficiency or effectiveness (that is, how well resources have been used and what results have been achieved). Another reason is that aid agencies have been treated as less important because they have served foremost as implementation intermediaries with no or little direct role in the physical implementation of specific aid projects or programmes. Their role has been treated as secondary, and thus of relatively little significance for the outcome of foreign aid activities. A third reason is that aid agencies have typically been responsible for commissioning studies of foreign aid operations. As such, little effort has been made to study this particular set of actors. Implicitly, if not explicitly, they have been treated as only part of the solution of foreign aid, not as a problem associated with this activity. We consider this to be not only an academic shortcoming but also a practical political inadequacy because, as we suggest in the concluding chapter, any future reform of foreign aid must involve a more systematic and thorough review of the way aid is being disbursed. Donor behaviour and strategy, therefore, is at the centre of tomorrow's debate about foreign aid.

The purpose of this volume is to correct existing trends in scholarship in this field by focusing on the role that the aid agencies themselves play in the process of providing foreign assistance to developing countries. More specifically, this project has three objectives. The first is to provide a mode of analysis that allows us to compare the strategy and behaviour of this type of agency in the context of providing aid. In this study we have chosen to compare over a 30-year time period the way American, Chinese and Swedish aid agencies have operated in Tanzania, a country which has received assistance from these three countries since the early 1960s. The conceptual and theoretical framework guiding this project has been evolved with a view to enabling others both to understand the particular features of foreign aid agencies and to replicate studies of these agencies in other contexts. In the conclusion of this volume we make an evaluation of the framework used in this volume so as to provide some guidance to others interested in pursuing similar studies.

The second objective is to provide a better understanding of the rationale that has dominated foreign aid in the three countries. We believe, for example, that American aid during the Cold War period was very much determined by the perceived competition with, or threat from, communism. Similarly, Chinese aid was strongly influenced by one-sided perceptions of Western powers. We do not argue that these perceptions were false but that the policy reality was much more complex and the rationale, therefore, often different from the way it was perceived by outsiders. We hope that, with the benefit of hindsight, we can demonstrate this point and thus help bring about a revised interpretation of the images of foreign aid that prevailed in the days of the Cold War.

The third objective is to provide a recipient's perspective on foreign aid. Although the impact of foreign aid on recipient countries is not a new topic, what is still lacking is an attempt to understand the role of foreign aid agencies in the policy process of these countries: in other words, how they are perceived by the recipient country officials and what traces or legacies they leave behind. It is important, for donor and recipient alike, to know these things.

Tanzania was chosen for this study because it has always been a major recipient of foreign aid. In fact in 1995 it was one of four countries – Mozambique, Nicaragua and Uganda being the others – whose ODA: GDP ratio was less than 1:4. In other words, more than 25 per cent of the country's GDP consisted of money provided by foreign donors. It was also chosen, however, because it was the only country that we could identify where the three donors covered by this study, the People's Republic of China (PRC), the Kingdom of Sweden, and the USA, had been active donors throughout a 30-year period.

HISTORY OF THE PROJECT

This project was originally conceived in 1991 in discussions between Goran Hyden of the University of Florida and Rwekaza Mukandala of the University of Dar es Salaam. Preliminary agreement was obtained from Ai Ping, a Research Fellow with the Chinese Association for International Understanding (CAFIU), in Beijing during a visit by Hyden to China in 1992. Dr Ole Elgström, a Senior Lecturer in Political Science at the University of Linköping in Sweden, who subsequently joined the Department of Political Science at the University of Lund in the same capacity, joined the project in 1993. These four researchers, with Mukandala as chairman and Hyden as secretary, have constituted the steering committee of the project, which received funding to the tune of \$342 000 from the Swedish Agency for Research Cooperation with Developing Countries (SAREC)[1] for a five-year period beginning in 1993. The project wishes to extend its warm thanks to SAREC for making this research possible.

The group has conducted much of its business by correspondence but it has organized an annual meeting of the steering committee to enable members to stay in touch, exchange views in a more personal way, and take stock of the progress. The first meeting was organized in Beijing in September 1993 and was hosted by Ai Ping of CAFIU. The second meeting was held in Dar es Salaam in July–August 1994. A certain number of field interviews and visits were organized in conjunction with that meeting: for example, the group visited projects funded by China, Sweden and the USA. In addition, interviews were held with a select number of senior Tanzanian officials who over the years had been involved in managing external assistance in the Government. The third meeting was held in October 1995 in Gainesville, Florida, at which meeting first drafts of chapters for this volume were presented and reviewed. The final meeting was held in Stockholm in April 1997, where the project findings were presented at a public seminar.

In addition to the four researchers mentioned above, this project has also sponsored three doctoral students supervised by Goran Hyden at the University of Florida. These three students – Stephan Snook, American, Laurean Ndumbaro, Tanzanian, and Zeng Menghua, Chinese – were selected because of their own interest in the issues of foreign aid and have been working on their own doctoral dissertations dealing with a more specific set of issues associated with the operations of US assistance to Tanzania (Snook), Swedish aid to Tanzania (Ndumbaro) and Chinese assistance to Tanzania (Zeng). Because Snook was ahead of the other two in getting started on his field work, he was able to complete it in time for the publication of this volume. As a result, he is the author of Chapter 3, which focuses on US aid to Tanzania. We are also grateful for his participation in helping to hammer out the conclusions from this project. Elgström has written the chapter on Sweden and Ai the one on China. This project has also benefited from the advice and participation by Kenneth Mease, a University of Florida political scientist, who has helped out on the methodological side and who also shared in formulating the conclusions of this volume (see Chapter 6).

ORGANIZATION OF THIS VOLUME

The first chapter, by Hyden and Mukandala, sets out the analytical framework that has guided this research. It places foreign aid in the context of the broader development theory and argues for the need to combine a resource dependency and institutionalist perspective in the study of foreign aid agencies as organizations. It indicates what makes these agencies different from firms operating in the market place but also from other administrative agencies operating in the domestic context of the respective donar countries. The chapter identifies a framework for the comparative analysis of aid agencies and comes up with a set of hypotheses related to what the authors call the of 'traps' of foreign aid operations. These hypotheses are related to four forces that are seen as driving the agencies: (1) the domestic political process of the donor country; (2) the political and economic context of the recipient country; (3) the dynamics of the international donor community; and (4) the aspiration of the donor agency itself to insulate itself from outside influences and pursue an autonomous line.

The second chapter by Mukandala is appropriately sub-titled a 'A Recipient's Tale'. It discusses the behaviour and strategy of donor agencies from a Tanzanian perspective. To provide a local context for understanding the operations of these agencies, this chapter also introduces the main features of Tanzania's post-independence development. By thus setting the empirical stage for the remainder of this volume, Mukandala identifies the most important local factors which over the years have influenced donor behaviour and strategy in Tanzania.

The following three chapters are case studies of the behaviour and strategy of the respective aid agencies in Tanzania. Each author was asked to stay within the framework introduced in the first chapter, but they were also permitted to give their contributions the tilt that their own professional interest encouraged and the material they came across dictated. Thus these three chapters are internally different, although the conclusions they draw address the main intellectual concerns expressed in this introduction.

Snook identifies three main time periods in the history of US foreign assistance to Tanzania. The division is very much determined by changes in domestic US politics. There is generally little evidence that what went on in Tanzania influenced American ideas about foreign aid in a positive manner. To the extent that events and policies in Tanzania affected US policy, it was in a negative way. For example, Tanzania's state socialist policies became a reason for reducing foreign aid in the early 1980s when the US Government expected adherence to the neo-liberal ideas of Structural Adjustment Programmes (SAPs) advocated and imposed by the international finance institutions. Snook shows how American aid flows to Tanzania have changed dramatically over the years. An interesting and somewhat unexpected finding is that socialist Tanzania received its largest inflow of American aid during the presidencies of Richard Nixon and George Bush, both Republicans. With specific reference to how the United States Agency for International Development (USAID) operates as an agency, Snook examines the influence of ideology, and argues that USAID's policy counsels are divided. He interprets USAID's behaviour as a clash between the competing propensities of conservative realism (or the use of foreign aid as bribery to get developing countries to accept US foreign policy positions), and liberal altruism (or the use of foreign aid as philanthropy in service of humanitarian principles). The antithetical tendencies interact within the agency at different levels and at different strengths. He shows that altruism is overshadowed by realist concerns. Conservatives who view foreign aid as a tool in the diplomatic negotiations kit dominate the making of high-level policies, particularly those that govern funding decisions. Altruism inhabits whatever cracks and crevices of the policy structure are not covered by realist concerns. The liberals within the agency are essentially relegated to making the comparatively minor decisions surrounding programme design and implementation. Snook terms the net effect 'pragmatic altruism'.

Elgström's chapter deals with the experience of Swedish aid's attempts to provide assistance on the recipients' own terms. He emphasizes the role that ideas play in shaping foreign aid policy. He tries to understand why Sida has been able to operate quite autonomously in relation to domestic Swedish actors and thus adapt its course to factors in the Tanzanian situation and, in the last ten years, also within the international donor community. Particularly interesting is his account of how the agency, for quite some time in the first half of the 1980s, ignored the negative economic trend in Tanzania and stood by the position of the Tanzanian government although there was a growing global consensus that something needed to be done to get the economic wheels of the country to move forward again. The period since 1984 has been characterized by an increased 'mainstreaming' of Swedish aid. This means that it has been much more closely coordinated with other donors, in particular the World Bank and the International Monetary Fund (IMF) which have taken the lead in demanding macro-economic reforms in Tanzania (as in so many other countries).

Ai Ping's chapter on China divides his country's assistance to Tanzania into two periods, both determined by policy changes in China itself. During the 1960s and 1970s Chinese aid was characterized by the principle of 'proletarian internationalism' or solidarity among non-aligned states, particularly those ready to follow a revolutionary socialist path. After Mao's death and the emergence of a new economic policy in China 1979 (market socialism), Chinese aid to Tanzania has increasingly become driven by economic and commercial principles. The Chinese have been interested in extending the aid, not so much as an act of solidarity – even if that principle has not vanished completely – but as a way of achieving tangible economic results that benefit both donor and recipient. Thus, for example, in the 1990s it has been common for Chinese projects to be organized as joint ventures, the assumption being that in such contexts the Chinese can help ensure a positive outcome. One reason this strategy has not always been successful in Tanzania is that the Chinese have not insisted on its implementation against the wishes of their local counterparts. One of the hallmarks of Chinese foreign aid policy to Tanzania (and other countries) has been to respect the principle of state sovereignty even if this means that their aid has not always been as effective as it otherwise could be. Ai Ping concludes, however, that the principle of mutual benefit is now being more strongly advocated by China and this means that it provides a powerful counterweight to the principle of respect for state sovereignty in the 1990s.

The concluding chapter is an attempt to draw together the main insights from the case study chapters and take stock of what the analytical framework used in this study tells us about the aid agencies and how they can be studied. Thus the principal overall findings of this project are summarized. The conclusion is not particularly encouraging. The study shows that the three major donors to Tanzania have all experienced difficulties in their operations that cannot be ascribed to conditions in Tanzania. It is rather their *modus operandi* which is responsible for a performance that can only be described as discouraging. Hyden and Mease argue that a more self-critical examination of the way these aid agencies operate is called for. They also draw attention to possible alternative ways of providing foreign aid.

Note

1. SAREC was incorporated into the Swedish International Development Cooperation Agency (Sida) in 1995 and constitutes a department with its own academic board inside that organization.

References

Esman, Milton J. and Norman T. Uphoff (1984) *Local Organizations as Intermediaries in Rural Development*. Ithaca, New York: Cornell University Press.

Kottak, Conrad P. (1991) 'When People Don't Come First: Some Sociological Lessons from Completed Projects', in Michael Cernea (ed.), *Putting People First: Sociological Variables in Rural Development*. Washington, DC: The World Bank.

Lele, Uma (1990) *Foreign Aid to African Agriculture: A Quarter Century of Experience*. San Francisco: ICS Press.

Riddell, Roger (1995) *Aid Dependency*, Monograph prepared for the 2015 Project of the Swedish International Development Cooperation Agency (Sida), Stockholm.

1 Studying Foreign Aid Organizations: Theory and Concepts

Goran Hyden and Rwekaza Mukandala

INTRODUCTION

In the early 1990s some US$50 billion were transferred from donor to recipient countries every year in the form of ODA, making bilateral and multilateral agencies very important actors in international relations and the national politics of many Third World countries. Although ODA constituted on average only one-third of a per cent of the gross national product (GNP) of the member countries of the Organization for Economic Co-operation and Development (OECD), the relative importance of the ODA contributions on the recipient side was very significant, especially in low-income countries in sub-Saharan Africa. Berlage and Stokke (1992:1) note that, in 1988–89, these countries received ODA equalling 14.2 per cent of their GNP. This compares with just a little over 1 per cent of GNP for countries such as Thailand and Mexico. By the mid-1990s, the situation in many of these African low-income countries was such that over half of the annual government budget was being financed from external sources. Much of it was being used to keep the day-to-day affairs of the government going. According to *Family Mirror* (August 1992), a respected private newspaper in Dar es Salaam, the major urban centre in Tanzania, foreign aid there constituted about two-thirds of the national budget in 1992. As in many other African countries, foreign aid had become the life-line of the Tanzanian government.

Foreign aid has been the subject of a relatively large number of studies where the objective has been to examine its ideological and philosophical rationale (Riddell 1987), the extent to which it works (Cassen *et al.* 1986; Lele and Nabi 1991), and how it is being evaluated (Berlage and Stokke 1992). Although individual donor agencies have been scrutinized by public review commissions or national audit bureaus, and have often undergone internal reorganization, we know remarkably little about these organizations given their significance in the context of resource flows to the low-income countries of Africa such as Tanzania. What we do know is that they find it very hard to meet the objectives set for them. For example, Uma Lele concluded in a multiyear study of external assistance to the agricultural sector in six African countries that donors had made a surprisingly small contribution to agricultural development in these countries. Those receiving most aid – Tanzania being one of them – had performed the least well, as 'external finance has substituted for a sound diagnosis of development problems' (Lele 1990:9).

The purpose of this study is to obtain a better understanding of how donor agencies operate. In this respect, we go beyond the boundaries of studies in the field of international relations which concentrate on the role of foreign aid as an instrument of foreign policy (for example, Hook 1994). We start from the premise that donor agencies act independently and that one of the factors which determines their behaviour is an interest in augmenting their autonomy. We argue that in order to understand the problems facing foreign aid it is important to improve our understanding of the operational characteristics of the donor agencies. Volumes by Stokke (1984 and 1991), Forss (1985), and Elgström (1992) give us some insights into their operations. We want to deepen this knowledge and make a contribution to the debate about the ways foreign aid might be structured in the future.

We are less interested in the outcome of specific aid projects or programmes than the generic effects of the presence of donors as international actors with a limited (but all the same significant) degree of operational autonomy. To be able to say something about this we have adopted a 30-year time perspective: 1965–95. The starting date for this period coincides more or less with the initiation of foreign aid to Tanzania, which became independent in 1961 and became a united republic, made up of Tanganyika – the mainland – and Zanzibar, the islands off the coast in the Indian Ocean, in 1964. By bringing the study up to 1995 we are able to connect with the ongoing debate around the world about how foreign aid may be restructured in the future.

The empirical material for this study is drawn from three countries that have been providing foreign aid to Tanzania throughout this 30-year period: the PRC, the Kingdom of Sweden, and the USA. They were chosen to represent three different perspectives on aid and therefore so would also include varying operational implications. It is the first time the agencies administering foreign aid in these three countries have been the subject of comparison. We are particularly pleased that it has been possible to incorporate the Chinese experience in this study. Sweden and the USA are members of the OECD's Development Assistance Committee (DAC) which monitors ODA. In this respect they may be described as 'mainstream' donors.

China does not belong to this 'club' and has operated its aid programme overseas largely independently of the rest of the donor community. One of our empirical concerns is how the donor agencies of these three countries have responded to their respective domestic constituencies, and another is how the donors have been influenced by interaction among themselves.

We are also interested in how conditions and policies in Tanzania have affected the behaviour and strategies of these three donors. Tanzania constitutes an interesting arena for the study of foreign aid. As we discuss in greater detail in Chapter 2, Tanzania was for a period in the late 1960s and early 1970s a special favourite of the donor community because of its policy of socialism and national self-reliance, two concepts that played a prominent role in development theory in *Ujamaa* (Swahili for 'familyhood'); this was acceptable to the donor community because it was not Marxist and emphasized both poverty alleviation and national development based on domestic (as opposed to foreign) resources. Donors shared the expectation in this period that these goals were achievable within a relatively short time span. If governments only showed the political will to move in such a direction, the donors could complement their efforts and accelerate the process of development. By the end of the 1970s, it was becoming increasingly clear that these goals were not being achieved. In fact, the socialist policies were now being viewed as impediments rather than facilitators of national development. During the 1980s, therefore, Tanzania underwent a painful process of adjustment which by the end of the decade had caused an almost total reversal of the policies from the late 1960s. The neo-liberal paradigm of development has become even further entrenched in the 1990s. It is now the market rather than the state which is treated as the principal mechanism for allocating resources.

In short, Tanzania constitutes the empirical universe for answering three simple but basic questions about the role that the Chinese, Swedish and US aid agencies have played in international politics and public policy-making in recipient countries: (1) what drives these agencies; (2) how do they operate; and (3) what legacy do they leave behind? We believe that by making this study comparative, we enhance our chances of finding interesting and valid answers to these questions. We hope that this study will help us to grasp little understood dimensions of decision-making strategies and behaviour in the donor community.

DONOR AGENCIES AS ORGANIZATIONS

In designing this study we have been particularly influenced by the literature in the fields of organization theory and policy studies. We are trying to fill the conceptual and theoretical space in the study of foreign aid that has been left by students of international relations and economists carrying out evaluations of its efficiency and effectiveness. Much of the literature on organizations does of course take its inspiration from studies of the firm, in which the boundaries between economic and sociological considerations are transcended. Theories of the firm postulate that because it operates in the market place it is subject to certain kinds of structural influences which make its behaviour predictable; hence, human behaviour in organizations can be analysed in terms of straightforward criteria such as attention to the principles of return on capital and benefits exceeding costs. This is not to suggest that every study of the firm starts from the premises of rational choice. There are many that stress the role of the 'human' factor and the need to adjust organizational structures to suit human needs and aspirations. One of the most well known in this genre is the study of corporate excellence in America (Peters and Waterman 1982). Regardless of what premise is chosen, however, these studies tend to have one thing in common: successful organizations are capable of manipulating the causes of inefficiency well. Managers fashion organizations to accommodate environmental uncertainty (Stinchcombe 1990). For example, in the 'new institutionalist' perspective which has become influential in recent years the emphasis is on understanding the factors that determine transaction costs: that is, the price paid for getting things done in a particular organizational set-up (Williamson 1985; North 1990).

Not all organizations, however, operate in a market context. Administrative or bureaucratic organizations such as government departments are largely insulated from the market and thus different. Their principal stimuli come from rules and regulations established by political authority: for example, in a democracy the legislature passes laws within which the executive branch of government subsequently issues directives that apply to more specific situations. The main difference between the firm and the bureaucratic agency, therefore, is that the former operates in a competitive environment, where insensitivity to its ramifications may bring collapse, while the latter performs in an environment which is uncertain not because of competition for scarce capital or technology but because of organized interest and political rivalry. Capital and technology are variables that can be controlled and manipulated in the interest of the organization without any apparent cost to others. Even if not all exchanges in the market place are positive for every actor involved, transactions are often Pareto-optimal in the sense of leaving both parties feeling satisfied with the deal. In short, it is possible to turn exchanges in the market place into positive-sum games.

Organized interest and politics, on the other hand, are social forces which are independent and much more difficult to control. The uncertainty is not objective in the same sense that capital and technology are. Because it is subjective in that all actors tend to perceive each issue from the point of view of how it affects their status and feelings as human beings, the probability of conflicts becoming zero-sum games is much higher in this kind of situation than in the market place, where capital and technology provide a more consistent and objective set of evaluative criteria. It is no coincidence, therefore, that the literature on bureaucratic types of organization tends to focus on conflict. The bulk of it suggests that such organizations dominate society at the expense of popular influence. There are others, though, who emphasize the influence of outside actors on the implementation of organizational objectives. Selznick's classic study of the Tennessee Valley Authority (1949), in which powerful local interests capture the organization for their own benefit, remains one of the most insightful in this genre.

Donor agencies fall within the category of bureaucratic agencies and can be expected to have many of the same characteristics as those listed above. At the same time they constitute a unique type of bureaucratic organization because they are not only responsive to demands and pressures exercised in the domestic political arena but also to those originating outside the domestic jurisdiction. Thus the conflicting pressures being brought to bear on the operations of these agencies are special and more complex than is the case typically with agencies operating only in the domestic arena. Particularly significant is that these agencies are embedded in social and political environments where its individual administrators usually are strangers. They do not necessarily speak the native language and they often have difficulties relating to the culture of these foreign countries. To be sure, many aid administrators learn much in the course of their assignment in a foreign country, and some even become enthusiastic advocates of the country in question. Such learning notwithstanding, there typically remains a cultural gap between the representatives of the donor country and those of the country receiving the aid. An aid agency therefore cannot be evaluated on the same terms as an agency operating only within the jurisdiction of a donor country. Achieving the goals of a particular project is much easier in such an environment than it is where the goal is often also to instil new knowledge in fellow workers in the recipient country. In trying to develop a better understanding of aid agencies we proceeded in an inductive fashion, trying to build a theoretical framework from the bottom up. We have decided that the best way to move ahead is to analyse the variables that are likely to influence the aid agency and examine how it tries to deal with them in order to enhance its own control of its social, economic and political environment. We argue that there are three dimensions of the environment which are particularly significant and thus worth treating as independent variables: (1) the domestic political actors in the donor country; (2) the policies of the recipient country; and (3) the donor community as a corporate entity. The politicians back home set the policies, control the financial resources, and insist on the accountability of the agency to them. They call the tune, but we disagree with those who argue that aid agencies are totally dependent on what domestic policy-makers decide. Recipient countries also have an influence. Although it is typically more subtle and less formal, there is plenty of evidence to suggest that policy statements and interventions made by recipient country governments have an influence on donor behaviour and strategy. For example, in this study we hypothesize that the Arusha Declaration, which helped launch Tanzanian socialism, is one case in point. Its reversal after 1986 when an agreement was signed with the IMF to liberalize the economy is another such event. Finally, with the growth of the aid business over the years, the donor community itself has become an actor of some significance. This is particularly true for the member countries of the OECD which tend to coordinate their strategies and approaches in such places as the annual meetings of the Washington-based international finance institutions (the IMF and the World Bank), the Global Coalition for Africa or the special consultative meetings organized under the auspices of the so-called Paris Club, a forum made up of all major governments providing ODA. Individual bilateral donors have at times played leading roles in certain sectors or in designing new approaches to aid administration, but in recent years the lead has come primarily from the multilateral agencies, notably the World Bank and the IMF.

Donor strategy and behaviour, then, is constrained in several different ways. Access to financial resources is often hampered by the perception, both real and imaginary, that donor funds are not very effectively used. This becomes an issue particularly in those contexts where fraud or deliberate misappropriation of such funds has taken place. Donor strategy and behaviour is also inhibited by the fact that its operations often challenge the sovereignty of the government or people of the recipient country. Even if the official rhetoric in the mid-1990s implies the donor's right to set conditions of both an economic and political kind, there are definite limits to how far these conditionalities can be effectively put into practice. For example, structural adjustment policies have been acted upon by recipient governments only with a high degree of scepticism. The same is true in most countries which have been subjected to pressures to adopt multiparty democracy. Donor strategy and behaviour, finally, is also limited by the pressures that often arise in the donor community to adopt a common stand on key issues. For example, the donor community's ability to have some credibility in its demand that recipient governments adopt certain kinds of policies depends very much on the extent to which donors take a united stand.

Even if donors' hands are often more tied than appears to be the case at a first glance at the donor-recipient country relations, the donor agency typically has more opportunities than domestic bureaucratic agencies to develop its own agenda. A major reason for this is that these agencies can play one actor against the other. Another is the fact that there is so much controversy about what criteria should apply to evaluating the performance of these agencies. Donor agencies can manipulate these ambiguities to their own advantage, thereby enhancing their autonomy *vis-à-vis* other actors: for example, where an ideological or moral commitment to assisting developing countries exists, the opportunities for turning even adverse feedback into a political asset are particularly great. In trying to understand the constraints and opportunities that aid agencies face, it is important also to examine how the ideological climate in which these agencies operate has evolved over the period covered in this volume.

DEVELOPMENT THEORY AND FOREIGN AID

Foreign aid is expected to promote social and economic development, so it is not surprising that development theory has played an important role in shaping the discourse on foreign aid. The experience of foreign aid, in turn, has fed back into the theorizing about development (Hyden 1994; Norwegian Institute of International Affairs 1994). Like many similar broad concepts, such as democracy, 'development' means different things to different people. In this respect, the concept is user-friendly (Black 1992). Nevertheless, development theory is centred around two separate axes: one focuses on the overall objective of development, and the other on the means to achieve the objective. The conceptual realm of development theory, therefore, tends to be confined to a distinction between whether growth or equity is being particularly emphasized as the overall goal, and whether the mechanisms to achieve development concentrate on a directed, top-down approach or a participatory, bottom-up one.

Development theory as applied to the international arena dates back to the 1950s. Much of it arose in the wake of the Marshall Plan, the transfer of US capital for the reconstruction of Europe after the Second World War. In this huge project, governments or states played a key pump-priming role by creating jobs for the rebuilding of public infrastructure and housing. The lessons learnt from this venture were reflected in the first international development theories that evolved in the mid-1950s. Not surprisingly, economists were in the forefront of this exercise. Their interest was in how to accelerate economic growth in countries where private capital was scarce. Their inclination was to emphasize the importance of national development plans which could serve as general guidelines for how scarce domestic and foreign resources should be allocated. This insistence on comprehensive plans inevitably gave the state a particularly important role in promoting development. The assumption that development theorists made in those days was that foreign aid would complement local savings. With an increased level of resources at their disposal, governments in developing countries would be able to accelerate economic and social development. What had taken Europe and North America hundreds of years to achieve, development theorists assumed (in their more optimistic moments) could be done in decades by the developing countries, if only with the help of sufficient foreign aid.

This approach may be best described as 'the big push'. Development was treated largely as an economic matter, with technology transfer also playing a role: many developing countries lacked skilled manpower, so the provision of technical assistance in the form of experts in specialized fields would fill this gap. For most analysts in those days, development was an exercise in social engineering, the difficulties and complexities of which were largely ignored. No one really doubted the feasibility of doing what was being planned. In the specific case of Africa, the political euphoria prevailing in the 1960s after national independence reinforced this feeling. It certainly was present when China, Sweden and the USA began providing aid to Tanzania.

As the 1960s came to an end, the mood among development practitioners changed. Foreign aid had not been able to achieve the anticipated progress. The gap between promise and practice was becoming an increasingly obvious embarrassment. The answer that development theorists provided, however, was not to change the overall approach but to see what could be done in order to make it more effective. This modification followed two separate lines, and one was to emphasize the need for greater attention to redistribution of resources to the poor. In the earlier period, when all attention had been on accelerating growth, the principal agents of change outside government were believed to be those already endowed with some wealth. These persons were viewed as entrepreneurs who could serve as innovators. Because many of them were also believed to be respected persons in their communities, it was assumed that others would imitate their behaviour. Innovations, in short, would be diffused through the already well-endowed. Even though there may have been something to this assumption, diffusion did not work fast enough to satisfy critics of this theory. The latter argued instead that the poor must be given a better share of the available resources so that they could improve their education and health. By doing so they would also be in a better position to take advantage of the development opportunities arising. Some of the bilateral donors, including Sweden, were among the first to put these new ideas into practice, but by the early 1970s they had been adopted by virtually all donor governments. Also, the World Bank changed its tune to concentrate capital on more integrated development projects targeting poorer regions or communities.

The other line of reform was to revamp public services so as to make them more efficient and effective in implementing development projects and programmes. Much attention was being paid to improving terms of service for state employees, adopting modern management methods, and decentralizing authority to lower echelons of government. This last element became particularly important as the notion was that decentralization would bring government closer to the people and therefore enhance the opportunities for effective implementation. As we shall see in subsequent chapters, Tanzania became a fertile testing ground of these ideas because of its home-grown socialist ideology which stressed the very values that development theory in the early 1970s advocated.

The lessons learnt from both the 1960s and 1970s were incorporated into the revised development theories that began to emerge in the early 1980s. Economists were now abandoning the Keynesian premises on which development economics had been based throughout the previous decades. Instead, they advocated a 'return to basics' (that is, liberal market philosophy, according to which the most efficient mechanism for promoting development is the market, not the state). This new theorizing emphasized the rationality of the individual. Peasants were no longer viewed as traditional and backward but as fully capable of making rational choices about how to improve their livelihoods. Thus, side-by-side with the macro-economic reforms that paved the way for deregulation, privatization and adjustment of overvalued local currencies, the neo-liberal theory of development assumed that individual actors would obtain more opportunities to take responsibility for their own development. This point had become particularly significant as critics of foreign aid argued that it was fostering relations of dependence. Recipient governments were beginning to take foreign aid for granted, seeing it not just as a complement to, but as an integral part of, their own resource base. Individuals and communities targeted by government policies, in turn, were beginning to interpret development as a gift from outside. For these reasons, neo-liberal theorists were ready to argue that foreign aid in many circumstances was counter-productive. Instead of facilitating or promoting development, it was impeding it. Many maintained that trade rather than aid would be beneficial. This criticism notwithstanding, foreign aid continued throughout the 1980s, but with less going to governments and more to non-governmental organizations and private entrepreneurs.

This shift away from governments as recipients of foreign aid in the early 1980s was the most significant consequence of the new development theory. It led to the 'discovery' of new actors which had not been accounted for in previous theorizing. These included women's groups, community-based organizations and informal sector entrepreneurs, all of whom were being described as the true promoters of development. This institutional diversification complicated the task of channelling aid. Most donor governments insisted on giving support for these non-governmental actors in developing countries only through non-governmental organizations in their own countries, thus taking away much of the value of the bottom-up approach that these indigenous organizations practised. The new approach was institutionalized through the establishment of SAPs in many poor and debt-ridden countries in Africa, Asia and Latin America, Tanzania being one of them. SAP advocates insist that these programmes take time to be successfully implemented, and that giving up half-way only prolongs the pain. For this reason, and in the absence of any alternative economic theory, the neo-liberal paradigm remains dominant to this day.

In addition to economic neo-liberalism, the 1990s is being characterized by the integration of political liberalism into development theory. Development was for a long time considered a non-political exercise. In fact, development practitioners were adamant about drawing a definite line between politics and development, the argument being that politics was the prerogative of the sovereign nation-state and thus outside the purview of donors. Although this notion was not always strictly adhered to in previous decades, it was only in the 1990s that the gauntlet was thrown down and political conditionalities introduced into development theorizing. Some theorists and practitioners are convinced that development is only possible with safeguards for individual civil and political liberties. In short, a democratic system of government, resembling that of Western countries, is a necessary (if not sufficient) condition for development. This approach has been adopted by most Western donor governments in the 1990s. The multilateral agencies which are made up of representatives of governments around the world have been more cautious in their approach: for example, the World Bank has refused to appear as an advocate of a particular form of government and has instead adopted the concept of 'governance' to indicate its interest in political reform. This concept is used in a loose sense and refers to the overall management of the national economy, in which both economic and political reforms are necessary. The overall effect of this new twist to development theory is to limit the options that governments in developing countries have. Their sovereignty over political matters is no longer beyond question. For example, when governments fail to show respect for human rights or their political opponents, donor government register their protest by threatening to withhold aid or, in some blatant cases, actually suspending it altogether.

What this brief overview of development theorizing in the post-Second World War period suggests is that ideas have shifted quite frequently. It seems no paradigm has really lasted longer than a decade. A major reason behind this inconsistency is the dynamics inherent in the gap between theory and practice that has characterized every period to date. Development theorists have set ambitious targets but practitioners have never been able to achieve them, thus giving fodder to critics who are anxious to revise existing theory. The situation in the 1990s is no different, and we can only continue to expect new paradigms to replace the old ones even in the future.

Of special interest to us here is how the donor agencies have reacted to these changes in development theory and what the implications are of success or failure in adjusting to the calls of new theories. We hypothesize that the two members of OECD – Sweden and the USA – are likely to be particularly challenged by shifts in the development paradigm, while China should find itself more independent of any such pressures. Development theory constitutes an important backdrop to foreign aid strategy and behaviour, but these are also determined by the way that such agencies are constituted and charged to operate by their political masters. It is around these issues that our study has been principally designed.

THEORETICAL AND CONCEPTUAL FRAMEWORK

The premise of this study is that donor agencies, like other organizations, strive for control of their environment by trying to insulate organizational tasks from influences that complicate programme and project management. Agency officials are likely to take this position both to protect their own power and to promote goal achievement. The strategy and behaviour that these officials adopt, however, do not emerge in a vacuum. What they do and what they decide is influenced by their ability to command resources and by the rules that have been institutionalized as guides for agency behaviour and decisions. In this study, therefore, we are combining a resource dependence and an institutionalist perspective on organizations.

The resource dependence model of inter-organizational relations assumes that organizations, in order to survive and prosper, depend on their ability to acquire and maintain resources. Resources must be obtained from other actors. These transactions constitute relations of dependence. Dependence is viewed as inversely related to power. Actors that control needed resources exert power over a dependent organization's structure and activity (Echeverri-Gent 1992:347). An organization's ability to modify such relations of dependence is a function of the extent to which these resources are abundant or not, concentrated or dispersed, critical or not critical to the organization, as well as its ability to provide resources of value to other actors. If, for example, resources are scarce, under monopoly control, yet important to the organization, it is reasonable to assume that the organization's autonomy is limited. Strategy and behaviour are likely to reflect this high level of dependence.

To fully understand the way organizations operate in their environments, however, it is important to recognize that resources which matter may be of different kinds. We distinguish between three types: (1) economic, (2) political, and (3) informational. Control over economic resources gives some actors power, but organizations can counter these by mobilizing political support to oppose these actors, withhold important information or circulate information which reflects positively on their operations and negatively on others. For example, corporate organizations often have the upper hand over customer organizations, but the latter can challenge corporate power particularly in situations where a product is deemed hazardous on health or safety grounds. Information circulated by customer organizations on this product could force the corporate entity to change its strategy and behaviour.

As implementing bodies, donor agencies are typically highly dependent on resources provided by the Government Treasury. Donor agencies do not raise their own revenue and are thus unable to counter the power of Treasury officials with their own economic might. Donor agencies have to rely on their ability to build and maintain political support and disseminate information about their work which convinces others that it is worthwhile. Support for foreign aid – and thus the power of individual donor agencies – has for a long time rested on two principal premises: (1) that the rich countries have a moral obligation to assist the poor ones; (2) that it is in the national interest of the donor country to give foreign aid. The relative stability of these assumptions, at least until the 1990s, has strengthened the autonomy of these agencies and given them the means to challenge the economic power of the resource provider. Donor agencies have typically been able to survive criticism of their performance which would have had more devastating effects on sister agencies in the government working exclusively in the domestic arena. It is only in the 1990s that matters have begun to change. Even those constituencies which for a long time gave foreign aid their full blessing have now become more critical of its rationale and usefulness.

Resource exchanges, however, only explain part of the strategy and behaviour of donor agencies. Institutionalized rules are as important. By 'institutionalized rules' we mean those rules that have gained general acceptance for policy uses. The activity of government agencies is generally more subject to the constraints imposed by institutionalized rules than are other organizations. When we say that such agencies are 'bureaucratized', the implication is that their operations are extensively dependent on institutionalized rules. Such rules, however, do not always impede the work of an organization. It can convincingly be argued that without such rules the organization would lose its ability to achieve its publicly stated goals.

Institutionalized rules shape policy implementation through coercive, mimetic and normative mechanisms. Coercive pressures occur when organizations adapt institutionalized rules because their prescriptions are sanctioned by legislatures or other bodies with the capacity to impart or withdraw funding and legitimacy. If these rules become too detailed they may confine the organization's ability to perform and thus undercut its ability to achieve stated goals. These rules, then, limit the power of the organization. In the case of donor agencies, the extent to which coercive rules are detailed varies from country to country. It seems clear that the more general and flexible coercive rules are, the greater the opportunity of the agency to exercise its own influence over strategy and policy.

Mimetic pressures occur when uncertainty encourages imitation of other organizations perceived to be more successful and legitimate. If one organization has found a way of doing things right, it is likely that others which are struggling to survive will copy its strategy or behaviour: for instance, donor agencies, although they are in competition with each other and moulded culturally by their roots in the national political scene of the donor country, have sometimes accepted the lead of others. The most obvious case in point is their general acceptance of the call by the international finance institutions for economic reforms in the early 1980s. As we shall see in subsequent chapters, these pressures were more easily accepted in the USA than they were in Sweden, where rules indicating that there was a distinct Swedish way of giving foreign aid had been institutionalized. By the mid-1980s, however, all donor countries, including Sweden and its Nordic neighbours, had come to accept structural adjustment as the right strategy for ensuring better use of external resources in developing countries.

Normative pressures are created through general socialization, the training and selection of personnel, and the creation of interpersonal networks that are part of the pursuit of certain public activities. Organizations develop their own corporate cultures which influence the way individuals make decisions and behave. Donor agencies, for example, tend to differ in terms of where their staff are recruited from. Their strategy also tends to be influenced by the extent to which staff see themselves as having a specialized career as opposed to just one of many which they can select. For instance, in the case of Sida, normative pressures developed within the organization which complicated and delayed its adaptation to the new economic situation of the 1980s, as suggested above.

Institutionalized rules have cognitive as well as normative consequences. They condition decision-makers' intuitive understanding by defining implementation problems in particular ways. In the process, they prescribe some practices and proscribe others. In the case of donors, these rules may lead agencies to adopt specific approaches, such as turn-key projects, 'concerned participation' or conditional aid. Thus, the strategy and behaviour that individuals in these organizations adopt are directly influenced by the culture that these institutionalized rules constitute. We suggest that resource dependence and institutionalized rules stand in an interactive relationship with each other. While resource dependence conditions the development of these rules, the latter also shape the nature of resource exchanges.

To understand fully what drives donor agencies and dictates their operational mode, we have identified a number of independent and intervening variables which differ in terms of being structural or behavioural. In making this distinction we have been largely guided by Giddens' structuration theory (Giddens 1984) which treats structure and human agency as complementary rather than contradictory, in that structures are created by human beings and hence subject to change by people. A structural variable in this study, therefore, means something determined by rules set by political actors, while a behavioural variable means something not determined by rules set by political actors. The latter is the 'agency' in the agencies we study here.

The specific challenge that donor agencies face is to strike a balance between organizational autonomy and responsiveness, especially to the environment in the recipient country. The competing demands for autonomy and responsiveness in order to carry out their work effectively is at the centre of this study. We treat the choices that agency staff make between these values as critical to the strategy and behaviour that they evolve. Autonomy is defined as the legal ability or authority to exercise discretion. It is a structural variable in that discretion is granted by political authorities. Autonomy can be studied both at the field level and at the headquarters level. Field-level autonomy is the freedom of the mission to act independently of the demands of the ambassador and the political authorities of the recipient country. Headquarters-level autonomy is the extent to which agency operations are free from intervention by domestic political actors. The level of autonomy directly influences the degree of responsiveness, primarily in the form of laws and regulations. It also has a bearing on the relations that the agency has with organizations in the recipient country and other agencies in the donor community. It influences the strategy adopted by the agency to the extent that high autonomy enables strategic planning to be more flexible. Finally, the level of autonomy also influences agency behaviour to the extent that increased autonomy enhances the level of discretion enjoyed by the agency and by individual officers.

Responsiveness is defined as the agency's collective willingness to change the official norms and values which find their expression most overtly in the directives which employees must follow, and more subtly in the organization's career incentives, to enhance the possibility that agency resources are being used to achieve its developmental objectives. Conditions in the recipient country and pressures from other donor organizations are likely to determine such decisions. Responsiveness is a behavioural variable which is influenced by external autonomy: that is, by the agency's legal authority to change directions and priorities. The degree of responsiveness, in turn, feeds back independently of the political authorities through various bureaucratic mechanisms, and this allows the agency to petition political authorities for change. Responsiveness is also likely to influence strategy through lessons learnt, and behaviour through the practice of innovation and a readiness to embrace change. Responsiveness, therefore, has an influence on how stable and predictable the behaviour of individual officials is likely to be.

In sum, the two intervening variables of autonomy and responsiveness are hypothesized to exert influence on each other. We hypothesize further that autonomy and responsiveness have an individual as well as a combined effect on agency relations with the political authorities in the domestic arena, other donors and recipient country institutions. We also anticipate that these two variables have an individual and a combined effect on the two dependent variables, strategy and behaviour as indicated in Figure 1.1.

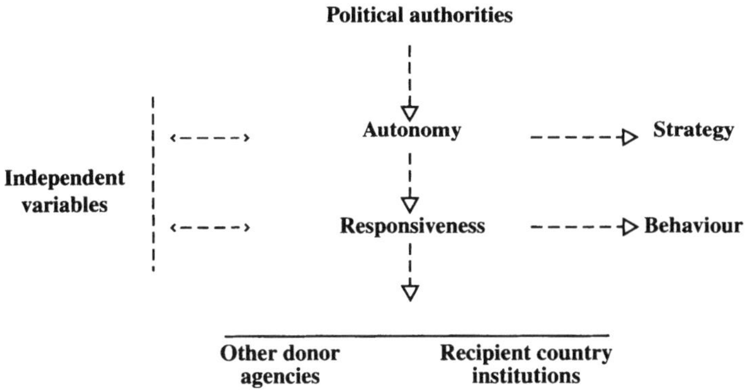

Figure 1.1 Relations among intervening and dependent variables

Drawing on what we have said above about organizations and how they interact with the environment, we have identified five independent variables that we believe are particularly significant for understanding donor agency strategy and behaviour: (1) sources of aid objectives; (2) basis for the provision of aid; (3) structure of agency; (4) staffing of agency; and (5) type and use of feedback. These are all expected to influence the extent to which strategy objectives and behaviour are likely to be stable or unstable.

We now turn to a discussion of our independent variables. The first such variable is defined as the extent to which agency policies are derived from the agency itself, the legislature or the executive in the donor country, or from the recipient nation. It is a structural variable because rules set by political actors limit the number of possible objectives and mandate certain objectives. We expect to find differences among the three donor countries studied here in terms of how they come to adopt certain kind of aid objectives. Much of it depends on how key actors in the policy-making circles in the donor country perceive development. We also expect to find differences over time as donor countries respond to the shifting paradigms of development described earlier in this chapter.

The second of our independent variable – basis of the provision of aid – refers to the extent to which its provision is conditional upon the recipient country's strategic importance and/or the extent to which the country meets certain criteria. The level of conditionality a foreign aid agency attaches to its assistance is a structural variable because the key conditions are determined by political actors. The basis of the provision of aid is likely to be shaped by the perception that policy-makers in the donor country have of the recipient country. In the case of Tanzania this was influenced in the 1960s and 1970s by its foreign policy stand as a non-aligned nation wishing to follow a development path of its own, and in later years by its image as a country ridden by corruption and inefficiency.

Structure of agency, our next variable, is defined as the extent to which the internal structure of the donor agency may be classified as centralized or decentralized. Again, this is a structural variable because decisions about this matter are made by political authorities. This variable has two dimensions of interest here. The first is the extent to which the central offices of the agency are more influential than their field offices. Budgetary concerns tend to favour centralization, while programme management typically demands decentralization. We expect to find differences among the three agencies covered here and possibly also variation over time. The second is the extent to which the agency programme is project-based or organized around broader sectoral support funding. Sectoral support tends to favour decisions at the central level as money is transferred directly to organizations in recipient countries. Project support, on the other hand, tends to favour the field offices, because they are closer to the place where funds are ultimately used and thus more strategically placed for the purpose of designing and developing specific projects.

Staffing of agency is defined in terms of where it looks for its personnel and what sort of qualifications and experience it seeks. It is a structural variable because the rules governing hiring and firing of staff and consultants or contractors are set by political authorities outside the agency. We expect that there will be differences among the American, Chinese and Swedish agencies in terms of whether staff are endogenously or exogenously recruited. Are officials in the agency largely an 'exclusive club' who make up a career service of their own, or do they move in and out of the foreign aid business? Are the principal implementers found within the organization or are they outsiders contracted to perform specific tasks on behalf of the agency? We are interested not only in tracing similarities and differences between the three agencies but also over time.

Type and use of feedback constitutes our fifth independent variable and is defined as the extent to which feedback, or information from the field, is incorporated into the decision-making process. This is a behavioural variable; it is not rule-bound. The type and use of feedback is determined by agency personnel. Feedback use is of critical importance to our analysis because if it is found to be high (that is, if the agency stresses the importance of using feedback and incorporates information provided by feedback into the decision-making process), all variables will exert greater influence on each other than if feedback is low. In other words, we anticipate

Table 1.1 Summary of analytical framework

Independent variables	*Intervening variables*	*Dependent variables*
Sources of objectives		
Basis of the provision of aid	Responsiveness	Strategy
Structure of agency	Autonomy	Behaviour
Staffing of agency		
Type and use of feedback		

that this variable has a great impact not only on the other independent variables but also on how agency personnel respond to the competing demands for autonomy and responsiveness and thus on how their strategy and behaviour eventually evolves. We expect there to be variation among the agencies in terms of how frequently evaluations and feedback information are used and also what kind of feedback information is being sought: quantitative or qualitative, output or process-based.

We can now summarize the analytical framework we are using to study donor strategy and behaviour as shown in Table 1.1.

We conceive the five independent and two intervening variables as lying along seven continua with the end more likely to yield stable strategies and behaviour on the right, as illustrated in Figure 1.2. The alignment, with the end *less* likely to yield stable strategies and behaviour cited first, is as follows: donor versus recipient-based objectives; high versus low conditionality; decentralized versus centralized decision-making; exogenous versus endogenous staffing; high versus low use of feedback; high versus low autonomy; and high versus low responsiveness. A particular donor agency may lie to the left on the continuum of one variable, but fall to the right on another. We hypothesize, however, that our three cases will fall consistently on the same location and that we can talk of three different models of foreign aid: an American, a Chinese and a Swedish, with the first lying to the left, the Chinese to the right and the Swedish falling in the middle.

According to this model we expect to find, for example, with regard to USAID that: (1) its objectives come from the agency itself and it believes it knows what is best for the recipient country; (2) it conditions its assistance based on the recipient country's strategic importance and/or its acceptance of the capitalist economic system and pluralist democracy; (3) it is decentralized and contracts outside consulting firms or awards grants to non-governmental organizations (NGOs) to implement and

← United States —— Sweden —— China →

I. Source of Aid Objectives

Agency-derived	Country-derived
Objectives are set by the agency, which assumes it knows what is best for the recipient country.	Objectives are set by the recipient country, which is assumed to know what is best for itself.

II. Basis for the Provision of Aid

Conditional	Unconditional
Aid is given to countries based on their strategic importance and to bolster democracy and capitalism.	Aid is intended as a sharing of wealth to foster international solidarity.

III. Structure of Donor Agency

Decentralized	Centralized
The agency uses secondary and tertiary organizations to carry out its policies and to evaluate outcomes.	The agency sets and carries out policies itself or simply transfers funds to the recipient country.

IV. Staffing of Donor Agency

Exogenous	Endogenous
Agency hires from the outside. Prior overseas experience and technical expertise is stressed.	Agency hires from within. Technical expertise alone is stressed.

V. Type and Use of Feedback

Quantitative/High	Qualitative/Low
Feedback is in the form of quantitative variables and is frequently sought.	Feedback is in the form of qualitative variables and is seldom sought.

VI. Level of Autonomy

High	Low
Agency has considerable autonomy from political actors.	Agency has little autonomy from political actors.

VII. Degree of Responsiveness

High	Low
Agency is extremely responsive to change.	Agency is not very responsive to change.

← Unstable —— Stable →

Figure 1.2 Hypothesized models of donor strategy and behaviour

evaluate its policies; (4) it hires its staff from within, but also brings in outside experts and deems technical expertise as an important qualification for being hired while treating previous overseas experience as a plus but not a requirement; (5) it relies on a mixture of quantitative and qualitative variables to measure success; (6) it enjoys more autonomy from political authorities than its Swedish and Chinese counterparts; and (7) it is more responsive to change than these other two agencies. We expect that the net effect of these variables is that US strategy and behaviour in Tanzania will prove to have been more unstable than is the case with the Chinese and Swedish agencies.

DONOR AGENCIES AND THE PROBLEMS OF FOREIGN AID

We know a good deal about the pathologies of economic exchange: depression, inflation, unemployment, maldistribution of income, inadequate public goods, and so on. We know very little, however, of the characteristics of one-way transfers of resources, a phenomenon that Boulding (1981) calls 'grants economics'. This study is not primarily economic but is all the same an attempt to get a better understanding of grants economics, especially the role that one set of principal actors – the donor agencies – play in shaping it (Hyden 1986:273). They are at one and the same time both part of the problem and the solution. Their mode of operation strategy and behaviour is important in determining the outcome of the foreign aid. When a donor agency gets too bogged down in one particular aspect of its operations, foreign aid gets trapped and fails to achieve its anticipated objectives. As these agencies try to cope with the challenges and pressures in their environment, we anticipate that there are at least four traps in which foreign aid can get lost.

The first of these we label the *accountability* trap. Foreign aid is part of public expenditure and thus money that comes from tax-payers. Donor agencies are likely to vary in the degree to which their managers will feel threatened by politicians who insist on results and frequent reports of what happens. We hypothesize that accountability considerations are evidence of a low degree of organizational autonomy. This becomes a trap where the following conditions are present in the donor country: (1) citizens have many avenues to articulate their opinion on public issues; (2) public tolerance of taxes is low; (3) foreign aid is tied to security and commercial interests; and (4) domestic issues are viewed as more important than international ones. When these conditions are present, politicians will be particularly anxious to keep a close eye on the foreign aid operations and intervene to direct their orientation. Rules and regulations will be issued in plenty to ensure that full reporting is achieved, even of quite detailed aspects of the operations. We expect that this trap is a more probable threat to the effectiveness of foreign aid in the case of the USA than it is in the other two.

The second is the *solidarity* trap. Foreign aid is meant to benefit its recipients and many believe that such aid becomes meaningful when it is given unconditionally in response to priorities and needs identified by the recipients. The problem is knowing what these priorities and needs are. For a long time, donor agencies have tried to deduce these from official documents such as national development plans and policy statements, but experience has shown that what recipient government officials produce as public or national goals often bears little relationship to the way resources are eventually allocated. We hypothesize that foreign aid conveyed as an act of solidarity indicates a high level of responsiveness to recipient country institutions, but that it reduces organizational autonomy and easily becomes a trap when the following conditions are present: (1) the extent to which the recipient government is representative of and accountable to public opinion is ignored; (2) foreign aid is given in the form of government-to-government transfers; (3) foreign aid is viewed as an act of international solidarity; and (4) the process of developing local capacity is treated as more important than obtaining quick results from foreign aid. We expect that this trap will apply more to the cases of China and Sweden than to that of the USA.

The third trap that we have identified is the *coordination* trap. Donor agencies believe that foreign aid can be made more effective if they coordinate their own efforts and avoid rivalry and duplication. While this argument is valid in many circumstances, the effect of such coordination is often to strengthen the hands of the donors and leave recipients with fewer opportunities to influence donor strategy and behaviour. For example, one of the few ways in which recipient institutions have managed to affect donor decisions has been to play one against the other. With greater coordination, the chances of doing so are reduced. Calls for greater coordination in the donor community tend to have the effect of making the agencies more interested in themselves than in the recipient country institutions. We hypothesize that coordination efforts make donor agencies responsive primarily to their own corporate community and reduce organizational autonomy when the following conditions prevail: (1) donors agree that recipients need to change policy; (2) there is a sense of the need for greater efficiency in the use of aid money; (3) ideological differences among donors are insignificant; and (4) the capacity of recipient country institutions is limited. We expect this trap to apply particularly to Sweden and the USA because of their membership of the OECD and the prominent role that both have tended to play in global development, and much less so to China which has continued to give aid without much interaction with other donors.

The fourth is the *insularity* trap. Donor agency officials are expected to ensure that their organizations achieve results; that something tangible is evident on the ground in the recipient country. If outside pressures on the agency to follow certain policy directives are weak, or the managers are capable of overcoming such pressures because of trust or personal power, the tendency is for the agency to become inward-looking. The organization becomes insular and locks out influences from the environment, whether it is the recipient country institutions, other donors, or the domestic political authorities. We hypothesize that this orientation becomes a trap when the following conditions are present: (1) project implementation is seen as successful by relevant political authorities; (2) the agency initiates few outside evaluations of its own activities; (3) the agency's structure is highly bureaucratic; and (4) its interaction with other donors is limited. We expect that this scenario will apply more to the Chinese case than to the other two.

The concept of trap implies that there are at least four different routes along which donor agencies can go astray in their effort to assist in recipient country developments. We assume that in examining three very different agencies, we will find that their internal dynamics differ and that it is wrong to assume that there is a single explanation of how such agencies work.

CONCLUSIONS

This chapter has indicated how we expect to go about answering our three research questions posed: What drives donor agencies? How do they operate? What legacy do they leave behind? Answers to these questions, we hope, will provide additional insights into the problems of foreign aid and provide the basis for assessing more carefully what works and under what conditions. We assume that decisions by donor agency officials are typically influenced by pressures from other organizational actors, whether these are coercive, mimetic or normative. All the same, structures created by others to guide foreign aid are not our only concern. We also want to assess how far behavioural variables play a role: that is, the extent to which agency officials themselves make a difference to the fate of their organization. It is in this context that the concept of organizational trap becomes interesting: do these officials become too preoccupied with one aspect of their mission with the result that they undercut their chances of achieving the stated goals of their organization?

References

Berlage, L. and O. Stokke (eds) (1992) *Evaluating Development Assistance: Approaches and Methods*. London: Frank Cass.

Black, Jan Knippers (1992) *What is Development*? San Francisco: ICS Press.

Boulding, Kenneth E. (1981) *A Preface to Grant Economics: The Economy of Love and Fear*. New York: Praeger.

Cassen, Robert *et al.* (1986) *Does Aid Work?* Oxford: Oxford University Press.

Echeverri-Gent, John (1992) 'Between Autonomy and Capture: Embedding Government Agencies in Their Societal Environment', *Policy Studies Journal*, Vol. 20, No. 3, pp. 342–64.

Elgström, Ole (1992) *Foreign Aid Negotiations*. Aldershot, England: Avebury.

Forss, Kim (1985) *Planning and Evaluation in Aid Organizations*. Stockholm: IIB, EFI, Stockholm School of Economics.

Giddens, Anthony (1984) *The Constitution of Society*. Cambridge, England: Polity Press.

Hyden, Goran (1986) 'The Pitfalls of Development Aid', in Pierre Fruhling (ed.), *Swedish Development Aid in Perspective: Policies, Problems and Results Since 1952*. Stockholm: Almqvist & Wiksell International.

Hyden, Goran (1994) 'Changing Ideological and Theoretical Perspectives on Development', in Ulf Himmelstrand, Kabiru Kinyanjui and Edward Mburugu (eds), *African Perspectives on Development*. London: James Currey; New York: St Martin's Press.

Lele, Uma (1990) *Foreign Aid to African Agriculture: A Quarter Century of Experience*. San Francisco: ICS Press.

Lele, Uma and Ijaz Nabi (eds) (1991) *Transitions in Development*. San Francisco: ICS Press.

North, Douglass C. (1990) *Institutions, Institutional Change and Economic Performance*. Cambridge: Cambridge University Press.

Norwegian Institute of International Affairs (1994) *North-South Relations and Development Cooperation*, Forum for Development Studies Nos 1/2. Oslo: Norwegian Institute of International Affairs.

Peters, Thomas J. and Robert H. Waterman (1982) *In Search of Excellence: Lessons from America's Best-Run Companies*. New York: Warner Books.

Riddell, Roger (1988) *Foreign Aid Reconsidered*. London: James Currey.

Selznick, Philip (1949) *TVA and the Grassroots*. Berkeley, Cal.: University of California Press.

Stinchcombe, A.L. (1990) *Information and Organizations*. Berkeley, Cal.: University of California Press.

Stokke, Olav (ed.) (1984) *European Development Assistance: Policies and Performance*, Volumes I and II. Tilburg: European Association of Development Research and Training Institutes.

Stokke, Olav (ed.) (1991) *Evaluating Development Assistance: Policies and Performance*. London: Frank Cass.

Williamson, Oliver (1985) *The Economic Institutions of Capitalism*. New York: The Free Press.

2 From Proud Defiance to Beggary: A Recipient's Tale

Rwekaza Mukandala

INTRODUCTION

Tanzania is fascinating to students of international development because of what she has said, done, and undergone with regard to aid and donors. First, Tanzania took a very unequivocal stand against aid conditionality (or aid with strings). 'The first responsibility of the Government, its first principle', said President Nyerere, 'is the protection of Tanzania's independence and its freedom to determine its own policies – both internal and external' (Nyerere 1966:2). In pursuit of this position the country lost aid from Germany and several other countries in the 1960s. Emphasizing this principle, especially after the way the French made an example of Guinea in 1958, demonstrated either foolhardiness or principled commitment of the highest order.

Second, in 1967 Tanzania proceeded to openly denounce or denigrate aid (and donors) as the engine of development. Said the Arusha Declaration: 'The development of our country is brought about by people, not by money. Money and the wealth it presents is the result, and not the basis, of development. The four prerequisites of development are (i) people, (ii) land (iii) good policies, (iv) good leadership' (Nyerere 1967). Socialism and self-reliance was the way to go. The government added a few years later that 'reliance on foreign assistance has already been demonstrated to be a myth' (United Republic of Tanzania, or URT, 1981). These strong statements led initially to a notable loss of aid to the country. However, the amounts of aid flowing into the country picked up, especially during the period of intense radicalism in the late 1960s and 1970s, to a point where Tanzania soon became one of the leading recipients of aid in the world. It gradually abandoned its suspicion of aid and became so addicted to it that in the 1990s Tanzania has become more like a shameless beggar. At the meeting of the Paris Club in March 1994, the government was almost on its knees. 'We seriously urge donors to understand and assist the government to redress the situation ... the external resource flow is most critical in redressing the current macro-economic imbalances.' It continued: 'We request donors to disburse with dispatch the resources pledged'

(URT 1994). Denunciation of conditionality and strings is now forgotten. The irony is that the country has undergone serious economic deterioration despite the massive aid flows. Tanzania is now considered one of the six poorest countries in the world!

It is these factors that explain the fascination mentioned above. How could a poor country take such radical principled positions against aid and aid conditionality, and how could it stand up to the big, especially Western, powers? How could a country so committed to independence and self-reliance and opposed to aid end up so dependent on it? How could massive inflows of aid coexist with massive economic deterioration? This chapter hopes to shed light on these paradoxes by seeking answers to three sets of questions. First, what was Tanzania's perception of aid and donors? Did the country have an aid strategy? If so, how effective was it in practice, and to what extent did it reflect the dominant perceptions? Second, what have been Tanzania's actual experiences with donors? How was aid solicited or granted, received and managed? Finally, what is the perceived impact of aid on Tanzania, and what impact has Tanzania had on the donors?

The following sections tackle each of these issues. Before doing so, however, it is important to introduce a theoretical perspective which is helpful in understanding and appreciating the dynamics of aid in countries like Tanzania.

THEORETICAL PERSPECTIVE

Studies pertaining to Tanzania reveal a tendency to personalize Tanzania's public policy in general and its foreign and aid policy in particular. Many studies of Tanzania's foreign aid policy centre on President Nyerere to the exclusion of other actors in the polity (Niblock 1972; Shaw and Msabaha 1981; Green 1995; Msabaha 1995). There has been a concentration on Nyerere's ideals and principles which Msabaha elevates to 'doctrines' (1995:165). There has been little attempt to situate Nyerere's statements and actions in the material realities and the material forces shaping society. Mushi (1981, 1982) has been the notable exception to this trend.

Consequently, many studies also personalize the notable about-turn in Tanzania's behaviour towards donors. Some attribute the change to Nyerere's departure from the presidency in November 1985 and his succession by Ali Hassan Mwinyi. Yet, as Svendsen correctly observes, 'the basic reason for the policy change, and later for the Economic Recovery Programme of 1986, was the realization that foreign financing was necessary in order to avoid political collapse' (1995:121). Donors also now personalize factors behind the extreme acquiescence of Tanzania's government to donor demands and conditionalities. 'They seem tired. That fight of earlier years is gone' (Helleiner *et al.* 1995:26). Yet even if there is tiredness, its cause is not explained.

From our perspective, the most critical starting point for a serious attempt is to understand and appreciate Tanzania's experience with donors is to underscore the importance of what Max Weber (1978) called 'means of administration and coercion' (MAC) and how they are sustained by the state. Mouzelis elaborates MAC as 'macro-institutional, organizational ensembles that, on the level of the whole polity, link rulers and ruled (for example, types of state administrations or military apparatuses, techniques of taxation, of national accounting, of mass mobilization and ... forms of political incorporation)' (1990:51).

The statement refers to what the state is: the institutions and organizations, ranging from rules, armies, civil service, and parastatal organizations, to what the state does and the work processes: administrate, adjudicate, collect taxes, regulate, provide critical infrastructure and social services, and defend its boundaries and sovereignty; and also the means with which it does the above: means of destruction, techniques of accounting, finances, skilled and experienced personnel, technologies and techniques, knowledge, and so on.

These MAC can be divided into two parts in the context of our discussion. There are those that are critical to the very functioning and continuing existence of the state, and then there are those functions and activities that are important, but not critical (these include developmental activities). To borrow from Thompson (1967), the former activities comprise the technical core of MAC. What needs appreciation is the extent to which the ruling classes are able to produce and reproduce these critical means of administration and if they can sustain them: that is, whether they have the capacity, resources (money), manpower, and technologies to sustain the critical core functions of this apparatus.

The central proposition of this chapter is that a country's autonomy, or that of its ruling classes, is at its maximum if it can produce and reproduce its MAC in a sustainable fashion. A self-reliant country in terms of capacity to sustain its MAC enjoys autonomy and prestige, especially in its dealings with external forces including donors.

This self-reliance, or lack of it, is reflected in a country's budget, which contains its anticipated amounts of revenue and their sources on the one hand, and proposed expenditure for certain items and purposes on the other (Wildavsky 1979). The budget would reflect self-reliance if it is balanced (that is, if anticipated revenue matches anticipated expenditures), or better still, if there is a positive imbalance (that is, anticipated revenue exceeds planned expenditures). The reverse situation impacts negatively. Imbalanced budgets in and of themselves, however, need not spell doom for a country. It all depends on the part of the budget that has a deficit. The expenditure side of the budget can be broken down into the recurrent budget which covers the government's ongoing activities, and the development or capital budget which is the public capital programme. In current terms one may say that the recurrent budget goes to fund the core state functions, while the development budget funds new activities into which the state decides to expand. A deficit in the recurrent budget is therefore more critical in terms of its erosion of autonomy than a shortfall in the development budget, the activities of which may in fact be frozen, scaled back, or abandoned.

The last point relates to mechanisms that the state may resort to in order to balance its budget and shore up its autonomy. Domestic borrowing, either from the public in terms of expanding the national debt outside the banking system or borrowing from banks through a judicious monetary expansion, is preferable to resorting to external sources. The latter also ultimately undermines autonomy.

It may even be said that a country's bargaining position in the international arena declines as its capacity to sustain its MAC weakens. The failure of a state to keep itself going erodes its position and prestige in the international arena. The old adage applies very well: beggars cannot be choosers. Tanzania's relations with donors, past and present, must be evaluated from this standpoint.

PERCEPTIONS AND STRATEGY

The underlying perception of aid as welcome but dangerous was anchored by a relative autonomy in the early years of the Tanzanian state. This autonomy was a result not only of Nyerere's personal character and preferences (because these were still unchanged even in 1985) but also of the Tanzanian state's capacity to finance its recurrent budget autonomously. As this ability declined, so did the list of things that the Tanzanian state was unable to accept and the humiliation that it was not willing to suffer. Tanzania's aid strategy, or lack of it, was also contingent on the above factors. Most importantly, Tanzania's experiences with donors reflects this point. Tanzania's perception of aid and donors has undergone several changes and gone through phases, just as donor perceptions of Tanzania underwent change, as will be shown in subsequent chapters.

Tanzania's perception of aid has been dominated by two major elements. One is the notion of aid as necessary and important in order to augment the country's development, and lately, its efforts to survive. In spite of the political rhetoric, Tanzania has never rejected aid altogether. As we will see below, however, it has not accepted it at any price. In an essay clarifying the Arusha Declaration (the major policy statement which launched Tanzania's key programme of socialism and self-reliance on 7 July 1967), President Nyerere emphasized that 'the policy does not say that Tanzania refuses outside aid, or that there is something wrong in receiving it' (1967). This acceptance of aid, though, has since undergone substantial change from wary or guarded solicitation and acceptance of aid in the 1960s and 1970s to desperate begging in the late 1980s and 1990s. Material realities occasioned this shift which will be explored below.

The second major element is the notion of aid as a necessary evil. Aid has always been perceived as a danger to the country's independence and sovereignty, as a danger to the country's economy and development efforts, and finally as dangerous in terms of its being a superficial ameliorative, a poor substitute for fundamental structural changes in the international economic order.

Right from independence in 1961, the government of Tanzania maintained that 'we want aid without strings on our political or economic policies' (Mushi and Mathews 1981:221). This position came into sharp relief in 1964–65 when Tanzania's intention to establish relations with all countries in the world led to a crisis with West Germany, whose Hallstein Doctrine prohibited relations with any country which had relations with East Germany. West Germany sought to prevent Tanzania from granting Consular General Status to East Germany. Tanzania refused to let West Germany determine with whom it would have relations, applying a policy that had been in place for some years. As Niblock correctly observes, this was, 'a genuine attempt at pursuing independence-minded policies, based on the tenets of non-alignment ... made before 1964' (1981:24).

By 1967 enough experience had been gained to enable the government to crystallize its position even more clearly. In the Arusha Declaration, aid was discounted as the main panacea of curing the country's woes: 'It would be stupid for us to imagine that we shall rid ourselves of our poverty through foreign financial assistance rather than our own financial resources.' There were several reasons for this statement. First, aid did not come in sufficient quantities and at the right time. This had disastrous consequences, as Tanzania realized when it tried planned development. In early 1962, it had been decided that the country's development efforts would be pursued through a series of five year development plans starting with the First Five Year Development Plan of 1964–69. Fifty-two per cent of the necessary resources for implementation of the plan were expected from foreign sources. According to Pratt (1973:20), 'within a matter of months after the production of the plan, development planning as a continuous process ceased to exist in Tanzania'. Lack of resources from abroad was regarded as one of the major reasons behind this breakdown in planning. Said Nyerere (1968:77), 'Our failure to reach many of the goals of the plan was due mainly to our having received a lower level of outside help than we had expected.' Regarding timing, Nyerere noted that 'the newspaper announcements of loans and credit are usually months and sometimes years in advance of agreements on the detailed project and the actual money comes a long time after that'.

There was a recognition that too much dependence on aid would endanger the country's sovereignty and independence. As president Nyerere noted:

> How can we depend upon gifts, loans and investments from foreign countries without endangering our independence? The English people have a proverb which says: He who pays the piper calls the tune! How can we depend upon foreign governments and companies for the major part of our development without giving to those governments and countries a great part of our freedom to act as we please. The truth is that we cannot.

Also, aid could 'have the effect of weakening or distorting our own efforts' (1968:240–1).

The third factor paramount in Tanzania's perception of aid was the realization that the nation's ability to repay loans was not limitless. 'When we borrow money from other countries it is the Tanzanian who pays it back ... Tanzanians are poor people. To burden the people with big loans, the repayment of which will be beyond their means, is not to help them but to make them suffer' (Nyerere 1968:239–40).

Fourth, aid was approached warily not only because it could never suffice, but also because it diverted attention from the more basic fundamental solutions to the effects of what was seen as a 'monstrous world' (URT 1974:297). Terms of world trade, world financial flows, and the general economic structures were seen as tilted against what was then called the Third World. Consequently, Tanzania and other countries had to fight for fundamental changes in these structures, and supported the demand for the New International Economic Order (NIEO). Relatedly, as Mushi correctly observes, 'aid, both financial and technical, is viewed as a right rather than charity' (Mushi 1981:46). While accepting the handover of the Kibaha

Education Centre from the Nordic countries in 1970, Nyerere spoke of 'a practical recognition that the wealthier nations of the world have a responsibility to contribute to the development of the poorer nations' (Nyerere 1974:143).

One perception, though latent in earlier phases, has become very manifest during the latest one (1986–96). It views donors as unrealistic, if not ignorant, in their demands and impatience, excessively intrusive in the country's internal affairs, hypocritical in their failure to acknowledge their role in earlier policy failures, constantly shifting conditionality, concealing vital information, not owning up to structural factors in their own countries behind their reduction in aid to Tanzania, and predisposed to circumvent the governmental system by creating project 'islands' of their own (Helleiner *et al.* 1995:2).

Tanzania had very distinct perceptions of the three donor agencies and their countries whose strategy and behaviour is the major focus of this study. Interviews with several former and current senior government officials indicate that the PRC was perceived as a 'comrade in arms'. One senior official added that the relationship between China and Tanzania was driven by 'solidarity and comradeship'. China in many ways constituted the ideal donor from the Tanzanian perspective. It fully accepted the principles of 'our equal dignity and humanity' (Nyerere 1974:41). China was perceived to be on the correct side in international affairs. It identified itself, particularly during the years of Mao Zedong, as belonging to the Third World, denounced imperialism, and embraced fully the anti-colonial struggles then raging in Southern Africa.

The perceptions of China, however, went further; its own struggle embodied something that was lofty, novel and attractive to a newly independent nation committed to self-reliance. 'Tanzania is enriched by this friendship', said Nyerere on his second visit to China in three years in 1968 (Nyerere 1974:40). Nyerere found the ideas and example of the Chinese leadership appealing, particularly their spiritual strength, the simplicity of their technology, and their unassuming method of leadership:

> In February I went to … China, and there I learned one very important thing … They are a frugal people, they husband their resources very carefully indeed, and only spend money on things which are absolutely essential … There are hardly any private cars in China, people go to work by bus or on bicycles … This attitude we have to adopt too. (Nyerere 1974:332)

Tanzania also sought to help champion China's cause and help it out of its isolation imposed by the USA and also in part by the Soviet Union. This was epitomized in the exclusion of China from the United Nations (UN). 'This great people's Republic must be able to join this world organization', Nyerere emphasized time and time again (Nyerere 1974:325).

Tanzania's perceptions of America were almost the exact opposite of the above. The USA had not had colonies in Africa, and had at times supported struggles for independence. It was therefore in good will that President Nyerere visited America in July 1963 and developed good relations with President John F. Kennedy. However, America being a superpower and leading member of the North Atlantic Treaty Organization (whose fellow-member, Portugal, was waging wars in Africa) made it difficult to sustain the USA as a friend. America came to be perceived as the leading imperialist power in the world and the main bulwark against peoples' liberation and, through its leadership of an inequitable international, economic order, as an impediment to Tanzania's economic development. Thus, if the Chinese system was envied because of the strength of its spirit, the American system of capitalism came to be despised because of its meanness, its government's propensity to push other countries around, to interfere in other countries' international affairs, and to use aid as a tool of foreign policy. This perception has since mellowed, but the relations with the USA have never reached the level of cordiality.

Sweden was perceived as driven not by ideological or solidarity pressures but by 'humanitarian' factors. Sweden (together with other Nordic countries) was seen as being motivated by a genuine desire to transfer wealth to people in need in order to alleviate poverty. Sweden was admired for 'the internationalism of the majority of the people of Sweden, and especially of its Government' (Nyerere 1974:336). Sweden was not neutral towards the great moral issues of the day: poverty and freedom. It supported 'humanity and justice'. Added Nyerere, 'Swedish people support human equality and oppose imperialism' (1974:336). There was admiration for Olof Palme, Swedish Prime Minister from 1969 to his assassination in 1986, because he had had 'a little trouble' as a result of his stand on issues like Vietnam and human equality. Nyerere spoke fondly of 'our warm feelings towards Sweden' (Nyerere 1974:332). Although the terms of Swedish aid have changed in the 1990s, Tanzania has continued to regard Sweden as its friend.

Drawing on these rhetorical statements, certain elements stand out as particularly important in Tanzania's perception of aid and donors: (1) diversifying the aid flow in order to avoid dependency on any one source and to keep non-aligned; (2) searching for aid without strings in order to safeguard the country's independence and sovereignty; (3) searching for financial resources free of interest, or those granted on very liberal terms, including low interest rates (so-called soft terms); (4) seeking aid that supplemented and encouraged people's own efforts rather than substituting or subverting them; (5) preferring aid that supported projects and programmes deemed important by the Tanzanian state and often included in the long term and short term plans; and (6) jealously guarding its MAC from donor and aid penetration and influence.

Interestingly, these elements were never consolidated into a coherent official strategy. According to Mushi (1981), 'negotiators for aid had no firm guidelines, save for the well-known but vague cautions that they should look for low-interest rate loans, avoid loan or grants with many strings, and approach donors who are interested in planned projects'. A top bureaucrat concurs: 'Tanzania has never had an aid strategy.' The broad ideological guidelines were never systematized into a policy and concretized into a strategy.

EXPERIENCES WITH DONORS

Various studies by both Tanzanian and non-Tanzanian scholars periodize the country's experiences with aid and donors differently. Mushi (1982) divides the years since independence into three phases: 1961–66, which he calls the politics of unity internally and politics of non-alignment externally; the 1967–71 Mwongozo phase; and the post-1971 phase, which he calls consolidation internally and collective self-reliance in external relations. Unlike Mushi, the majority of studies base their periodization on the quantitative flows of aid. They thus identify periods when aid flows were high (for example, from 1975 to the 1980s and 1986 until now), and periods of low aid flows (for example, the period between 1980 and 1985). Two recent student dissertations – Killian (1994) and Kahendaguza (1995) – as well as Lipumba (1994) and Crouch (1987), all belong to this category.

Yet the above periodizations beg many questions. Even if the criteria were Tanzanian government positions and donor responses, a further question is: what enabled Tanzania to stake out positions and hold on to them stubbornly in one period and give up on them completely in another? Relatedly, why did donors succeed in forcing Tanzania to conform to their conditionalities in the 1980s, when they had failed to do so in the 1960s and early 1970s? The key to the above riddle is Tanzania's capacity to produce and reproduce its MAC in a sustainable fashion.

This study divides the period under study into three phases. The first is the phase of surplus and proud defiance, 1961–78; the second, the phase of deficits, crisis and desperation, 1979–85; and the third, the phase of acquiescence and dependency, 1986–95.

Surplus and Proud Defiance, 1961–78

The first period was the time when the country managed to sustain its MAC successfully. As can be seen in Table 2.1, the country had an overall budget surplus until 1978–79 when a deficit appeared, which has persisted ever since. During this phase also recurrent revenue was more than adequate to cover recurrent expenditure. Moreover, the Government was able to contribute to the development budget in a meaningful way. The state managed to fund its organizational core without recourse to external sources, and proudly staked out and implemented its own positions during this phase. The country could defy donors and still manage to pay its civil servants a living wage, pay for essential imports, and service key infrastructure. This became impossible in subsequent phases resulting in serious consequences, as will be shown below. During this phase, the state defined several needs in society as core needs, especially poverty, health and education, and set out to treat these and their eradication in a consistent fashion. Donors were then invited to participate in these activities. China chose to engage in poverty eradication, Sweden opted for health and education, while the USA chose a mixture of projects covering several sectors, as will be shown in subsequent chapters. Also during this period, aid was used almost exclusively to fund the development budget. A recurrent deficit was covered by recourse to domestic borrowing. Finally, the amounts of aid were low though increasing gradually, especially in the 1970s when they reached US$424 million in 1978 (as shown in Table 2.2). The debt service burden was also low, reaching US$38.2 million in 1978 (as shown in Table 2.3).

This was a phase of proud defiance. It began with Tanzania gaining independence from the UK on 9 December 1961 and ended with Tanzania's invasion of Uganda to remove the brutal government of Idi Amin in late 1978. In the intervening years, the country had tussles with West Germany over the representation of East Germany in 1964 (as already noted) and with Great Britain over South African membership of the Commonwealth in 1961, raising objections because of its policy of apartheid. In June 1965 Tanzania led a number of African countries in breaking off diplomatic relations with Britain when the latter failed to take decisive action against the regime of Ian Smith which had made a Unilateral Declaration of Independence in Rhodesia (now Zimbabwe). The two countries also clashed in 1968 over pension payments to former

Table 2.1 Trend of expenditure (Million Shillings)

	1963/64	*1967/68*	*1975/76*	*1978/79*	*1982/83*	*1986/87*	*1987/88*	*1988/89*	*1989/90*
A. Recurrent revenue	718	1130	3946	6812	13135	34500	56530	71789	95113
B. Recurrent expenditure	709	1106	3716	8295	14872	39310	61765	92262	118553
surplus (A − B)	8.7	21.4	230.3	(1483)	(1737)	(4810)	(5235)	(20473)	(23440)
C. Development revenue	145	344	2253	4741	5146	11833	15091	15747	22696
Local sources	(94)	(260)	(1222)	(2313)	3294	6378	8467	6153	11200
Foreign sources	(51)	(84)	(131)	(2427)	1852	5455	6624	9593	11496
D. Development expenditure	145	344	(2253)	(4741)	5146	11832	15091	15747	22696
Total expenditure (B + D)	854	1452	5969	13036	20017	51142	76856	108009	141249
Total revenue (A + C)	863	1474	6199	11553	18261	46333	71621	87537	117809
Overall deficit/surplus (A − (B + D)	8.7	21.4	230	(1483)	(1737)	(4809)	(5235)	(20473)	(23440)
% of Development expenditure (D/(B + D) × 100	17.0	23.7	37.7	36.0	25.7	23	20	14.6	16.1

Note: Figures in brackets represent deficits.
Source: Statistics from the Review of the important Economic Indicators for the Period 1961–1987, Appendix to the second five year Union Development Plan 1988/1989–1992/1993.

Table 2.2 Foreign aid disbursements to Tanzania, 1970–92 (million US$)

Year	*ODA net loans**	*Total grants*	*Total aid gross*	*Grants as % of total*	*Technical cooperation grants (A)*	*Foreign aid net of (A)*	*(A) as % of total*
1970	24	28	51	54	21	30	42
1971	32	31	62	49	24	39	38
1972	17	45	61	73	35	26	57
1973	35	65	100	65	41	59	41
1974	63	99	163	61	48	115	29
1975	114	188	302	62	60	242	20
1976	71	196	267	73	77	190	29
1977	125	215	340	63	80	260	24
1978	−33	457	424	108	106	318	25
1979	101	487	588	83	138	450	24
1980	9	658	666	99	173	494	26
1981	193	509	702	73	176	526	26
1982	194	490	684	72	181	503	27
1983	164	430	594	72	174	420	29
1984	128	430	558	77	139	419	25
1985	79	408	487	84	136	351	28
1986	102	578	680	85	260	420	38
1987	71	811	882	92	250	632	28
1988	69	906	975	93	285	690	29
1989	180	738	918	n.a.	202	n.a.	n.a.
1990	288	887	1175		209		
1991	170	914	1084		209		
1992	413	933	1346		233		

n.a. = not available.
*Concessional loans less principal repayments.
Source: OECD Development Cooperation annual DAC figures 1970–93 in Lipumba (1994).

colonial officials in Tanganyika who were British citizens, and over the nationalization of commercial real estate in 1971.

The USA also had its share of fights with the Tanzania Government, 'once when we believed it to be involved in a plot against us, and again when two of its officials misbehaved and were asked to leave Tanzania' (Nyerere 1966:230). Apart from these tussles Tanzania was generally in a state of cold confrontation with Western powers led by the USA and Great Britain over the Congo Crisis, Vietnam, and the liberation of South Africa and the Portuguese colonies. Nyerere described Tanzania's relationship with the USA as one of 'uncooperative coldness' (1981:73). In these years

Table 2.3 Total debt service (million US$)

Year	*Total*	*Official*	*Private*	*Official/total (%)*	*Private/total (%)*
1974	23.4	12.2	11.2	52.1	47.9
1976	27.7	18.0	9.7	64.9	35.1
1978	38.2	27.1	11.0	70.9	29.1
1979	39.1	34.3	4.8	87.7	12.3
1980	51.2	43.5	7.7	84.9	14.1
1981	47.3	41.9	5.4	88.6	11.4
1982	53.4	44.9	8.5	84.1	15.9
1983	77.8	56.8	21.0	73.0	27.0
1985	89.0	60.0	4.0	93.8	6.2
1986	86.0	63.0	3.0	95.5	0.5
1987	95.0	75.0	0.0	100.0	0.0
1988	91.0	69.0	0.0	100.0	0.0
1989	73.0	66.0	0.0	100.0	0.0
1990	103.0	94.0	0.0	100.0	0.0

Source: Kilindo (1993).

Tanzania prevailed in all these conflicts by consistently sticking to her position even if it meant the loss of aid.

Relations with the USA were complicated also by such factors as the visit by Zhou Enlai, China's Premier, to Tanzania in 1965 and the Arusha Declaration, the socialist blueprint, in 1967, and also by its support for other Western governments that Tanzania opposed. For example, the invasion of Guinea in 1970 by mercenaries supported by Portugal, a member of NATO, coupled with the overthrow of Uganda's President Obote in 1971, an action supported by the UK, drove relations to a sour point. Where the Arusha Declaration had denigrated aid, Mwongozo, another major policy statement made in 1971 in the wake of the above developments, denounced imperialism. 'For Tanzania it must be understood that the imperialist enemies we are confronting are British imperialism, Portuguese colonialism, the racism and apartheid of South Africa and Rhodesia' (Mwongozo 1971). The USA was not mentioned specifically but its diplomats could not have missed the point.

The USA's assistance to Tanzania dates back to the years before independence. Chapter 3 records the highs and lows of American aid to Tanzania, especially through USAID. Between 1963 and 1966, $39.7 million were obtained for aid project and programme assistance. The amount declined to $31 million during the period 1967–70, before slightly rising to $32.3 for the period between 1971 and 1974. A high point of $40.2 million was reached in 1975 before the level of inflow declined again in subsequent years. Between 1963 and 1984 a total of $363 million was obtained from the USA. This is quite a considerable amount given the tense relations between the two countries for much of the time.

American aid to Tanzania accounted for 3 per cent of total net receipts in 1963 and multiplied to more than 55 per cent by 1969. A substantial share of American aid was received during the years 1967, 1968 and 1969, averaging 54.6 per cent of total net receipts. This high percentage reflects payments for building the main highway to Zambia. Thereafter there was a decline to 34.5 per cent in 1970 and then to 12 per cent in 1972. After picking up to 24 per cent in 1975, a continuous downward trend in the USA's share was observed between 1975 and 1982 which recorded a less than 10 per cent share. During the period 1989 and 1993, the USA's share of total bilateral aid has not exceeded 5 per cent.

US technical cooperation for the years that data is available has hovered between 0.1 to 3.1 per cent of total assistance received from donors. Compared to the figure for Sweden which has ranged above 10 per cent most of the time, the US contribution is meagre.

As Adam *et al.* (1994:15) correctly note in the early years of this phase, the 'UK alone and in some years together with the USA supplied all bilateral aid to Tanzania'. Beginning with the post-Arusha Declaration period though, Sweden emerged as the major bilateral donor except for a few years (Adam *et al.* 1994:15–16), as is shown in Table 2.4.

Recollections of the times and contemporary interviews point to the fact that US aid was (and still is) perceived as politically driven. In the early phase it was driven by the desire to have Tanzania in the Western camp within the context of the Cold War. This involved political support in international fora and the pursuit of economic policies that promoted capitalism. Americans were also seen as calculating and arrogant, if not downright racist.

Aid was not concentrated in any one area, but was dispersed. Money was put into agriculture, infrastructure, education and training, public administration, and industry. It was as if there was a constant search for the most strategic point where the American contribution could have the most effect. Perhaps most importantly, American aid always came across as not being triggered by Tanzania's needs or even demands, but by America's. To paraphrase one interviewee, American aid was driven more by the need to influence, especially in the context of the Cold War. It was widely perceived as heavily ideological, as aimed at the erosion of Tanzanian socialism (interviews). Consequently, there were serious regular disagreements and a fair amount of American aid was forfeited. Tanzania remained

Table 2.4 Summary data: net ODA by main donor (million US$)

	1970s	*1980s*	*1990/1992*	*Total*	*% of total aid*
Bilateral, of which:	1865	5419	2416	9700	74.15
Sweden	422	780	386	1588	12.4
Netherlands	246	607	202	1055	8.07
Germany	252	533	205	990	7.57
Norway	150	566	271	987	7.55
Denmark	194	475	263	932	7.13
UK	102	441	197	740	5.66
Italy	4	486	210	700	5.35
Japan	51	453	171	675	5.16
Canada	177	300	96	573	4.38
Finland	70	291	127	488	3.73
USA	167	174	101	442	3.38
China	n.a.	n.a.	80		
Multilateral:	476	1632	1159	3267	24.98
IDA	175	736	584	1495	11.40
UN	129	308	156	593	4.43
EC	82	342	195	619	4.76
OPEC	11	97	4	112	0.86
Total	2352	7148	3579	13079	100

n.a. = not available.
OPEC = Organization of Petroleum Exporting Countries.

peripheral to American interests, just as American aid remained peripheral to Tanzania's political economy. It was always regarded with suspicion. American personnel were often seen as Central Intelligence Agency (CIA) men and women, a perception that grew stronger as Dar es Salaam became a haven of liberation movements, leftist scholars, and radicalism (Saul 1973).

There were structural barriers to easy and friendly relations between America and Tanzania. They were always on opposite sides on the most divisive issues of the day: Vietnam, African liberation, racism and apartheid in South Africa, the NIEO, the liberation of Palestine, and the admission of the PRC to the UN. Relatedly, they were divided by ideologies. The USA was the flag bearer of capitalism while Tanzania denounced capitalism as 'animalism' *(unyama).*

Sweden and the other Nordic countries were appreciated for their genuine desire to alleviate poverty and to transfer wealth to the countries of the South. This commitment to Third World development was evident in the substantial amounts of aid they committed, the sectors in which they engaged (water, health, education), and the way they provided support through programme assistance, most of which belonged to the core challenges identified by the Tanzanian state. The grant element compared to loans was very high. Also the *modus operandi* of Nordic countries, in general, and Sweden, in particular, was appreciated. They took on projects and programmes that were identified as priorities by the recipients. They did not try to micromanage the projects themselves. They showed trust in the Tanzanian government. Above all, the social democratic ideology that held sway in the Nordic countries was seen as having similarities with Tanzania's *Ujamaa*. Close relationships developed between Tanzanians led by President Nyerere, and Swedes led by Premier Tage Erlander, and, later, Olof Palme. Sweden also held the same position as Tanzania on many controversial global issues: non-involvement in the Cold War conflict, support for African liberation, support for populist anti-imperialist struggles (Vietnam, Palestine), and so on. Some Tanzanians feel that the Nordic countries looked to Tanzania for guidance, especially on African issues.

China had also been one of the sources of development assistance since the early 1960s. Among the major projects that benefited from Chinese aid are: the military, a joint shipping line, the Friendship Textile Mill, the Tanzania–Zambia Railway (TAZARA), Ubungo Farm Implements Ltd (UFI), Mang'ula Mechanical & Machine Tools Company Ltd, Mbarali and Ruvu rice farms, and numerous extension stations.

Chinese aid, like that of Sweden, was very much appreciated, but for different reasons. Aid relations with China generally were cast in the light of international politics. While the opening to China was seen as a sign that 'Tanzania has gone communist' by the Western countries or organizations with which Tanzania was locked in ideological and political struggles, the Chinese agreement to finance and build the TAZARA project after it had been branded unviable by Western powers was seen as a great act of solidarity. Inaugurating construction of the railway, Nyerere was very clear: 'We are extremely grateful to the Chinese People's Republic for their [*sic*] help in railway project; we are grateful for the spirit in which the offer of assistance was made, and for the manner in which this assistance is given' (Nyerere 1974:235). The Chinese provided an interest-free loan to build the railway and purchase rolling stock; there was a fifteen-year grace period, and payment was staged over 30 years. Also, it was not conditional: 'the Chinese people have not asked us to become communists in order to qualify for this loan … they have never at any point suggested that we should change any of our policies – internal or external' (Nyerere 1974:235).

The Chinese also showed maximum commitment to, and trust in, Tanzania. They funded what was requested. Apart from the railway most other projects were in line with Tanzania's core wishes and long-term plans. Tanzania's major socio-economic objective was to build a socialist self-reliant economy with enough backward and forward linkages to be capable of generating self-sustained growth. Such an economy, it was argued, had to be based on a capital goods sector organically linked to agriculture (Rweyemamu 1974; Thomas 1975). The UFI and Mang'ula Mechanical & Machine Tools must be seen in this light. The Friendship Textile Mill also fitted very well into these plans.The rice farms were critical in assuring self-sufficiency in food production. A joint shipping line symbolized attempts at liberation from the international economic structures. All the Chinese projects were in areas that were considered critical if Tanzania was to achieve its lofty developmental goals. Chinese involvement in Tanzania's military was also of fundamental importance. The Chinese came in with a military doctrine and organization that was appreciated and fully adopted by Tanzania. The earlier military doctrine, inherited from the British, had led to a mutiny and a humiliating disarming by a British intervention force in 1964 (Nyerere 1967). The newly constituted army became the Tanzania People's Defence Force (TPDF), and recruited trainers from the Chinese People's Liberation Army. TPDF was integrated into the country's overall political structure and organized along populist participation principles under which distinctions in rank and status were minimized. Also, Chinese weaponry was preferred. The SAR 56 (a semi-automatic rifle first manufactured by China in 1956) became the basic assault weapon in the Tanzanian military. The creation of a peoples' Militia after the Uganda coup of 1971 represented a further adoption of the Chinese military doctrine (Masero 1995).

Finally, it needs to be appreciated that chinese aid was a product of the context and era of the 1960s. If its commencement was symbolized by Premier Zhou Enlai's visit in 1965, its internationalist reciprocal nature was played out at the UN in New York in 1971 at the time of China's admission when Tanzania's Permanent Representative, Salim Ahmed Salim, danced with glee on the floors of the UN while the then US Ambassador, George Bush, was addressing the General Assembly. The US government, and especially George Bush, never forgot that dance, and Salim Ahmed Salim paid the price several years later in the 1980s when threat of an American veto denied him the post of UN Secretary General.

In these early years all donors assumed that Tanzania had an effective and even efficient organization to plan, solicit, receive, deploy, monitor and evaluate performance and feedback. Little attention was paid to aid organization and delivery, efficiency, or accountability and operationalization.

The foremost characteristic of Tanzania's aid management in this phase is that it lacked clear guidelines. While it is true, as pointed out above, that aid guidelines called for aid that was untied, enhanced self-reliance and independence, diversified sourcing, and was repayable, these principles or guidelines were never turned into an enforceable policy on aid. There was never a checklist of which conditions an aid package should fulfil before it was accepted. Neither was there an indicative scale of what a project had to score on several constituent elements before it was deemed acceptable. According to a seasoned top government official, Tanzania never had an aid strategy. Consequently, as Mushi (1982:43) noted, the bureaucrats and technocrats were never guided by the policy of socialism and self-reliance, and 'in their efforts to harness external relations ... they concentrated on the usual issue of economic growth'. Lack of aid strategy was related to lack of a comprehensive rational aid organization.

The numerous government institutions and their subsidiaries pursued projects on their own with little coordination at the public enterprise or sectoral ministerial level. While the Loans, Guarantees and Grants Act, 1974 (Act no. 30 of 1974), which was to regulate foreign borrowing and guarantees by government, conferred competence to raise foreign loans on behalf of government to the Minister for Finance, other ministries and organizations also raised loans and only informed the Treasury. With regard to debt service, the same Act charged the Minister to ensure that

> the aggregate of the service cost becoming due and payable in respect of all outstanding foreign loans during that financial year and the four succeeding years does not exceed 15 per cent of the average annual foreign exchange earnings computed on the basis of the annual foreign exchange earnings of the proceeding three financial years. (Kibola 1990:110)

Observing the above requirements became increasingly difficult. The ratio of total debt service to exports of goods and services increased from 4.8 in 1974 to 6.1 in 1978 (Kilindo 1993:208).

To sum up the main features of this phase, it was one in which Tanzania, buoyed by its budgetary self-reliance, projected its autonomy in international relations and diplomacy, including aid. Tanzania was able to discriminate between good and bad aid, and to reject both political conditionality, and tied aid. At the level of operationalization and implementation, however, it fell far short of its lofty aspirations.

Deficits and Dependency 1979–85

If the earlier phase was symbolized by the raising of the Tanzanian flag in Dar es Salaam in 1961 and in Kampala in 1979, there were signs towards the end of the first phase that things were beginning to change for the worse. Starting in 1977, a combination of forces led gradually to a budgetary crisis. These included the collapse of the East African Community in 1977, the war with Amin's Uganda 1978–79, and the second oil price shock of 1979. The chief defining feature of this phase is the fact that it became increasingly difficult for Tanzania to pay for its MAC. Recurrent revenue could no longer cover recurrent expenditure. The overall budget surplus also disappeared. A deficit appeared in 1978–79, as shown in Table 2.1, and persisted throughout this period. Budgetary deficit is one of the key characteristics of this period. It necessitated increased domestic borrowing. Overall domestic credit increased by 31 per cent from 1977 to 1982, which resulted in more inflation and consequently pressure on balance of payments. Even so, the deficit could not be filled and the government had to resort to using aid not only to finance development expenditure, as had been the practice during the first phase, but also to finance part of recurrent expenditure.

The second defining feature of this phase was confrontations with the donors over the role played by the international finance institutions, the IMF and the World Bank. Those organizations had always been seen by Tanzanians as instruments of the major Western powers. Throughout the 1960s and 1970s Tanzania, because of its financial health and strength, had been able to keep them at arm's length. During Robert McNamara's term as President of the World Bank (1968–80), the institution demonstrated a readiness to respond to Tanzania's needs. The amounts of disbursements from the Bank and IDA increased accordingly during these years. Tanzania also continued to draw on the IMF's short-term facility until 1979 when the country needed an extended facility, and approached the Fund for the first time. The IMF insisted on structural adjustment as a condition before extending any loans (Malima, 1986:131; Biermann and Wagao 1986:140–7). President Nyerere disagreed and fired off the first shots in a public quarrel with the IMF and the World Bank in early 1980 when he rhetorically asked who had appointed the IMF to be the International Ministry of Finance. He said he regarded the Fund's attempts to exploit the country's balance of payments difficulties as 'strange and repugnant' (Sobhan 1995:76).

The second phase is characterized by the ascendancy of multilateral aid. Financial assistance from the World Bank and the IMF eventually became a significant part of the total inflow of aid. As can be seen in Table 2.5, the World Bank (IBRD) and IDA aid rose nearly nine fold, from almost $11 million in 1970 to slightly less than $95 million in 1979. While Sweden and Norway continued to provide significant amounts of aid in the early 1980s, the prominence of the World Bank and the IMF went much further

Table 2.5 Gross aid disbursements to Tanzania, 1969–82 (US$ million)

	1969	*1970*	*1971*	*1972*	*1973*	*1974*	*1975*	*1976*	*1977*	*1978*	*1979*	*1980*	*1981*	*1982*
Loans (Total)	19	41	48	99	98	143	232	106	175	148	143	153	176	213
Bilateral	11.7	30	33	80	85	121	164	67	96	70	48	75	68	86
Canada	0.4	0.7	0.7	1.5	5.6	25	19	15	2.5	–	–	–	–	–
China	n.a.	9.7	6.2	59	54	60	75	4.5	15	3.6	3.6	n.a.	n.a.	n.a.
Denmark	1.2	2.2	2	1.4	1.1	9.4	14	11	30	16	5.3	9.6	0.3	0.8
West Germany	0.1	–	2.4	1.2	1.7	8.4	15	4.5	12	33	–	–	–	–
Netherlands	0.1	–	0.6	0.9	3.7	5	11	4.6	8.8	0.8	–	5.8	5.4	5.4
Sweden	5.3	5.6	8.6	12	5.5	2.8	1.7	0.9	–	–	–	–	–	–
UK	0.1	–	–	0.8	–	–	–	–	–	–	–	–	–	–
USA	3	4.7	7	4.6	2	2.8	19	9.5	14	0.1	7.3	8	8	5
Soviet Union	n.a.	1.2	0.3	0.4	0.5	0.4	0.5	–	2.5	–	–	n.a.	n.a.	n.a.
Other (Ii)	1.5	5.9	4.7	3.5	5	3.8	8.5	16	11	16	32	51	54	74
Multilateral	7	11	15	19	13	22	68	39	79	78	95	78	108	128
IBRD	–	1.2	7.2	13	9	8.3	39	10	24	27	33	12	2.8	0.4
IDA	7	9.4	8.1	2.7	3.1	5.9	20	29	40	24	39	35	78	99
IMF Trust Fund	–	–	–	–	–	–	–	–	5.2	16	16	14	0.1	–
Other	–	–	–	2.5	0.5	8.2	7.8	–	11	11	6.7	17	27	29

Grants (Total)	4.7	6.2	6.8	9.8	24	52	128	119	135	214	325	485	332	308
Bilateral	4.3	5.9	6.4	9.6	23	50	104	106	123	192	198	459	295	277
Canada	0.1	0.1	0.7	0.8	0.8	1.6	13	5.2	5.7	26	25	17	25	33.8
Denmark	0.1	0.2	0.1	0.6	2.3	5.2	3.2	6.5	3	10	15	3.6	6.2	7.8
West Germany	–	0.1	–	0.1	–	0.5	1.2	2.6	0.9	–	34	181	26	31
Netherlands	–	–	–	–	–	0.2	1.6	11	24	29	46	62	53	32
Sweden	0.4	0.2	0.5	3.2	11	27	50	46	52	54	70	60	63	63
Norway	0.4	0.9	1.9	1.7	5.4	8	13	7.1	15	25	35	32	31	42
UK	0.1	–	–	–	–	–	4	7	7.5	25	27	54	37	28
USA	3	4	2	3	3	5	14	19	13	10	19	10	10	5
Other (Iii)	0.2	0.4	1.2	0.2	0.5	1	4.2	1.5	1.5	13	27	40	44	35
Multilateral	0.4	0.3	0.4	0.2	0.3	1.5	24	14	12	22	27	26	37	31
EEC	–	–	–	–	–	–	15	5.7	10	20	n.a.	n.a.	n.a.	n.a.
UN	0.4	0.3	0.4	0.2	0.3	1.5	8.8	7.8	1.7	1.4	6.7	n.a.	n.a.	n.a.
Total	23	47	55	109	121	195	360	225	310	362	468	638	508	521

Source: Crouch (1987) with data from OECD, *Geographical Distribution of Financial Flows to Developing Countries, and World Bank Debtor Reporting System.*

than the amounts of money they dispensed. Especially critical was their certificate of approval of how the economy was being run.

The ascendancy of the Fund and the World Bank triggered off almost all the danger signals mentioned in the preceding section of Tanzania's perception of aid. They were seen to be threatening the country's independence and sovereignty. They were charged with interference in the country's internal economic and political policies. These two institutions were seen as pursuing policies which aimed at blunting or even reversing the country's chosen path of *Ujamaa*. Malima notes that 'as one examines the political implications of one IMF condition after another, the argument that the IMF's main preoccupation is with technical recommendations becomes less and less plausible' (Malima 1986:131). In his view, they sought to perpetuate the world economic structures that would lock Tanzania into poverty and weakness forever. Another observer, Reginald Green (1995), notes: 'The President objected both to some elements of the Bank/Fund package proposals and to their neo-liberal rhetoric, as well as more basically to their rather overt attempt to introduce comprehensive external vetting of, rather than advice on, economic and social policy' (Green 1995:84).

In the early years of this phase, aid continued coming and, as can be seen in Table 2.2, aid disbursement during the period rose from $424 million in 1978 to a record $702 million in 1981. Both bilateral and multilateral donors stepped up aid to Tanzania (Sobhan 1995:77). The World Bank became Tanzania's largest donor in 1982 for the first and last time in the country's history, disbursing $98 million through IDA. The Bank, however, was also undergoing a transition under Mr Clausen, who was replacing Robert McNamara as president. Conditional lending would soon gain ascendancy, egged on by the USA's newly-elected President, Ronald Reagan.

Tanzania desperately looked for alternatives. A team of independent advisers led by Ernst. Michanek, former head of the Swedish aid agency, Sida, was appointed and submitted a report in April 1982 with recommendations that did not differ greatly from the IMF/World Bank position. The Government launched its own National Economic Survival Programme which centred on austerity and export promotion, but it did not work. This was followed by a home-grown SAP in 1981–85, which also came to naught because of failure to secure foreign assistance.

A third distinguishing feature of this phase is the fact that the economic, social and political situation was going from bad to worse. Economic decline and macro-economic imbalances continued. Real per capita GDP declined starting in 1981, growth in agriculture averaged only 2 per cent, industrial output fell by 15 per cent per year, and industrial capacity utilization fell to less than 25 per cent. There was a serious deterioration in infrastructure and communication, and serious shortages of consumer goods, which led to severe black marketeering and corruption (Mans 1994:352). The balance of payments situation also got worse. Total aid fell to $487 million by 1985 (Table 2.2). Even Sweden's aid reached its lowest point since 1976 in that year (Sobhan 1995:77).

The positions of USAID, Sida and China varied substantially in these years. USAID pressured Tanzania very heavily to abandon its autonomous policy posture and accept IMF conditionality. As a result, American aid was reduced, beginning in 1979. This trend accelerated under President Reagan, whose administration was seen by Tanzanians as ultra-conservative. Finally, aid reduction gave way to what the AID Mission called a 'winddown'. No new aid commitments mere made beginning in 1982, and soon afterwards, AID began to close down all projects already under implementation.

For Tanzanians American pressure was felt not only through bilateral communication: Tanzanians detected a heavy and obvious American hand in the hardening IMF and World Bank position concerning their conditionalities. This hardening was especially evident after the election of President Reagan. The substantial influence of America in these two bodies was brought to bear to ensure Tanzania's capitulation. Ronald Reagan and Margaret Thatcher, then Prime Minister of the UK, regarded the struggle against state socialist projects and Third World solidarity as a crusade. In this regard, they took every opportunity to denounce and attack development policies like those of Tanzania. Organizations that had sprung up to champion Third World solidarity and the NIEO, such as UNCTAD and the 77 Group, were marginalized. Others, especially UNESCO, were more unfortunate, with these Western powers withdrawing support until they saw a significant turn-around in its policy posture and the departure of its Director General.

China occupied the other extreme. She stuck to her position of non-interference in the internal affairs of other countries and totally refrained from involvement in the ongoing policy debate. Aid continued to flow into its projects. For example, a lot of new machinery was delivered to the Mbarali rice farm in 1984. Although there was a drop in total Chinese aid compared to the earlier phase because of the completion of the huge TAZARA, the UFI and the Friendship Textile Mill, China was seen to sympathize with Tanzania's crisis.

Sweden occupied a middle position. First of all, there was no serious drop-off in the amounts of aid. Indeed it was felt in the early years that Sweden, through continued aid, tacitly supported Tanzania's position against the IMF and World Bank complex. But after the submission of the Michanek report, the Swedish position (together with those of other Nordic countries) hardened and edged closer to that of the IMF and the World Bank. Sweden came to accept that the Tanzanian economic policy was unsustainable and had to be adjusted. The domestic Tanzanian efforts, to which the Swedes had initially pinned their hopes, were not producing any tangible improvements. In 1984, therefore, at a meeting held in Tanzania, Sweden and the other Nordic donors communicated their decision that it was in Tanzania's interest to reach an agreement with the IMF.

Aid management during this phase was not a critical issue. Although a government-initiated study did point out serious weaknesses in budget management (Premchand 1978), aid management did not feature in the intense debates that went on at that time. Indeed, donors closed their eyes and plugged their ears to anything other than the macro-economic policies of the government. There was an attempted *coup d'état* and a politically motivated hijacking of an Air Tanzania aircraft which was flown to London, but these had no discernible impact on donor behaviour. Yet the confusion and lack of coordination continued, and in fact increased. As the economic crisis intensified, inflation soared and real wages declined.

Acquiescence and Dependency, 1986–95

If President Nyerere started off the previous phase in angry defiance, his successor Ali Hassan Mwinyi began the third phase by giving in to pressure from international financiers. He said: 'Tanzania was forced to reach an agreement with the IMF because of the worsening state of the economy' (Tegambwage 1990:11).

In June 1986, the Minister of Finance outlined to Parliament details of an Economic Recovery Programme (ERP) aimed at liberalizing the economy and stabilizing its finances. Since then, a series of agreements between the Tanzanian government, the Fund and the World Bank have further reinforced those economic and financial trends. Western donors have all supported these moves and endorsed them at such occasions as the annual consultations under the auspices of the so-called Paris Club, a forum made up of all the OECD government donors. Although China has not participated in these gatherings, its own aid policy has shifted towards commercialization of the aid relation. The message to Tanzanians, therefore, has been clear: reform or perish.

The third phase was initially characterized by increased aid flows from 1986 to 1993. An especially steep rise occurred in 1992 when aid increased almost 200 per cent. During the ERP alone, Tanzania received almost $6 billion in net foreign assistance. In nominal terms this represented an increase of nearly 60 per cent over net ODA received during the previous crisis period (Mans 1994:391).

Swedish disbursements to Tanzania remained almost constant throughout the late 1980s. They rose sharply during 1989–90 and were followed by a further 33 per cent increase during the following year, as is shown in Table 2.6. Swedish disbursements declined by nearly 7 per cent in 1992 and by a further 33 per cent in 1993. This declining trend has continued. Swedish aid during this phase was concentrated in energy, public administration, women in development and environmental issues. In the 1990s the development of economic infrastructure remained a priority, including energy, telecommunications and transport. Sweden has also been active in the social sector, including education and balance of payment support. The broad aims of the Swedish aid policy have been to promote economic growth and alleviate poverty, rehabilitation and development of social services, promotion of economic reforms and democratization.

USAID resumed activities in Tanzania following the reaching of an agreement with the IMF and World Bank in 1986. Disbursements have fluctuated, peaking in 1988 at US$64.2 million and hitting zero in 1991 during the Gulf War. USAID during this phase concentrated on agricultural transport, family planning, liberalization of markets and politics ('governance'). Training has also received some limited support. The broad aim has been the promotion of economic growth, rural infrastructure, strengthening of the private sector, family planning, and AIDS prevention.

Date on actual financial flows from China are not very complete. For the period spanning 1988–91 a total of around US$12 million were received from China. In spite of Tanzanians failing to manage Chinese-aided projects, the Chinese never abandoned any of the core projects which they had started. Part of the funds mentioned above were used to supply spare parts, working capital, and technical assistance to the Urafiki Textile Mills, Mbarali and Ruvu rice farms, and UFI. Relatedly, though they adopted a commercial orientation in terms of new project ventures, *mutuality of interests* between Tanzania and China became a cornerstone of their engagement. The state still played an important role. According to one interviewee, the Chinese continued to support projects in which the state was involved during a period of time when the Americans were insisting on Tanzania's conversion to market-led strategies. Normally, agreement was engineered at state level, and only details of implementation were worked out at lower levels. Lately efforts have been made to develop relations between the Chinese and Tanzanian private sector partners.

Table 2.6 Summary of external assistance disbursements by donor (in US$ thousands)

Donor	*1990*	*% change 1990–91*	*1991*	*% change 1991–92*	*1992*	*% change 1992–93*	*1993*	*1994 plan*
Multilateral								
UN System								
DTCD		–		–	30	0.0	30	
FAO	2448	–65.3	849	–33	569	90.9	1086	2846
IAEA	303	10.9	336	–22	262	152.3	661	
IBRD	5.454	–	–	–	4674	–		
IDA	131398	38.3	181705	–31	125797	6.4	133829	
IFAD	170	204.1	517	841	4865	–	–	
IMF	203	–	29161	209	89957	–100	463	
ITU		–	2	–	37	113.5	79	
UNCDF		–	505	24.6	629	100	1258	
UNDP	13789	49.4	20604	0.2	20635	0.6	20769	13
UNEP	1227	–	–	–	530	72.6	915	
UNESCO		–	183	–		–	–	
UNFDAC	92	8.7	100	–		–		
UNFPA	4448	42.6	2553	–21	2026	–89.8	207	
UNHCR	326	116.6	706	71.2	1209	28.6	1555	
UNICEF	18808	–14.6	16062	13.8	18275	–27.9	13179	
AFDF	15044				38033	13.3	43105	
CFTC	2	–	239	7.5	257			
EC	34960	139.9	83873	59.3	133605	–10.5	119520	316
EIB	3955	–		–				
OPEC	168	–	7799	–25.0	5848	–60.9	2286	840
Total	54582	68.4	91911	93.4	177743	–7.2	164911	1156

Bilateral								
Australia	2162	−55.9	954	30.2	1242	−19.9	995	
Austria	1860	236.4	6257	−35.5	4033	174.5	11071	
Belgium	10424	13.5	11834	51.4	17917	−7.4	16597	3583
Canada	66451	−51.0	32573	−33.4	21697	37.5	29836	
China	2294	3.0	2362	−4.1	2266			
Czechoslovakia	10082							
Denmark	64408	38.8	89381	−10.9	79642	4.9	83553	
Egypt	527	−0.6	524	47.3	772	24.1	958	
Finland	51000						13574	
France	556	29.3	719	235.3	2411	−81.8	439	
Germany	48538	14.0	55334	−18.6	45053	8.6	48948	1209
Hungary	300	0.0	300	−16.7	250			
India	664	437.2	3567					
Iran	1200							
Ireland	6452	−16.7	1000	−19.4	7479	−39.5	4528	
Italy	44176	−2.9	6262					
Japan	42138	−14.3	37853	68.9	55347	2.0	56446	47
Netherlands	41407	−22.3	32761	29.1	63024	−19.0	51031	
Nigeria		17.9	48813		3475			
Norway	102138	−15.4	86394	−0.4	86078	−4.1	82579	
Poland	32	25.0	40					
Spain	6845	−6.3	6412					
Sweden	94060	33.6	125627	−6.6	117324	−32.6	77906	57
Switzerland	21342	−26.5	15691	71.4	26896	−41.1	15836	
UK	22915	43.7	32918	54.6	50879	−35.5	32804	
USA	31008	−0.3	30930	−0.3	30846	−16.7	25702	
Total	672979	−6.6	628506	−1.9	616631	−10.1	552803	4896

Source: UNDP, Development Cooperation 1993 Report.

Despite the increase in gross aid, budgetary deficits during this phase have continued, and even increased. The overall deficit more than trebled during the 1988–89 fiscal year and increased by a significant amount in the following year, as shown in Table 2.1. The country's total debt also more than doubled, from US$3 billion to $7 billion in 1996. According to Shimwela, this was more than 200 per cent of the GDP, estimated at $3 billion (*The Guardian*, 2 February 1996:3). This was in spite of the rescheduling of $1.6 billion and cancellation of another $152 million of debt by few financiers between 1986 and 1992 (Sobhan 1995:80). It is important for our argument to note that it continued to be difficult for the country to underwrite its MAC. Recurrent deficit as a percentage of recurrent expenditure doubled from 10 per cent in 1985 to 22.5 per cent in 1989. Donors were now financing not only part of development expenditure, as had been the case in the first phase, but they were effectively contributing to the recurrent budget as well. According to Sobhan (1995:23), throughout the 1990s around 50 per cent or more of aid was being diverted to recurrent expenditure. Also, aid has been funding almost 50 per cent of development expenditure throughout this period. The development budget is now entirely hostage to the preferences of Tanzania's donors (Sobhan 1995:56). The numerous 'agreements' reached during this phase between Tanzania and the donors, and the increasing conditionalities, must be seen from this perspective. An important distinguishing feature of this phase is the institutionalization of discourse with donors led by the Fund and the World Bank over economic and social policy, and later politics. As Green (1995:102) puts it, after 1980 'The Fund and Bank were rapidly building up gatekeeper and coordinator roles so that they significantly influenced all official transfers not just their own.' This has been a phase characterized by donor ascendancy and IMF/World Bank leadership in aid management. In this function the IMF has coordinated overall balance of payment support while the World Bank has coordinated sectoral support. Benchmarks and schedules of implementation have been prepared and included in the policy framework paper originating in Washington that recommends how harsh reforms will be.

Apart from controlling the design of reform, the IMF/World Bank complex also controls the evaluation of progress. According to Sobhan (1995:100), 'The Bank defines the methodology as well as selects and interpret the facts which determine the evaluation of performance. The Bank thus performs the task of both advocate and judge.' Sobhan concludes that 'every major policy initiative put in place in Tanzania in recent years appears to have originated out of initiatives of the World Bank and IMF' (1995:128). Also, according to the same author, their 'good housekeeping seal of merit' is considered a necessary pre-condition by all other bilateral donors. Their position has been strengthened by their monopoly over documentation prepared for the aid consultative meetings (1995:98).

Ultimately the IMF/World Bank dominance has emanated from lending, but mostly from their intellectual power. The World Bank has confined Tanzania's aid consortium by dint of its intellectual authority as the apostle of market-driven reforms. Western bilateral donors, including USAID and Sida, not only have accepted as legitimate the prescription of policy solutions to Tanzania and imposed them through conditionalities, but they also have acquiesced to the leadership of IMF/World Bank complex in this regard. Some (such as Germany) have gone further and legislated that formal agreement with IMF over reforms is a *sine qua non* for commitment of aid. Most bilateral donors have not attempted to develop any alternative policy packages.

The conditionalities imposed by the Fund and the Bank, as well as individual donor countries, have been many and occurred on an accelerating scale in the mid-1990s. The reasons have been a combination of perceived wrong policies or actual mismanagement by the Tanzanian government. Incidents include the following:

1. The delay of the consultative Group meeting in 1989 until the government adopted a more realistic exchange rate.
2. Withholding of the second tranche of the two World Bank sector adjustment credits in 1990–91 until policy conditions were met.
3. Withholding funding for the Open General Licence (OGL) in 1992 until there was improvement in fund accountability (Mans 1994:392).
4. Suspension by Sweden and Norway in late 1994 of disbursements of NKR100 million and SEK90 million respectively, earmarked for balance of payments support until the Government improved its tax collection. A main reason was the discovery by an audit of illegal import exemptions being issued to private traders. Other donors followed suit, affecting aid amounting to US$1.1 billion. A planned Consultative Group meeting in Paris was postponed. Plans for an ESAF programme with IMF and a World Bank structural adjustment credit (already agreed) 'was put on hold' (Helleiner *et al.* 1995:1).
5. Pressure by donor governments also in late 1994 to remove the Minister of Finance on grave suspicion of having issued illegal exemptions to gain personal rewards (*Daily News*, 19 November 1994).
6. Strong conditions issued by donor governments at a Consultative Group meeting in Paris in February 1995 to deal with tax exemptions

and evasions, establishment of macro-economic stability, and acceleration of structural reforms as pre-conditions for new aid commitments.

7. A decision by Germany in April 1995 to block DM70 million following failure to conclude Enhanced Structural Adjustment Facility (ESAF II) talks with the IMF.
8. A threat by donors in May 1995 to abandon projects in Mbeya region if they were not assured of their safety.
9. A decision in May 1995 by the US State Department to slash US$17 million in scheduled aid to Tanzania because of failure to liberalize the insurance industry.
10. A threat by the World Bank in May 1995 to withdraw a credit facility of $200 million if the Railway Corporation did not close down feeder railway lines which the World Bank considered unprofitable.
11. A decision by donors led by Denmark in May 1995 to impose election conditionalities.

From the Tanzanian perspective, donors fell victim to the familiar problems of the corruption of absolute power. First, they insisted on policies whose correctness was not proven and whose long-term impact was uncertain. According to Mans (1994:357), an IMF official then stationed in Tanzania, donors concentrated on import liberalization rather than export promotion; as a result local industry was put at a disadvantage compared to imports. Also, their policies 'favored trading over direct production activities including exporting', and the OGL operated for six years without an effective management and accounting system. Second, donor behaviour was seen as lacking forthrightness: donors' claims, for example, that conformity with their conditionalities was the critical factor in determining levels of aid was seen as lacking in truth. Tanzanians knew that in actual fact donors faced domestic pressure in their own countries to balance their budgets and reduce public expenditures, including aid. The donors also faced the pressure of new demands for support from important 'new pastures' in Eastern Europe and South Africa. Aid to regions of the world less vital to the Western powers was therefore bound to decline.

Another case in point is the reluctance to accept responsibility for earlier projects and programmes that had failed. Bilateral donors tended to attribute all responsibility for failure to Tanzania, even where historical facts proved otherwise. Admissions such as the following have been rare. A World Bank study admitted that 'there are countless examples of badly chosen and poorly designed public investments, including some in which the World Bank has participated'. A 1987 evaluation revealed that half of the completed rural development projects financed by the World Bank in Africa had failed (Pasfitt 1990:27).

The point needs elaboration. Tanzanians involved in the aid business feel that most bilateral donors lack transparency and openness. They disclose as little information as they can. Bilateral donors have their own interests, which they pursue relentlessly. Not all aid to development expenditure can be shown in Tanzanian government books because only 50 to 60 per cent is ever received. It also takes significantly long periods of time to materialize, even after commitments are made. Technical assistance is another mysterious arena. The amounts paid to Western experts is seldom disclosed to recipient countries, and less than 20 per cent of technical assistance funds disbursed by donor governments actually end up in Tanzania. Lack of transparency was also evident in the concealment of information from recipient countries, incomplete records of direct donor disbursements to certain projects, and donor operations of special offshore accounts for projects (interviews).

Finally, there was always a contradiction between donor words (intent) and actual behaviour. Helleiner and his colleagues note that donors want recipient governments to assume more ownership of donor programmes but at the same time resist recipient government pressure to do so. They quote a donor official as saying, 'we have *pressured* them to accept ownership of ...' (emphasis added). Another is quoted as having stated: 'we want them to take ownership but of course they must do what we want. If not they should get their money elsewhere' (Helleiner *et al.* 1995:12). A similar contradictory attitude was manifest in the donors' propensity to invoke sanctions when Tanzania failed to fulfil a conditionality, whilst they (for example, the World Bank) routinely renege on agreements and unilaterally introduce new conditions (Helleiner *et al.* 1995:12). In 1995, donors were said to have provided only one-quarter of what was promised to finance Tanzania's parliamentary and presidential elections that year.

TANZANIA'S IMPACT ON DONORS AND DONOR IMPACT ON TANZANIA

The impact of aid and donors on Tanzania is pervasive and fundamental. On a positive note , the vast amounts of money, technologies and personnel have had an undeniable impact on production, commerce, communication and transportation, agriculture, education, health, and public administration, to mention but a few sectors. Aid kept the government open and functioning when the going got tough, starting in the second phase and continuing to the present day. But it is the negative impact that stands out. Aid contributed to an overexpansion of the state and its functions, thus making its means of administration and coertion unsustainable.

Unable to sustain and reproduce its own MAC, the Tanzanian government has been made to eat its own words, to bend, fall on its knees and beg. The Helleiner study cites one donor official saying (tongue in cheek) 'they seem tired. That fight of earlier years is gone' (1995:26). Most commentators seem to agree that the leadership lacks a unifying and illuminating vision (Mukandala 1995).Tanzanian political leaders have failed to generate their own policy alternatives. They are buried in piles of donor demands and conditionalities, trying to salvage whatever pride they can by passively resisting some of the most radical outside initiatives, such as civil service reforms, through delays. Donors, recognizing this fact, have recently been lamenting the lack of 'political commitment' (NORAD 1995).

The above situation has also led to the pre-emption of Tanzania's key policy institutions. While African and Africanist political scientists deplore the domination of the executive over other branches of government in Africa, the executive has at times been subordinated to donors. The December 1994 government reshuffle in Tanzania was clearly at the behest of donors. Furthermore, Parliament has also been reduced to a rubber-stamping function as far as economic policy is concerned. The now perennial underbudgeting which inevitably leads to mid-year mini-budgets is a result of wishing to present a budget frame that is acceptable to the IMF/World Bank even if it is totally unrealistic (Helleiner *et al.* 1995:31). More seriously, instances have been recorded where the World Bank presented budget estimates to the Consultative Group meetings in Paris which showed a surplus and then presented different figures to Parliament in Dar es Salaam which showed a deficit, whilst the Tanzania delegation, which was present throughout, kept quiet. The usurpation of power and the resulting confusion were obvious at the meeting in Paris in February 1995 (Helleiner *et al.* 1995:31).

The pre-emption of Tanzanian institutions was also plain during the run-up to and during the October 1995 presidential and parliamentary elections. Several key demands by the opposition were ignored by the ruling party and government until they were backed by donors. The call for vote counting at polling stations was a non-starter until donors made it their condition. The National Electoral Commission decided to invite representatives of donor governments and international organizations (such as the UN, Organization of African Unity and the Commonwealth Secretariat) as observers after the government had relented under donor pressure.

Even then, foreign invitees of Tazanian NGOs – churches, universities and so on – were excluded. They were deemed unimportant finally when a crisis developed during the vote counting in Zanzibar. On election day in Dar es Salaam, there was constant dialogue between donors and the respective electoral commissions and government. Calls for dialogue from opposition parties went unheeded. A group of donors in fact became a semi-permanent body continuously monitoring events, pressuring government. There was no national dialogue. Aid and donors now threaten 'Tanzania's independence and its freedom to determine its own policies' to use the very words of President Nyerere (1966:2) quoted at the beginning of this chapter. Self-reliance, in the material but also intellectual sense (that is, ability to conceive and chart policy and strategy), has grown ever distant.

A good starting point in reversing the above trend may be to address the issue of the Tanzanian state's sustainability of its MAC. The latter should address itself to the task of maintaining a MAC that it can fund on its own. Only then can it start to recover some of its lost self-confidence and freedom of action. Donors can help in this process by enabling the government to reduce its work force. Credible hand-shake packages would attract many to retire, who may then join the private sector. Such a move would leave the government with fewer employees which it could pay well from its own coffers. For donors, this would be self-sustaining and productive aid. A process in this direction stalled during the years of the Mwinyi government but was restarted after President Mkapa was elected in 1995.

Finally, it is important to address the less obvious issue of Tanzania's impact on donors. Tanzania is likely to have influenced donors in three ways. First, donors like China have benefited from Tanzania's support in international forums. Reference has already been made to Tanzania's important role in China's fight to secure a seat at the UN. Second, Tanzania provided well-meaning donors with a prime recipient environment at least until the 1980s, because in those days the country was relatively free from corruption and mismanagement. This made it easier for aid agencies to justify expenditures and expanded budgets.

The third and most important impact of Tanzania on the 'aid industry' and donors consists of the country's intellectual leadership. If the World Bank and IMF now lead the donor pack, Tanzania, led by President Julius Nyerere, was a leader of the developing nations in the 1960s and 1970s. Tanzania's *Ujamaa* became a model that informed many debates on aid. Tanzanians played very prominent roles in two international commissions on international development. Minister Amir Jamal was a member of the

Brandt Commission in the 1970s, and Professor Justinian Rweyemamu served on the Secretariat. Subsequently, upon his retirement from the Presidency, Julius Nyerere chaired the South Commission in the late 1980s. Furthermore, Tanzania was at the forefront of the movement for an NIEO, and indeed hosted the Group 77 meeting of all the underdeveloped countries in Arusha in 1979.

CONCLUSION

This chapter has tried to show that Tanzania's early firm stand against aid conditionality and its success in resisting pressure to change was not only a result of the country's moral position, but most importantly a consequence of its healthy budgetary situation. Surpluses in state revenues enabled the state to produce and reproduce its means of administration and coercion. Ironically the firmly-held principled positions on aid and other issues of development and liberation attracted rather than repelled aid. Part of these massive inflows of aid funded the expansion of the state's MAC. This expansion, coupled with further pressures on state revenues arising from exogenous factors, gradually made it difficult for the state to pay for its MAC. This triggered struggles with donors over policy which Tanzania could not win, given its weakened position because of the budgetary deficits.

The chapter has also shown that aid was not guided by an explicit rational strategy, and its management was rarely efficient and effective. This in a way contributed to its limited impact on productive activities and the non-sustainability of many functions and activities that were funded. An irony is that while China and Sweden were for a long time Tanzania's favourite donors, the country still ended up following the policy prescriptions and directions of the USA, with whom it has had mostly cool relations. Finally, it has been argued that Tanzania has to restore its autonomy if it is to deal effectively with the poverty which afflicts the country. This restoration depends on recovering the ability to pay for its core MAC. Donors can help by financing the downsizing of this state apparatus to an affordable level.

References

Adam, C., A. Bigsten, P. Collier, E. Julin and S. O'Connell (1994) *Evaluation of Swedish Development Cooperation with Tanzania.* Stockholm: SASDA.

Biermann, W. and J. Wagao (1986) 'The IMF and Tanzania – a solution to the Crisis?', in P. Lawrence (ed.), *World Recession and the Food Crisis in Africa.* London: James Currey.
Crouch, C. (1987) *Western Response to Tanzanian Socialism and Self Reliance 1967–1983.* Avebury.
Green, R.H. (1995) 'Vision of Human Centered Development: A Study in Moral Economy', in C. Legum and G. Mmari (eds), *Mwalimu The Influence of Nyerere.* London, Dar es Salaam and Trenton, USA: Britain Tanzania Society, James Currey, Mkuki na Nyota, and Africa World Press.
Helleiner, G.K. *et al.* (1995) 'Report of the group of independent advisers on development cooperation issues between Tanzania and its aid donors' (mimeo).
Kahendaguza, R. (1995) 'The Unpredictability of Aid: Tanzania's Experience from Independence to the 1990s'. BA, dissertation, Department of Political Science, University of Dar es Salaam.
Kibola, H.S. (1990) 'The Debt Problem in Tanzania: Some Issues and Prospects', in H. Othman and E. Maganya (eds), *Tanzania's Debt Problem and the World Economy.* Dar es Salaam: Institute of Development Studies.
Kilindo, A.A.L. (1993) 'Budget performance and Foreign Indebtedness in Tanzania', in M.S.D. Bagachwa and A. Mbelle (eds), *Economic Policy under a Multiparty System in Tanzania.* Dar es Salaam: Dar es Salaam University Press.
Killian, B. (1994) 'Factors Informing Changes in Tanzania's Foreign Policy 1980–1990s', University of Dar es Salaam, MA Thesis, Unpublished.
Lipumba, N. (1994) 'Foreign aid and economic development', in G. Strom (ed.), *Change in Tanzania 1980–1994.* Stockholm: Sida.
Malima, K. (1986) 'The IMF and World Bank Conditionality: The Tanzania Case', in P. Lawrence (ed.), *World Recession and the Food Crisis in Africa.* London: James Currey.
Mans, D. (1994) 'Tanzania: Resolute Action', in I. Husain Farugee, *Adjustment in Africa Lessons from Country Case Studies.* Washington, DC: The World Bank.
Masero, (1995) 'The Military and Political Pluralism in Tanzania'. University of Dar es Salaam, MA Dissertation.
Mouzelis, N. (1990) *Post-Marxist Alternatives.* London: Macmillan.
Msabaha, I. (1995) 'Contribution to International Relations', in C. Legum and G. Mmari (eds), *Mwalimu: The Influence of Nyerere.* London, Dar es Salaam and Trenton, USA: Britain Tanzania Society, James Currey, Mkuki na Nyota, and Africa World Press.
Mukandala, R. (1995) 'Ideological Challenges of the Transition to Pluralism', in *REDET Reflections on the Transition to Democracy in Tanzania.* Dar es Salaam: Dar es Salaam University Press.
Mushi, S.S. (1981) 'The Making of Foreign Policy in Tanzania', in K. Mathews and S.S. Mushi (eds), *Foreign Policy of Tanzania 1961–1981: A Reader.* Dar es Salaam: Tanzania Publishing House.
Mushi, S.S. (1982) 'Aid and Development: An Overveiw of Tanzania's Experience', in S.S. Mushi and H. Kjekshus (eds), *Aid and Development: Some Tanzanian Experience.* Oslo: Norwegian Institute of International Affairs.
Mushi, S.S. and K. Mathews (eds) (1981) *Foreign Policy of Tanzania 1961–1981: A Reader.* Dar es Salaam: Tanzania Publishing House.
Niblock, T.C. (1972) 'Tanzanian Foreign Policy: An Analysis', *African Review,* Vol. 1, No. 2.

Niblock, T.C. (1981) 'Tanzanian Foreign Policy: An Analysis', in K. Mathews and S.S. Mushi (eds), *Foreign Policy of Tanzania 1961–1981: A Reader*. Dar es Salaam: Tanzania Publishing House.

NORAD (1995) *Civil Service Reform in Tanzania*. Oslo, Norway.

Nyerere, J. (1966) *Principles and Development*. Dar es Salaam: Government Printers; reprinted in S.S. Mushi and K. Mathews (eds) (1981) *Foreign Policy of Tanzania 1961–81: A Reader*. Dar es Salaam: Tanzania Publishing House, pp. 219–33.

Nyerere, J.K. (1967) *Ujamaa Essays on Socialism*. Oxford and New York: Oxford University Press.

Nyerere, J.K. (1968) *Freedom and Socialism*. Dar es Salaam: Oxford University Press.

Nyerere, J.K. (1974) *Freedom and Development*. Dar es Salaam: Oxford University Press.

Parfitt, T.W. (1990) 'Lies, Damned Lies and Statistics: The World Bank/ECA Structural Adjustment Controversy', *Review of African Political Economy*, no. 47.

Pratt, C. (1973) 'The Administration of Economic Planning in a Newly Independent State: The Tanzania Experience 1963–1966', in L. Cliffe and J.S. Saul (eds), *Socialism in Tanzania Vol. 2*. Dar es Salaam: East African Publishing House.

Premchand, A. (1978), *Survey of Government Financial Management System in Tanzania*. Dar es Salaam, mimeo.

Rweyemamu, J. (1973) *Underdevelopment and Industrialization in Tanzania: A Study of Perverse Capitalist Industrial Development*. Nairobi: Oxford University Press.

Saul, J. (1973) 'Radicalism at the Hill', in L. Cliffe and J.S. Saul (eds), *Socialism in Tanzania, Vol. 2*. Dar es Salaam: East African Publishing House.

Shaw, T. and I. Msabaha (1981) 'Tanzania and the New International Economic Order', in K. Mathews and S.S. Mushi (eds), *Foreign Policy of Tanzania 1961–1981: A Reader*. Dar es Salaam: Tanzania Publishing House.

Sobhan, R. (1995) *Aid Dependence and Donor Policy*. Stockholm: Sida.

Svendsen, K.E. (1995) 'Development strategy and Crisis Management', in C. Legum and G. Mmari (eds), *Mwalimu. The Influence of Nyerere*. London, Dar es Salaam and Trenton, USA: Britain Tanzania Society, James Currey, Mkuki na Nyota, and Africa World Press.

Tanganyika African National Union (1971) *Mwongozo*. Dar es Salaam: Government Printer.

Tegambwage, N. (1990) *Who Tells the Truth in Tanzania*. Dar es Salaam: Tausi Publishers Limited.

Thomas, Clive (1974) *Dependence and Transformation*. New York: Monthly Review Press.

The Daily News, Dar es Salaam, Tanzania

The Guardian, Dar es Salaam, Tanzania.

Thompson, J.D. (1967) *Organizations in Action*. New York: McGraw-Hill Publishing Company.

UNDP (1993) *Development Cooperation Tanzania 1993 Report*. Dar es Salaam: United Nations Development Programme.

United Republic of Tanzania (1974) 'Statement to the 6th Pan-African Congress, Dar es Salaam, June 1974' reproduced in S.S. Mushi and K. Mathews (eds)

(1981) *Foreign Policy of Tanzania 1961–1981: A Reader*. Dar es Salaam: Tanzania Publishing House.
United Republic of Tanzania (1981) 'Cooperation Against Poverty', in K. Mathews and S.S. Mushi (eds), *Foreign Policy of Tanzania 1961–1981: A Reader*. Dar es Salaam: Tanzania Publishing House.
United Republic of Tanzania (1994) Brief to the Paris club meeting, musch, mimeo
United Republic of Tanzania (1997) 'Civil Service Reform', mimeo.
Weber, M. (1978) *Economy and Society*, G. Roth and C. Wittich (eds). Berkeley CA: University of California Press.
Wildavsky, A. (1979) *The Politics of the Budgetary Process*. Boston, MA: Little, Brown.

3 An Agency under Siege: USAID and its Mission in Tanzania

Stephen L. Snook

INTRODUCTION

In this chapter the strategy and behaviour of USAID in Tanzania will be examined from 1961 to 1995. The evolution of the American foreign aid programme from 1944 to 1960 will be briefly reviewed. The different influences of USAID's cultural, task and political environments will be analysed. The history of the AID mission will be presented in three time periods, and the cross-case variables evaluated in each.

Broadly speaking, there are three basic theoretical perspectives on foreign aid. The first sees aid as what it purports to be, simple altruism. Foreign aid has served 'humanitarian and egalitarian principles' in a good-faith effort to establish 'a just international order in which all states [have] a chance to do well'. Wealthy countries give aid to poor countries for selfless, not self-interested reasons, under terms that are 'favorable to the economic development of the recipients and unfavorable to the use of aid for leverage by the donors' (Lumsdaine 1993:30, 102, 275).

In the second perspective, states are assumed to be rational entities in a conflictual world that act to protect their territorial and political integrity and to conserve and expand their share of power in the international system (Krasner 1985:28). This 'realist' perspective predominates in US foreign policy circles. It affords scant place for altruist sensitivities in the conduct of foreign policy (Brown 1984:115–21).

Realists typically are pessimistic about the prospects for development. A truly effective programme to accelerate world economic growth would require a massive transfer of wealth far in excess of what American taxpayers would ever accept. The amount of money actually available for foreign aid is inadequate for the task; world poverty is an intractable problem in the short term. This is not to say that foreign aid has no utility. It is a useful slush fund to 'bribe' Third World governments to support US foreign policy goals (Morgenthau 1962; Bandow 1988). For realists, aid to

Africa has never been anything other than a tool for geopolitical gain (Ungar 1993:385).

The third theoretical perspective considered here is radical criticism, which in recent years has lost much of its salience. Like realists, radical critics interpret foreign aid in instrumental terms. Like realists, they believe foreign aid has nothing to do with altruism. They too cast doubt on the development enterprise, but for different reasons. The problem lies not in the inadequacy of resources, but in the misguided liberal belief that poor countries can prosper in the international capitalist system. The faith is wrong. The system is permanently and unfairly tilted against the developing countries (Wallerstein 1979). Foreign aid is an instrument of capitalism, used by the donors to pierce and penetrate developing countries and open them up for exploitation by the donors' transnational corporations (Hayter 1971; Biersteker 1987).

A straightforward altruist perspective of aid does not hold up in the case of American aid to Tanzania. Declassified portions of the official record reveal that Washington's chief objective in establishing an AID programme in Dar es Salaam in 1961 was to head off Communist influence.[1] The USA has not always provided aid to Tanzania for purely charitable reasons.

Likewise, an unmixed realist view of aid as pure bribery is not tenable in the case of American aid to Tanzania. In the early 1970s the Nyerere government started becoming increasingly hostile towards the USA, and (consistent with the realist perspective) the Nixon and Ford administrations reduced new development assistance to the country in response.[2] Then the Tanzanian economy began suffering from the effects of the first oil shock, and in 1975 the country was stricken with severe drought. The threat of famine loomed. In response, the Ford administration reversed its policy and made a $24.4 million (in constant 1987 dollars) emergency loan. This did not result in any change in Tanzanian attitudes; the Nyerere government remained 'a thorn in the side of the U.S.' for two more years of declining relations (USAID, 'Appraisal', 1978). The increase of aid in 1975 was not a bribe to procure Tanzanian political support; it was done for humanitarian reasons.

The radical perspective also fails to explain the case of American aid to Tanzania. AID never functioned as an instrument of capitalist penetration in Tanzania, first all because Tanzania was never very attractive to foreign investors, American or otherwise, and second because its government from independence onwards was hostile to the interests of foreign capital (Bienen 1967). Aside from a NASA satellite tracking station in Zanzibar which it removed in 1964, the USA had 'no *major* compelling political, security or economic interests in Tanzania' (USAID, 'Appraisal', 1978, emphasis added). AID's mission in Tanzania never served to facilitate the entry of American corporations into the country.

The radical view of aid as an instrument of capitalist penetration cannot be sustained in the case of US foreign assistance to Tanzania, but the altruist perspective of aid as philanthropy and the realist perspective of aid as bribery both can in part. AID's behaviour can perhaps best be described as one of *pragmatic altruism*. AID's missions are guided by a general concern for helping; the design and implementation of development programmes reflect altruistic principles. But pragmatic considerations prevail in the three most important decisions AID must make: whether to provide aid to a country, how much to give, and for what. With the lone exception of 1975, the amount of new aid obligated to Tanzania each year changed according to the attitude of its government towards US foreign policy.[3] Twice in 1970 and 1988 the USA increased aid to Tanzania to reward it for cooperation, and four times – in 1972, 1976, 1983, and 1991 – it slashed aid to punish Tanzania for defiance.

AID's task environment is characterized by the same high degree of uncertainty as its political environment. There are uncertainties of supply. Which technology to provide? How to work effectively under ineffectual host country governments? There are uncertainties of demand. Excess demand for the benefits that development projects can provide may lead to violence. Inadequate demand, on the other hand, can turn projects into white elephants (Hirschman 1967). Success in international development demands experimentation and an institutional ability to learn. Unfortunately, these traits are not nurtured in AID's internal environment.

There are conflicts in all large bureaucracies between the individual and the organization (Downs 1967), but they are more serious than normal in AID. The fact that its resources come form Washington while its operations are conducted overseas necessitates a Janus-faced posture. AID must be alert to changing moods in Washington while, to succeed in its uncertain mission of assisting the poorest countries on earth, it is 'forced to be particularly reliant on its lower ranks for adaptive and innovative behavior' (Tendler 1975:24). However, the incentives AID provides for its employees do not encourage the spirit of innovation. AID is governed by the State Department's management system, with its 'tortuously slow apprenticeship' and its 'premium on conformity and on the patronage of superiors writing efficiency reports, who were in turn awaiting their own similar advancement through the ranks'. AID reflects the State Department 'culture in which the simple declarative sentence [is] regarded as risky' (Morris 1977:34, 36). Fear of the written word is pronounced.

A review of AID archives in the 1970s found them to consist of sanitized, technical and lifeless reports (Tendler 1975). A one page anonymous circular making the rounds in AID's Washington offices in March 1995 is instructive.

AID's culture, the memo declared, places the highest value on AID's employees' assumed stability in recipient countries. They are more comfortable dealing with economic issues than the political and social aspects of development. They believe that unpopular policies 'will go away if ignored'. Externally, AID resists 'being integrated with other donors', and internally 'responds vertically to bureau hierarchy, and has difficulty organizing horizontally'.

AID AND THE PROBLEM OF FEDERALISM

Much of AID's observable behaviour is a consequence of the unusual system of government under which it operates. American federalism was designed in the eighteenth century by men who were torn between a distrust of centralized power (acquired from the struggle for independence) and a rueful understanding of its necessity (gained from a failed experiment with confederacy). The failure of the Articles of Confederation to provide a viable central government was clear to the men who wrote the US Constitution. They understood the need for effective government, but they were more concerned with safeguarding against future tyranny than establishing a system of rational administration. The founders therefore created a government that, while able to control the governed, first and foremost is obliged to control itself (Rossiter 1961; Wilson 1989).

Federal agencies are far from helpless. The separation of powers has given them a substantial degree of *de facto* power that has grown as the federal government has grown. Meier (1979) goes so far as to argue that the federal bureaucracy has become an unintended fourth branch of government. It is commonly viewed as inefficient, dysfunctional, oligarchical and anti-democratic (Goodsell 1985:6–11), a far cry from the Weberian ideal. It is rather a government of strangers.

THE EVOLUTION OF THE AMERICAN FOREIGN AID PROGRAMME

The world's first peacetime foreign aid programme was born in the USA at a conference of high level planners form the Roosevelt administration and the Churchill government at Bretton Woods, New Hampshire, in 1944.

The delegates devised a strategy to prevent another world war from occurring by pegging world currencies to a gold-backed US dollar and crafting a set of international institutions – principally the World Bank and the IMF – designed to lower trade barriers and provide loans to governments to use either to finance long-term development projects or to remedy short-term balance of payment problems.

The high hopes for a permanent peace that followed the surrender of Japan in August 1945 were dashed in the dozen months it took Stalin to establish Soviet dominance over Eastern Europe, for the Communists to resume the civil war in China, and for war-ravaged Europe to begin to exhibit signs of renewed political extremism. It took the US government until 1947 to develop a policy framework to view these events. That year President Truman declared that the earth was being divided into a free world and a world enslaved by Communism, and challenged the American people to decide which side they were on (Freeland 1972).

Having identified Communism as a threat to American national security, the Truman administration devised a strategy to contain it by encircling the Soviet Union and Eastern Europe with a girdle of military alliances and by aiding the embattled Chinese nationalists (Acheson 1969). The nationalist movements which brought renewed war to Vietnam and independence to India and Pakistan inspired nationalist movements in every European colony in the world. Facing this extraordinary development, the Truman administration deemed that the desperate poverty of the people living in the colonized areas was likely to make Communist utopianism appealing to them. A foreign aid programme to improve global standards of living seemed justified as part of the effort to contain Communism.

Congress passed an Economic Cooperation Act in the 1948 which created the Economic Cooperation Administration (ECA) (Kindleberger 1987). The ECA was in place by the end of 1948 when, in the fourth point of his inaugural address, Truman called for the expansion of the existing foreign aid programme into all countries emerging from European colonialism (McCullough 1992). The 'loss' of China to Mao's Communist armies in 1949 spurred Congress to pass the 1950 Act for International Development which replaced the ECA with the Technical Cooperation Administration. The act was superseded by the 1951 Mutual Security Act, passed in response to the outbreak of the Korean War on 25 June 1950, which replaced the Technical Cooperation Administration with the Mutual Security Administration. In its first year in office, 1953, the Eisenhower administration reorganized that into the Foreign Operations Administration, then reorganized it again in 1956 as the International Operations Administration (Rondinelli 1987).

President Eisenhower was disinclined to support the nationalist movements rising in the colonies of America's allies. He was to describe nationalism in his memoirs as a destructive hurricane. This gave Senator John F. Kennedy an opportunity to make a name for himself by declaring his support for the right of self-determination (Mahoney 1983).

The Kennedy administration got the Foreign Assistance Act (FAA) through Congress its first year in office, replacing the International Operations Administration with the Agency for International Development. Kennedy then moved vigorously to win Africa to the free world by extending liberal amounts of aid and by appointing dynamic ambassadors. Kennedy himself cultivated a personal relationship with the new African leaders – many were as young as he – by receiving them with great fanfare at the White House (Noer 1989). Among these was Julius Nyerere.

THE THREE PERIODS OF AMERICAN AID TO TANZANIA

Twice since AID's inception in 1961 there have been particularly profound changes in the strategies it has pursued. These changes were caused by two significant political events in Washington: the 1973 congressional reform of the FAA, called the New Directions, and the 1980 election of Ronald Reagan. These two events divide the history of the AID mission in Tanzania into three distinct time periods, each characterized by a different dominant strategy and a different set of development objectives.

The first period lasted from 1961 to 1973. In its first thirteen years the AID Mission in Tanzania was guided by a '"foundation laying or stage setting strategy" [of] filling manpower and institutional gaps' (USAID, Field Budget Submission, 1974). Projects were designed 'to strengthen sections of ministries, to provide training and to support training institutions' (USAID, Development Assistance Program Revision, 1977).

The second period was from 1974 to 1980. The 1973 Congressional revision of the FAA, called the New Directions, required AID to concentrate on reaching the poor majority. In Tanzania, where 90 per cent of the poor were farm families, the AID mission began implementing programmes 'directly at the village level' (USAID, Field Budget Submission, 1974).

The third period covers the years 1981–95. The Reagan administration directed AID to support IMF policy reforms in Tanzania which aimed 'to erode government mentality of excessive reliance on the public sector for economic development' (USAID, Annual Budget Submission, 1989). Beginning in 1981 the USA started using its aid to Tanzania as leverage to force policy reform.

The First Period: Institution Building, 1961–73

AID's strategies for each country are expressed in formal plans. This planning method was established on the recommendation of a group of social scientists called the Charles River Group who met shortly after the founding of AID and urged that the project approach of AID's forerunners be abandoned in favour of comprehensive country programming (Packenham 1973).[4] In the 1960s AID country plans were called Country Assistance Programs (CAPs). They were revised on an annual basis. In 1972, under the Nixon administration, the name of the planning document was changed to the Development Assistance Program (DAP), and a multiyear planning framework was established.

AID opened a mission in Dar es Salaam in 1961. Nine projects were authorized that first year, and $22.8 million in spending was pledged. The Mission's first country plan was written from 1961 to 1962 and submitted in January 1963. The plan had two main thrusts: to improve Tanzania's physical infrastructure, its roads and urban water systems in particular; and to strengthen and build national institutions, particularly the civil service and institutions of higher learning (USAID, 'History', 1985).

Source of AID Objectives

Based on the work on institution building of Milton Esman and his colleagues, and on the 'gap theory' developed by Hollis Chenery at the World Bank, institution-building and gap-filling criteria shaped the selection of AID objectives in Tanzania in the first thirteen years (Riddell 1987; Rondinelli 1987). At another, higher level, however, AID was guided by what one former foreign officer was to describe as the State Department 'ideology of imperial benevolence' (Morris 1977:27). The objectives AID adopted in the first country plan came from a document entitled 'Tangayika, Department of State Guidelines for Policy and Operations'.

The State Department document established three key objectives: (1) to help build 'a strong and responsible government'; (2) to prevent Communist penetration of the government and the economy; and (3) to ensure 'the continued reliance of Tanganyika on Western sources for the major portion of its economic and technical assistance'. In recognition of the fact that the State Department objectives had no development component, the Mission added a fourth: 'economic development of a responsibly governed Tanganyika at a satisfactory rate' (USAID, CAP, 1963a).

The second country plan of September 1963 reaffirmed the Mission's objectives of 'continued growth of the present system of government under moderate leadership'. AID's first two country plans referred to Tanzania's own three-year and subsequent five-year development plans, but only to show how the Mission's objectives were in alignment with, and supportive of (but not derived from), Tanzania's national development goals (USAID, CAP, 1963a, 1963b, 1965, 1966).

The Conditions of American Aid

US foreign policy-making was dominated in the early 1960s by an East Coast establishment of Ivy League intellectuals and millionaires. Keynesianism, the lessons of the Second World War, the principles of the Truman Doctrine, and the experience of McCarthyism shaped their world view.

The elite circle recognized that Kennedy's 1961 foreign aid initiative would greatly increase their career opportunities by expanding the number of overseas assignments. But they disdained Kennedy's desire to link aid to democracy as naive (Lyons 1994). AID's planners in Tanzania stated outright in the first country plan that the administration's 'hopes for Tanganyika's tranquil political progress under a classic Western system of parliamentary democracy and civil rights are exaggerated'.

In the second country plan (submitted two months before Kennedy's assassination) the AID Mission informed Washington anew that it would not link American assistance to democracy, but rather would 'attempt to persuade Tanganyikan leaders to follow democratic processes'. The Mission believed that hectoring a proud and newly independent government would be unprofitable; 'any attempt to relate the level of U.S. assistance directly to political objectives would be violently resented and unproductive' (USAID, CAP, 1963b). This was reaffirmed in the third country plan of October 1964, submitted a month before Lyndon Johnson was elected President. It stated that 'any overt attempt to tie the level of U.S. assistance to political conditions would be both unproductive and resented by the local leadership we seek to strengthen' (USAID, CAP, 1964). At the same time, the Mission placed one condition on its assistance: that the Nyerere government not become pro-Communist.

The year 1964 was a watershed for the USA in Africa. After Kennedy's death, a rift formed in the State Department between the activist Kennedy appointees whom Lyndon Johnson inherited and the entrenched foreign policy establishment. A struggle for control of the agenda began (Lyons 1994). Meanwhile two events in January 1964 focused US attention squarely on Tanzania: the revolt in Zanzibar, and the mutiny of the Tanganyikan army. The mutiny, which occurred simultaneously in Kenya and Uganda, was put down in Tanganyika by the British at the request of Nyerere.

The Zanzibar Revolution, however, which threw off Arab rule and brought Abeid Karume and his Marxist adviser, Abdul-rahman Mohammed Babu, to power, was much more problematic.

The PRC moved quickly to exploit the situation. It made a nominal $14 million loan to Zanzibar and established a $31 million military training mission to Tanganyika. In office only two months, and governing a nation still in shock from the Kennedy assassination, the Johnson administration was hesitant to take action in Tanzania, feeling the best option was 'to remain engaged in a low-key manner and try to demonstrate the value of good relations with the West' (Lyons 1994:253). To this end the Johnson administration established relations with Zanzibar in February and sent Frank Carlucci as Chargé d'Affaires 'with the difficult mission of disabusing Karume of what he'd been told by Babu' (Attwood 1967:157). Carlucci quickly concluded his task was hopeless, and on 26 March cabled this opinion to Washington (Lyons 1994:253).

A week later the US ambassador to Kenya, William Attwood, made a statement in the press warning East African governments that the Chinese were setting up a 'non-African type of regime' in Zanzibar, and urged them to be on their guard. President Karume reacted angrily, and demanded that the USA remove the NASA tracking station. The station was moved to South Africa. As it was being dismantled, Carlucci attempted to disarm Karume by presenting the generator to his government as a gift (Attwood 1967:164).

As the Chinese presence grew, the US press played up speculations that Zanzibar was becoming 'another Cuba'. Julius Nyerere moved quietly and effectively to defuse the situation and persuaded Karume to merge Zanzibar with Tanganyika. In April the URT was formed. The Johnson administration expressed tremendous relief and hailed Nyerere's move as an example of Africans solving their own problems (Lyons 1994:263).

At the year's end US–Tanzanian relations took an abrupt turn for the worse. On 24 November 1964, in a military operation called Dragon Rouge in the Congo, American planes dropped Belgian paratroopers over Stanleyville (now Kisangani) to rescue white hostages, including four US diplomats, who had been taken by a Chinese-backed rebel force. African leaders reacted with outrage (Lyons 1994:256). Nyerere condemned the foray as 'another Pearl Harbor'. All through December the countries of the African bloc in the UN took turns criticizing the US with such venom that American donations to at least one private humanitarian organization in Africa dropped substantially that year (Attwood 1967).

The tension between the USA and Tanzania reached its height in January 1965 when Tanzanian security officers recorded the telephone conversation of two American embassy officials speculating about whether they had enough 'ammunition' to get a message sent from the State Department congratulating Karume on the anniversary of the revolution. Nyerere accepted the tape recording as evidence that the alleged American plot against Zanzibar was real.

The Mission believed that Tanzania was inclined to accept Communist assistance because of its 'preoccupation with the political liberation of the remaining territories of Southern Africa'. Tanzania was now the 'headquarters of the African Liberation Committee and of numerous refugee political organizations dedicated to bringing about political and social change in their homelands' (USAID, Congressional Presentation, 1967). The 'crucial question' in the Mission's view was 'whether progress can be achieved quickly enough ... to avoid the dangers of despair and a grasping at alternative extremist approaches' (USAID, Congressional Presentation, 1967).

The Structure of AID

AID is part of a veritable development industry: a coterie of private consulting firms, universities and non-profit humanitarian relief and development organizations that implement most of AID's programmes. In any given year, between 60 and 80 per cent of the funds AID disburses is returned to the American economy (Tendler 1975; *Washington Post*, 18 September 1993; Zimmerman 1993; ABC Television, 4 December 1995).

AID itself is a peculiar and not particularly effective mix of centralized and decentralized functions. Authorization, appropriation, budgeting and accounting are centralized functions subject at a minimum to Congressional oversight committees, the Government Accounting Office (GAO), and AID's Inspector General. Programme design and implementation, on the other hand, take place in the field. Although conducted with wide discretion, these functions are subject to an internal review process. Over the course of the 1960s, AID's internal review process became an increasing burden. By 1973 its weight was so heavy the Tanzania mission complained that 'as AID's project design techniques have grown in sophistication and standards have increased, no [mission] can hope to find the time or expertise to anticipate the questions raised by a multitude of reviewers at several levels in [AID headquarters in Washington]' (USAID, Field Budget Submission, 1973).

The Staffing of AID

Initially, most US foreign assistance was delivered through bilateral channels. In its early years, AID was the leading institution of the American foreign aid programme. However, over the course of AID's first decade of existence the bulk of US assistance was gradually shifted from bilateral to multilateral channels. This was done primarily to protect a larger proportion of foreign aid from the political process (Tendler 1975). AID lost its pre-eminence to the World Bank. From 1961 to 1970 American multilateral aid grew seven times faster than bilateral aid. While the World Bank's loan commitments quadrupled and its personnel doubled, AID's appropriations were reduced by 20 per cent and its personnel was halved (Wood 1986).

AID has three basic categories of personnel. The first is US direct hires. These are permanent American employees of the federal government with full diplomatic status and perquisites. The Second is foreign service nationals, permanent foreign employees of the federal government paid at local wage rates (which, in the case of Tanzania, have generally been about one-tenth of American salaries). The third is contractors and consultants. These can be Americans or host country or even third country nationals. There are various types of contracts that AID awards. These range from open-ended contracts for administrative work in the main office to close-ended contracts for the implementation of specific projects in the field.

AID in its earliest years was heavily staffed by direct hires.[5] This changed as AID underwent reductions; the agency became increasingly reliant on contractors.[6] Project implementation changed as a result. In the first seven years of the institution-building period, the Mission implemented about half of its projects itself and contracted out the other half. Of 39 projects launched throughout 1966, seventeen were implemented by AID or other federal agencies, while eighteen were implemented by American universities, private contractors, non-profit corporations, or other NGOs. The mix changed in 1967–73. Of 18 projects launched, AID or another federal agency implemented five, and NGOs implemented eight.[7] The tendency to use NGOs to implement projects, as with the growing reliance on contracted personnel, increased throughout 1973.

Feedback in AID

In the institution-building period AID relied on project output information to gauge project success. Examples of the sorts of statistics AID compiled and reported were kilometres of roads or numbers of buildings completed, and numbers of Tanzanians educated. The Mission's goals for aid to education, for example, were to achieve a 200 per cent increase in the annual number of secondary school certificate candidates and a 300 per cent increase in high school certificate candidates by 1968 (USAID, CAP, 1963a). The indicators established for the Masai Livestock and Range Management Project were 'the per-man and per-acre productivity of Masai herdsmen' (USAID, PBS, 1970) to be measured in terms of increased 'livestock off-take in the Masai District' (USAID, Field Budget Submission, 1974).

The success indicators of the first period were essentially output quotas. The idea of determining the effect of AID projects on people's lives was not considered. During the institution-building period the Mission did not look at the numbers of school graduates who were finding jobs or the type of jobs they were finding, for example. No one seems to have wondered whether the Masai herdsmen actually wanted to increase their 'livestock off-take'.

The Degree of AID Autonomy

AID's autonomy is relative to three separate sources of authority in Washington. The first is the State Department of which AID is a semi-autonomous branch. The second is the Congress, which controls AID's budget and oversees its activities. The third is the President, who conducts foreign policy.

The State Department: with the great increase in the numbers of US embassies that the Kennedy administration opened in emerging countries in Africa, State Department careers quickly became invested in the continent far out of proportion to Africa's strategic importance to the USA. A clientelist mentality took hold. State Department and AID personnel in Africa developed their own 'isolated and private view of foreign policy', and whenever necessary joined forces to commit 'little bureaucratic deceptions to conceal the client's failures lest [they] lose what meager call they had on Washington's programs and attention' (Morris 1977:18). Thus, in the first decade of its existence, the AID mission in Tanzania worked quite closely with the American Embassy to design and implement an aid programme that launched an average of four projects and obligated an average $19.2 million in constant dollar new spending each year from 1961 to 1973.

The Congress: during the early 1960s AID's missions selected which aspects of the FAA to implement in their countries. By 1965 there was growing concern in Congress about AID's lack of accountability and its apparent disinterest in empowering ordinary people to participate in their own development. The agency's heavy focus on big capital projects, such as the construction of urban water systems and college campuses in

Tanzania, led Congress to revise the FAA in 1966. The new act required AID to concentrate on public health and agriculture and, in Title IX – 'Utilization of Democratic Institutions in Development' – instructed the agency to encourage popular participation in its development programmes wherever national differences permitted (Packenham 1973).

The AID mission in Tanzania responded to the requirement for more emphasis on social services and agriculture. New spending obligated in these two sectors quadrupled from a combined $27.3 million in 1961–66 to $110.1 million in 1967–73. In the climate of the times, however, AID's Washington offices were uncertain what to do about Title IX. A proposal was put forth to create an Office of Political development to juxtapose against the CIA, but this was not adopted. AID did form a brief-lived Political Development Division (Packenham 1973).

In the mid-1960s the Vietnam War was coming under public criticism. Opposition to the war grew accordingly in Congress. In 1967, partly to show its displeasure with the President's Vietnam policy, Congress made a heavy cut to the AID budget. The effects were felt in Tanzania. Average new spending fell 89 per cent from $18.6 million in 1963–65 to $2.1 million in 1966–68, and then another 39 per cent to $1.3 million in 1968–69. The lean years made AID more attuned to the mood of the legislature. In the 1970 Congressional Presentation, AID's Africa Bureau declared its focus was now on 'improving the quality of life for the African people' three years before the New Directions (USAID, Congressional Presentation, 1970).

On some occasions during the institution-building period congress intervened in AID operations to *help* the administration pursue US foreign policy goals. For example, the Senate held up the entire 1972 foreign appropriations bill out of anger at Tanzania for an unseemly incident following the vote on the proposal to expel Taiwan. The vote was taken on 25 October 1971. UN Ambassador George Bush delivered a last minute appeal for support in the General Assembly, and then waited on the dais while the vote was cast. When the US defeat was registered, Tanzania's Permanent Representative Salim Ahmed Salim danced a gleeful jig under the eyes of Bush in front of the television cameras of the international media. The White House released a statement two days later saying that Nixon had been shocked by the spectacle. On 29 October, the Senate killed the entire foreign appropriations bill (Kissinger 1979:784–5). The following year, 1972, for the first time, AID obligated no new spending in Tanzania.

More typically Congress has tried to legislate limitations on the President's use of foreign aid as a foreign policy tool. The most substantial of these was the 1973 New Directions that required AID to concentrate on reaching the poor majority. The bill was reported out of the Senate Foreign Relations Committee over the opposition of Chairman J. William Fulbright who decried it as a 'face-lifting job' (Rondinelli 1987:73). The New Directions mandated six changes in strategy: (1) AID was to focus on technology and commodity transfers; (2) capital-intensive projects were to be replaced by labour-intensive programmes; (3) AID was to concentrate on food production, rural development and nutrition, population planning and health, education, public administration, and human resource development; (4) AID's highest priority would no longer be macro-economic growth, but programmes which improved the lives of the poor majority and increased their capacity to participate in their own development; (5) the agency was to begin supporting host country development plans; and (6) AID was to shift focus from public to private sector initiatives (Rondinelli 1987).

After passage of the 1966 FAA the Mission had begun restructuring its project portfolio. AID projects to build the agricultural college at Morogoro and the university campus at Dar es Salaam, and to upgrade the capital city's water system, had all recently ended. This fortuitously placed the AID Mission in Tanzania in conformance with five of the six New Directions mandates. The sixth, the mandate to place greater emphasis on private sector initiatives, could not be met. By 1973 Tanzania's private sector was coming under increased government control.

The President: AID was under three different administrations during the institution-building period of 1961–73. Kennedy created the agency in order to distinguish more clearly between economic and military aid. He acted in the hope that the economic aid would be used to support democracy. The activism of his administration produced a scattershot approach to development in Tanzania. From 1961 to 1963 an average of seven new projects were launched annually at an average of $18 million in new spending. Twenty-two projects were launched, totalling $54.1 million. The projects were mainly concentrated in three sectors: $13.0 million for social services, $21.7 for physical infrastructure, and $17.1 million for public administration.

Kennedy was assassinated just four months after Nyerere visited Washington in July 1963.[8] The man who succeeded Kennedy could not have been more different. Lyndon Johnson was unschooled, untravelled and unread (Tucker 1994:313). He was uncomfortable dealing with international affairs and with people from different countries. He was susceptible to prejudices. When in early 1968 television coverage of the starvation in Biafra began to galvanize public opinion to intervene, Johnson's lack of action drew sharp criticism from presidential candidate Richard Nixon and unfavourable commentary in the media. After one particularly compelling television report was aired, Johnson called the Under Secretary of State for Africa and angrily ordered him to send relief to 'get those nigger babies off my TV set' (Morris 1977:42).

Johnson's humble background made him deeply sympathetic with the plight of the poor, and thus more comfortable among foreigners of low station than suave foreign diplomats. On a visit to West Africa as Vice President under Kennedy he behaved like a politician on the campaign trail, enthusiastically wading into crowds and pressing the flesh. During a tour of rural India, Johnson described to a rapt group of peasants 'his boyhood experience drawing water from the well, showing how the rope occasionally slipped and burned the palms of his hands. The rubbed their palms too' (Heinrichs 1994:27).

However, Johnson's attitude towards Africa contrasted sharply with Kennedy's. Where the Kennedy administration had paid great attention to Africa and had tried to push new ideas through, the Johnson administration delegated responsibility for African affairs to the State Department and urged the European powers to accept overall responsibility for the continent. To Johnson, Africa was 'the farthest corner of the world ... the place to threaten to send indiscreet officials who drew his ire'. His administration wanted the USA to be the junior partner, to avoid playing the role of 'Mr Big' in Africa (Lyons 1994:245, 248). Africa became 'the last issue considered, and the first aid budget cut' (Morris 1977:17).

The AID mission in Tanzania launched the same average four new projects per year during Johnson's five years in office as during Kennedy's three years (from 1961 to 1963). However, the heavy budget cuts made by Congress in 1966 and 1967 resulted in lower average new spending commitments under Johnson: $7 million per year, less than half the $18 million under Kennedy.

Richard Nixon narrowly won the election from Vice President Hubert Humphrey in November 1968, entering office in January 1969. Like Johnson, Nixon came from a humble background. Like Johnson, he had a mediocre education, but (like Kennedy) he was well travelled. As Vice President to Eisenhower, Nixon had come to believe that the State Department could not be trusted, and that the foreign policy establishment had not served Eisenhower well. Unlike Johnson, who had plainly confessed his bafflement about foreign affairs, Nixon 'considered himself an initiate in the mysteries' (Morris 1977:66).

Nixon named as his National Security Adviser the Harvard professor Henry Kissinger, a man who shared the opinion that foreign policy should be conducted outside the State Department bureaucracy and shielded from domestic politics whenever necessary, even if that required lying to the public. Nixon and Kissinger also shared a near complete lack of interest in Africa. They both wanted Africa kept off the agenda in order to pursue the larger goals of extricating the USA from Vietnam, *détente* with the Soviet Union, and making an opening to China.

Nixon unilaterally abrogated Bretton Woods in August 1971 by ending the fixed-exchange rate, gold-dollar currency system which had allowed countries to exchange dollars for gold on demand (Strange 1991:114–15). Consistent with this policy to relieve the USA of some of the costs of serving as Free World hegemon, the Nixon administration retained Johnson's policy of encouraging Europe to take the leadership role in Africa and paid little attention to the continent. The exceptions were Nigeria, where the civil war continued to exact a horrible toll (having been a campaign issue, Biafra still held an interest for Nixon), and South Africa, which the Nixon administration wished to make as close an ally as Iran, but did not dare. By 1969 the USA's southern Africa policy was coming under fire from the African bloc in the UN and from civil rights organizations in the USA. The administration would have to make a new policy (Morris 1977:120; Schurmann 1987:330).

The new policy emerged from an amazingly wrong-headed National Security Study Memorandum on southern Africa that Kissinger circulated in November 1969, which declared, 'There is no hope for the blacks to gain the political rights they seek through violence' (Ungar 1993:388–9). After a review 'that was alternately childish, venomous, dull, colossally wasteful of official time, and very much the stuff of government in foreign affairs', Nixon settled on a policy of softened pressure on Portugal, 'limited association' with Rhodesia and South Africa, and continued lip service in support of the principle of majority rule. Foreseeing how the initiative would be received by the African bloc, Kissinger recommended an increase in aid to the front-line states. The policy was adopted with little discussion. It was promptly dubbed the 'tar baby option' by its critics at the State Department who recognized 'that its only real result would be to mire the United States deeper on the side of the oppressors' (Lake 1976; Morris 1977:111–19).

In the year after 'Tar Baby', American aid ballooned to $94.3 million. This was partly a response to the Chinese decision that year to build TAZARA. Forty per cent of the new AID spending went into the $37.2 million Tanzania-Zambia Highway project 621-0091, undertaken in conjunction with the World Bank and Sida.

In the five years under Nixon from 1969 until the 1973 New Directions, a total of $163.4 million in new spending was pledged in Tanzania.

The $94.3 million obligated in 1970 was fourteen times more than the $6.8 million promised the year before, four times the previous high of $23.7 million in 1963. Average new American aid spending in Tanzania for the five years under Nixon (from 1969 to 1973) was $33 million, four times Johnson's $7 million and nearly twice the $18 million average under Kennedy.

Interpreting the Strategy and Behaviour of AID, 1961–73

AID obligated a total of $255.9 million in constant 1987 dollars of aid to Tanzania during the thirteen years of the institution-building period, an average of $19.7 million per year. New spending pledges were not evenly distributed across time. Two-thirds of the total was promised in the second half of the period, 36.9 per cent in the single year of 1970.

In the six years 1961–66 the Mission obligated a total of $87.3 million in new spending in Tanzania, an average of $14.6 million per year. In 1967–73 the amount pledged almost doubled to $168.5 million, an average of $24.1 million. The increase was not evenly distributed across sectors. AID obligated a paltry $200 000 each for Tanzania's industrial and finance sectors. Two sectors actually lost funding. Support for public administration decreased sharply, from $23.0 to $9.7 million. Support for social services also declined, but less severely, from $25.1 to $21.6 million. Two sectors saw increases: the first was the agriculture sector. In a clear response to the 1966 FAA mandate, AID raised total new pledges in this sector from $2.4 million in 1961–66 to $88.6 million in 1967–73. But in an equally clear breach of the mandate to end capital projects, the Mission also increased support for the infrastructure sector, from $36.7 million to $48.4 million.

As already noted, the Mission finished all its straightforward construction projects as required, but Kissinger's 'Tar Baby' policy and the Chinese railroad initiative resulted in a fourteen-fold budget increase and the matching Tan-Zam Highway project. In addition to this, the Mission built large infrastructure components into many of the new agricultural projects, thus violating the spirit (if not the letter) of the law. For example, the $14 million Masai Livestock and Range Management Project launched in 1970 provided for the construction of water points, cattle dips, veterinary facilities, training centres, and 145 miles of feeder roads.

While the total amount of new spending obligated in Tanzania doubled from the first half to the second of the institution-building period, the total number of projects launched was halved, from 38 in 1961–66 to 18 in 1967–73. The net effect of the increase in spending pledges and the decrease in the number of projects was a quadrupling in the average cost of a project, from $2.2 million in the first six years to $9.4 million in the next seven.

The strategy and behaviour of AID in Tanzania was guided in part by altruistic principles. Some of the altruism came from within the Mission. The language of the Mission's planning documents is replete with expressions of concern about helping Tanzanians improve their lot, and there is no reason to believe these expressions were insincerely made.

Some of AID's altruism was legislated by Congress: the increased support for agriculture, for example. While the Mission would later claim that the changes it made in its project portfolio after 1966 were a response to the 1967 Arusha Declaration (USAID, 'History', 1985), a more compelling argument is that the Arusha Declaration happened to coincide with the 1966 FAA.

Some of AID's altruistic propensities came from higher levels in the agency. In 1972 AID decided that loans should be directed 'increasingly toward those countries financially capable of carrying them' and grants 'increasingly toward the least developed' (USAID, Field Budget Submission, 1972).

Most funding decisions were governed by national interest. American aid was originally provided to Tanzania to prevent it from going Communist. The Nixon administration increased and decreased the amount of new aid to Tanzania according to Tanzanian attitudes towards US foreign policy. New aid pledges rose to a height of $94.3 million in 1970 to counteract the Chinese railroad project and to make 'Tar Baby' more palatable to the Nyerere government. Two years later, in 1972, new spending was slashed to zero to punish Tanzania for the dance of Salim.

AID enjoyed substantial autonomy from Congress in its first few years. Missions selected which aspects of the 1961 FAA they would implement. The result was a significant reform of the FAA in 1966. However, the manner in which the AID mission in Tanzania found ways of circumventing the mandate to end big infrastructure programmes by packing construction elements into other projects shows that AID found ways to defy the will of Congress. AID could also thwart the will of the President. The Tanzania Mission resisted, for example, Kennedy's desire to link American aid to democracy.

In the early years AID worked hand in glove with the State Department establishment, which to all intents and purposes wrote AID's first Tanzania country plan. But AID maintained total autonomy from the other donors in Tanzania. The first AID country plan stated quite plainly that 'we do not consider it desirable for the external aid donors to do more than continue to keep in close touch, exchange information on their aid activities and avoid specific duplication' (USAID, CAP, 1963a).

The Second Period: Reaching the Poor Majority, 1974–80

The 1973 mandate of reaching the poor majority closely resembled the strategy of meeting 'basic human needs' initiated at the World Bank with an address by Robert McNamara to the Board of Governors in Nairobi that same year (Wood 1986). As we have seen, AID had been anticipating this change since 1970. The Mission in Tanzania was ready for it, and was quick to show it both understood and was obeying the New Directions. 'The current Foreign Assistance Act (FAA) clearly emphasizes rural development ... The target group and prime recipients of aid benefits are to be the rural poor' (USAID, Field Budget Submission, 1974). The Mission estimated the conversion from institution building to reaching the poor majority would take about five years. In 1977 the Mission submitted a progress report. Noting its previous emphasis on capital projects such as 'constructing the highly visible Tan-Zam highway', the Mission reported it had now begun 'to focus more on small farmers and livestock growers ... to reach out to villages ... from the cities and campuses' (USAID, DAP revision, 1977). Reaching the poor majority had become the dominant strategy, and by the first year of the Carter administration all the Mission's objectives inclined in that direction.

Source of Agency Objectives

Prior to 1975, the influence of the Tanzanian government on AID planning was extremely limited. AID accepted the broad sectoral objectives called for in Tanzania's national development plans but did not invite Tanzanian participation in AID planning. Eventually the Tanzanian government decided to take a more active role. In early 1975 it asked each donor to finance a regional development study 'with the implication that donors would subsequently finance a comprehensive regional development program for that region'. In the case of AID, the government suggested Arusha Region for the Americans, given AID's long involvement in the area (USAID, 'Appraisal', 1978).

Tanzania allowed the donors nine months to submit the study. The AID Mission replied that it would be impossible for it to obtain the necessary approval, recruit staff and prepare the plan at such short notice. The government withdrew its request (USAID, DAP, 1975).

Tanzania renewed the request after Carter took office in 1977, and this time it went through (USAID, 'Appraisal', 1978). The Arusha Regional Planning and Village Development Project, approved in 1978, committed \$24.2 million, fully 84 per cent of the \$29.0 million in new project spending that year.

The 1976 election ended eight years of Republican control of the White House and retained a Democratic majority in Congress. The Mission realized that a government unified under the Democratic Party was probably going to produce significant changes in US foreign policy, and proposed that a major strategy review session be held in Tanzania in early 1977 to be attended by high level officials from Washington. The Africa Bureau agreed to a review session, but did not agree to holding it in Tanzania, and recommended instead that the new strategy be 'hammered out' in Washington. The Mission 'declined the invitation, believing with considerable justification that such a strategy session should take place in Tanzania' (USAID, 'Appraisal', 1978). Incredibly, the dispute about where to meet could not be resolved, and no strategy review session was held at all. The Mission instead was told to revise the existing country plan, a task it completed by the end of the year.

Basis of American Aid

The conditions the USA placed on its aid during the period of reaching the poor majority changed from requiring that Tanzania should refrain from becoming pro-Communist to requiring that Tanzania demonstrate it was sufficiently poor. This Tanzania was easily able to do. Aside from the negative condition of its poverty, the growth in Nyerere's international stature as a consequence of his continuing support for the liberation struggles in southern Africa provided a positive justification for continuing American aid to Tanzania.

The policy of keeping out of other countries' internal affairs, begun under Johnson and sustained by Nixon, remained in effect during the Ford administration. The policy of non-interference began to come to an end in 1977 when the Carter administration pronounced its support for human rights and majority rule. The violation of human rights and inordinate levels of defence spending by a government became reasons for suspending or reducing American aid to developing countries (Brzezinski 1983). In making political reforms a condition for receiving American aid, the Carter administration restored a portion of the Kennedy vision of a foreign aid programme in support of democracy.

The Carter Doctrine did not have to be applied in Tanzania. The Nyerere government's 1973–76 Villagization Programme, the compulsory resettlement of 5 million or more Tanzanian peasants in the 'largest resettlement effort in the history of Africa' (Hyden 1980:130) was a clear and gross human rights violation, but it was a *fait accompli* by the time Carter took office. The Mission's 1978 budget submission stated that 'neither political human rights problems nor the level of defense expenditures requires special treatment or restrictions in AID programs' (USAID, Annual Budget Submission, 1978). In 1979 the Ambassador was able to enthuse, 'We are to a rare and happy extent free to make our development decisions for development reasons' (USAID, Country Development Strategy Statement, 1979).

Opinion about *Ujamaa* began to divide in the Mission as Tanzania's economic situation worsened in the latter part of the 1970s. Some saw a causal relationship between the crisis and *Ujamaa*. They wished to use American aid for leverage as a brake on Tanzania's radicalization. The 1975 country plan indicated the desire of this faction 'to try to influence policies and decisions in view of contributions being made', but the consensus in the Mission was that it would have been futile to try. The size of the AID mission in Tanzania was big compared to other AID programmes in Africa, but it was small compared to other donors in the country. AID's $26.7 million in new spending in 1975 amounted to just 5 per cent of the $609.8 million total foreign aid that Tanzania received that year. This amounted to $41 in foreign aid for every Tanzanian man, woman and child (Blue *et al.* 1976), a substantial sum of money in a country where per capita income was $305 (USAID, Congressional Presentation, 1976). The small size of the programme did not give the Mission much leverage to use had it wanted to.

The Structure of AID

The 1973 New Directions mandated changes in AID that had the effect of making the agency become a bottom-heavy organization (Tendler 1975). An unintended consequence of the increased reliance on the lower ranks to formulate and implement plans was the rift between AID's Africa Bureau and the AID mission in Tanzania that developed throughout the 1970s. The 1978 'Appraisal Report' found there was an 'absence of a constructive and imaginative dialogue' between headquarters and the field, 'particularly in terms of what constitutes conformance with the [New Directions]'. In the view of the Mission, the Africa Bureau in Washington interpreted the New Directions quite narrowly and reduced the Mission's discretion, yet it played no positive role in formulating an appropriate and focused strategy for Tanzania. For its part, the Bureau was 'uneasy' about the internal consistency of the Mission's strategy. It feared that the Mission was spreading itself too thin (USAID, 'Appraisal', 1978).

The most significant and most divisive issue in the Mission remained the question of what the proper attitude towards *Ujamaa* should be. Altruists were drawn to the Nyerere vision. They could see Tanzanian socialism as an appropriate response to an unfair world system. They found congruence between the broad goals of *Ujamaa* and the New Directions. In his foreword to the 1975 country plan the US Ambassador wrote:

> The dedication to equity among its citizens and current emphasis on food production bring Tanzania in close alignment with our own Foreign Assistance Act. Moreover, the direction and style used by Tanzania in pursuit of its development goals (including its concept of Ujamaa villages), while undoubtedly controversial, are nonetheless clearly stated and widely understood. (USAID, DAP, 1975)

Some in the Mission felt that Tanzania's belief that it 'does not receive a fair return for sales of its products abroad' justified its view 'that the developed world, with the U.S. in the lead, should take the initiative to right the wrongs and inequalities in the present international economic structure' (USAID, Country Development Strategy Statement, 1979). Some AID advisers seemed positively smitten by *Ujamaa*. A team of consultants came away from Tanzania 'convinced that Nyerere is one of the most creative thinkers on the subject of development in the world. We believe the effort ... is one of the most important experiments in the world ... more impressive than the Chinese model ... a successful and "authentically African" model of development' (USAID, Conceptual Framework, 1977).

Ironically, however, in supporting *Ujamaa*, its supporters in AID fell into the solidarity trap. The firm support *Ujamaa* gave to the principle of national self-determination barred AID's *Ujamaa* supporters from objectively considering the relationship between the policies of *Ujamaa* and the performance of the Tanzanian economy. In supporting *Ujamaa*, the altruists in the Mission found themselves maintaining the 'realist' fiction that politics does not matter in development.

The realists in the Mission, however, found *Ujamaa* to be contradictory to, not congruent with, the New Directions. Tanzania's 'attitudes toward private enterprise, individual freedoms and expropriation of private property are contrary to Congressional and AID criteria and are factors that mitigate aganist closer U.S.–Tanzania ties' (USAID, 'Appraisal', 1978). The realists believed *Ujamaa*, not the market, was the cause of Tanzania's worsening economic situation. 'Market forces, which it was assumed would regulate equity in LDCs (less developed countries), even if indirectly, in Tanzania are partly controlled or far too weak as a regulating device' (USAID, DAP Revision, 1977). It was no longer possible to ignore the effect of politics in Tanzania, 'a country where donor coordination is discouraged and where AID does not have access to bilateral dialogue on macroeconomic considerations and major development policy issues' (USAID, 'Appraisal', 1978).

The division of opinion about *Ujamaa* produced a deadlock in Mission planning. The final country plan submitted under the Carter administration acknowledged as much:

> The history of AID's attempts to develop its economic assistance strategy for Tanzania amply demonstrates the difficulty of achieving, within U.S. foreign assistance circles, a consensus on why we should be providing assistance, what form U.S. assistance ought to take, and what the levels ought to be. There are those who favor Tanzania's self-reliance with equity philosophy and there are those who fault its lack of pragmatism. (USAID, Country Development Strategy Statement, 1981)

The Staffing of AID

The trend towards greater use of NGOs as implementers and increased reliance on contractors continued throughout the period of reaching the poor majority. Of the 16 projects launched in the seven years 1974–80, NGOs implemented all but two, or almost 88 per cent of the projects launched in 1974–80 compared with not quite 47 per cent of the projects in 1961–73.

A comparison of two different years before and after the election of Jimmy Carter shows the extent to which AID increased its reliance on contractors. The Mission consisted of 37 direct hires and 53 contractors in 1975, and 44 direct hires and 99 contractors in 1978. The decline in the proportion of direct hires in the Mission from 41 per cent to 31 per cent in four years was a trend that would continue.

The change towards increased exogenous staffing had a down side. It produced a caste of project managers who, according to the 1978 'Appraisal Report', were unequipped to carry out programme analysis: 'Few staff members appeared to be qualified for the broader aspects of project management, especially with respect to guiding, analyzing and negotiating the overall direction of projects.' Worse, they 'sometimes form a screen between top USAID management and project implementers' (USAID, 'Appraisal', 1978).

The Type and Use of Feedback

By 1975 AID was beginning to develop indicators of programme success that differed from the project output statistics used in the previous decade. The new indicators were designed to measure effects more directly. The development of these indicators was pioneered in the Tanzanian Mission by the new and as yet quite junior division of Health and Human Population. As the focus of AID health projects changed to preventative from curative strategies, project results were no longer measured in output statistics such as the numbers of health centres constructed or personnel trained, but in terms such as 'the ratio of population to doctors and health facilities to population ... distribution and placement of health services in centers of population [and] the way in which health services are used by the people in the various parts of the country' (USAID, DAP, 1975). As the new way of thinking gained currency in the agency, the type of feedback the Mission sought in Tanzania slowly began to change from measures of output to measures of effect.

The Degree of AID Autonomy

By the time of the American bicentennial (1976), in the eyes of Tanzania and many other countries of the world, the USA had fallen in status from champion and defender of democracy to chief apologist for exploitative capitalism and right-wing dictatorship. The rancorous criticism that US foreign policy was drawing from abroad and from within Congress provided even more reason for AID to continue to pretend as it always had that politics had no influence on development.

The State Department: during the 1970s the Embassy ceased being directly involved in Mission planning, but it continued to play a role in setting the overall size of the programme. The Embassy 'insisted on a modest U.S. presence in Tanzania based primarily on the "show of interest" rationale and sufficient to provide an entree to diplomatic dialogue'. It 'quantified the AID role in terms of aid levels and USAID staffing' (USAID, 'Appraisal', 1978). In other words, the State Department kept US aid to Tanzania to a minimum.

The Congress: during the period of reaching the poor majority, Congress passed over 150 restrictions and prohibitions that reduced executive control over foreign policy (Tower 1988:152). In 1974, one year after the New Directions, Congress acted to limit both the President's role in the budget-making process and his powers to conduct foreign policy. In the same legislation Congress made the State Department the 'first cabinet department subject to annual authorization for its entire appropriation'

(Schick 1980:172). Henceforth AID would have to be re-authorized by Congress each year before it could receive funding. The combined effect of the various acts to reduce executive control over foreign policy on AID's capacity to plan and implement effectively was deleterious. In a section of the 1977 revised country plan tilted 'Limitations on Development Imposed by Congress and AID', the Mission complained 'of the limitations on our ability to respond to Tanzania priorities and critical development needs on a timely basis. The Mandate, while focusing AID upon the small farmer, limits our ability to reach him' (USAID, DAP Revision, 1977).

The President: when Nixon resigned in August 1974, Gerald Ford came to office with a popular image as 'a regular guy ... "superbly average ... like Ike"'. One of his first decisions as President was to retain Henry Kissinger in his dual role as both Secretary of State and National Security Adviser.

Following the Portuguese coup in April 1974 and the announcement by the new regime of a timetable for the independence of Portugal's colonies, Kissinger began secretly funding an anti-Marxist faction in Angola. This set in motion a series of events that soon engulfed Angola in civil war.

Predictably, the Nyerere government denounced the US actions in immoderate language, and then alarmingly announced plans to provide Soviet-run training bases for the Angolan Marxists (Stockwell 1978:202). Kissinger reacted to the prospect of a superpower confrontation in Africa by immediately opening negotiations with Nyerere to halt the escalation (Crouch 1987:162). US–Tanzanian relations reached rock-bottom. In reflection of this fact, the Ford administration cut new project spending in Tanzania from $26.7 million in 1975 to $547 000 in 1976.

In the combined final seven months of the Nixon administration and Ford's $2\frac{1}{2}$ years in office, AID obligated a total of $35.7 million in new spending in Tanzania. The three-year average of $12 million was one-third of the $33 million average under Nixon and two-thirds of the $18 million average under Kennedy; it was also one-third more than the $8 million under Johnson.

Carter combined traditional southern political traits with deeply held religious beliefs. He emphasized the breach of faith with the American people that had occurred under Republican rule and portrayed himself as someone who could be trusted to restore open government. 'I will never lie to you' was a theme of his campaign. He believed US foreign policy was 'stalemated on the level of power and excessively cynical on the level of principle' (Brzezinski 1983:81). He was especially critical of the secretive conduct of Kissinger, and pledged to restore basic moral principles to US foreign policy (Hargrove 1988). His administration made improved human rights a condition for receiving US aid. This became known as the Carter Doctrine.

It had no immediate effect in Tanzania. Carter entered office in 1977 when US–Tanzanian relations were at their low point. In Carter's first year in office AID obligated less than $1 million in new spending for the second year in a row. A year later Tanzania was still strongly opposed to many US foreign policy goals and was routinely demonizing the USA. Despite this the USA increased new spending in Tanzania from $940 000 to $29 million in 1978. The Mission's opponents of *Ujamaa* were overruled by a higher need to secure Tanzanian support for the administration's new southern Africa policy.

The increase in aid had the desired effect. In his introductory statement accompanying the 1978 country plan (the first written under the new Country Development Strategy Statement format of the Carter administration), the US Ambassador was pleased to note 'the sharply improved atmosphere of US–Tanzanian relations' and supported the increase in aid: 'It is appropriate that this improved atmosphere be reflected in an expanding assistance program.' The deadlocked division in opinion about *Ujamaa* had produced a situation in which the Mission was having trouble articulating 'a coherent and focused program in which goals are quantified and a relationship is drawn between strategy, activities and accomplishments'. Mission planning had become 'patchwork'. The result had been 'a drift in strategy, and an attempt to fashion a "program for all seasons"' (USAID, 'Appraisal', 1978). Now the deadlock was broken.

The second oil shock and the war with Uganda in 1979 were disastrous events for Tanzania. The government was forced to petition the IMF for relief. The IMF indicated its conditions, Nyerere rejected them, and a struggle began that would continue for the next six years.

In the first years of the dispute, the Nyerere government showed its resolve to 'pay the price of social and economic disruption, in order to lay the framework for a different type of society' (Blue *et al.* 1976). When negotiations with the IMF broke down, the Mission reported in the 1980 country plan that the 'Tanzanian leadership feels these measures … would require it to compromise its basic socialist philosophy and would not have the effect anticipated by the IMF in any case'. Undeniably the Tanzanian economy was 'in great jeopardy … At stake is the progress made in recent years in extending social and economic services and facilities to the mass of the population' (USAID, Country Development Strategy Statement, 1980).

During Carter's four years in office from 1977 to 1980, AID obligated a total of $83.0 million in new spending in Tanzania. The average of $21 million per year was less than the $33 million under Nixon, but more than the $18 million under Kennedy, the $12 million under Ford, and the $8 million under Johnson.

Interpreting the Behaviour of AID, 1974–80

There were several changes in sectoral spending over the course of the 1974–80 period of reaching the poor majority. Annual new spending for agriculture continued to rise, from an average $1.6 million in the years 1974–76 when the Republicans controlled the White House to $6.9 million in 1977–80. Average annual support for social services likewise rose, from $2.4 million in 1974–76 to $6.7 million in 1977–80. Support for public administration, in decline since the 1966 FAA, sharply increased in the period of reaching the poor majority from an average of $700 000 in 1974–76 to $3.8 million in 1977–80. Support in the finance sector, on the other hand, fell, from an average of $7.5 to $1.9 million. Meanwhile average annual new spending in the infrastructure sector declined to zero and remained there.

The average in total new spending for the full seven-year period of reaching the poor majority was 14 per cent lower than the average for the institution-building period. AID pledged a total of $254.5 million in the thirteen years from 1961 to 1973, an average of $19.6 million per year. It promised a total of $118.6 million in the seven years of reaching the poor majority, an average of $16.9 million.

The average number of projects launched per year also declined. On average four projects had been launched per year from 1961 to 1973. From 1974 to 1980 the average number was two. The average cost per project therefore continued its increase, from $4.6 million in the institution-building period to $7.4 million in the period of reaching the poor majority.

Congressional controls over AID multiplied during the 1970s in the form of mandates and the earmarking of funds. These measures were cumulatively debilitating for the Mission. The Embassy continued to play a role in 'quantifying' the size of the AID programme in Tanzania. Meanwhile the Mission remained as aloof from the other donors as it had been in the 1960s. A report in 1976 summed up the Mission's attitude in this regard. AID's programmes 'should be consistent, or not in conflict, with, and in some cases might be supportive of, programs of other donors. In general, however, they should not be dependent upon other donor programs for their management, operation, or success' (Blue *et al.* 1976).

The Third Period: Forcing Political Reform, 1981–95

Ronald Reagan entered office in 1981 with an advantage neither Nixon nor Ford had enjoyed: a Republican majority in the Senate. The new administration brought with it a new foreign policy agenda and a new approach to foreign aid that was first articulated in a speech by Reagan to the World Affairs Council in Philadelphia on 15 October 1981. The new administration's emphasis would be on 'guiding assistance toward the development of self-sustaining productive capacities' (Department of State 1981). At the Cancun summit a week later, Reagan described the perspective that would guide foreign aid under his administration. 'We are mutually interdependent', he told the assembled Third World leaders on 22 October, 'but above all, we are individually responsible' (Bandow 1988:146).[9]

The Reagan administration retained the Carter policy of making American aid conditional on political reform, but changed the conditions from insisting that recipient governments respect human rights to insisting that they free their markets. Congress greatly helped the administration in this endeavour by passing the Brooke Amendment to the FAA.[10]

The Source of AID Objectives

The AID programme in Tanzania was in severe jeopardy the moment Reagan entered the White House in 1981. AID's decades-old willingness to excuse recipient governments for political failure in order to shelter programmes and protect careers had rendered it 'often unable and usually not willing to withhold funding if policy reforms are not made' (Bandow 1988:148). This was not going to be the case in Tanzania. In each of its first three years in office the Reagan administration slashed new spending in Tanzania, from the $32.7 million in Carter's last budget to $17.4 million in Reagan's first, then to $3.6 million in 1982, and (for only the second time in history) to zero in 1983.

The cuts broke the deadlock in the Mission over whether, how, and at what level to support *Ujamaa*. Those who had favoured Tanzania's philosophy of self-reliance with equity had lost. Those who had faulted Tanzania's 'lack of pragmatism' had won, but it was a Pyrrhic victory. When they saw they would have to share in the task of terminating their own programme the members of the Mission closed ranks in opposition to the cuts. 'To have approved our Country Development Strategy Statement on the one hand at the same time deny us the financial and human resources necessary to effectuate that strategy strikes us as being capricious and wasteful' (USAID, Annual Budget Submission, 1981).

In 1983 new spending was cut to zero; the Mission declared itself in 'a very somber period' (USAID, Annual Budget Submission, 1983) and reluctantly initiated the 'wind-down scenario' for the termination of the programme. Still, it planned hopefully for a 'turnaround scenario' in case Tanzania came to an agreement with the IMF and AID funding resumed (USAID, Annual Budget Submission, 1984). The hoped for 'turnaround' began in 1984 when Sweden changed sides in Tanzaina's dispute with the IMF. Suddenly bereft of the support of his strongest ally, rather than give in to the IMF, Nyerere decided not to seek another term. In December 1985 Ali Hassan Mwinyi became Tanzania's second President.

Six months later in June, Tanzania initiated the IMF's ERP. In short order a Standby Agreement was reached with the IMF in August, a Paris Club debt-rescheduling agreement was signed in September, and a World Bank Multisector Rehabilitation Credit agreement was signed in November (USAID, 'Concept Paper', 1987). President Reagan immediately authorized a $12 million grant to Tanzania for a project called Transport Sector Policy Reform and Rehabilitation. Another $46.2 million was added to an ongoing project, Regional Transport Development, which was refurbishing the railways in Tanzania, Zambia and Zimbabwe. The following year, the $64.2 million Agricultural Transportation Assistance Programme was launched to rebuild a portion of Tanzania's rural roads (USAID, Annual Budget Submission, 1988; USAID, Tanzania Overview, 1995). The choice of objectives represented a significant change: infrastructure projects were back.

Under the Bush administration, the Mission added a $12.9 million training programme in 1989. Four projects totalling $32.6 million were begun in 1990. In the covering letter accompanying the 1990 Action Plan, the Mission Director declared 'the conclusion of the Mission's rebuilding phase'. A $49.6 million finance project was added in 1992. Under the Clinton administration, a $16.2 million health project was launched in 1993, and a year later a $16.0 million rural telecommunications project and also a $400 000 project to privatize real estate development.

Basis of American Aid

The conditions for receiving US assistance under Reagan became more stringent than ever. Tolerance of socialism evaporated. During the wind-down, the Mission repeatedly expressed doubts to Washington that the Tanzanian government would yield to the IMF, but Washington did not budge. In a cable on 13 April 1985, the Africa Bureau reminded the Mission that 'all AID resources ... are to be linked to our efforts to support policy reform'.

Although the altruist viewpoint disappeared from official channels after 1981, the altruists in the Mission left traces of their continued existence. Writing in the margins of the same 11 February 1987 cable from REDSO, an anonymous reader expressed doubts about the wisdom of forcing Tanzania to abandon *Ujamaa*: 'Reforms are only easy in hindsight if successful, not when you have to grapple with competing forces beforehand.'

The Clinton administration made AID an experiment in reinventing government, launching the most substantial reforms ever undertaken in AID. The Country Program Strategy Plan was renamed the Strategic Planning Framework. Changes were made to increase participation in planning, to establish planning by objective, and to decentralize AID. A contractor thought it was not working. The effort to bring 'beneficiaries in as stakeholders and partners' was not working because 'the "partners" don't have time for all the endless meetings'. Decisions were still made in advance. 'The "partners" are invited in to rubber-stamp the decision, to demonstrate "partnership."' An official at the Mission described how the process worked in Tanzania in terms that clearly revealed that the era of proud defiance was over. 'The Tanzanians', he said, 'are brought in at the end to stand there and nod yes'.

The Structure of AID

In the second year of the Brooke-induced wind-down, in a 5 December, 1984 cable to all missions worldwide, Reagan's administrator, M. Peter McPherson, declared that AID 'will place less emphasis on centralized control over planning and program design, and will rely on the extensive experience of field managers'. This signalled the advent of a new effort to decentralize the agency.

Three years later, in 1987, Congress revised the FAA once again by enacting the Development Fund for Africa (DFA), a reform intended to free AID's Africa Bureau of a certain amount of Congressional control first by fixing a level of funding for Africa[11] to relieve it of political pressures, second by removing certain regulations that locked AID into project assistance and tied it to American products, and third by encouraging AID to programme for strategic results (USAID, Growth Renewed, 1992). A cable from the Africa Bureau to all missions on 20 December 1989 announced that the twin reforms were having the desired effect: 'AID's decentralized, country-specific approach to the programming and implementation of development assistance has been judged, by analysts within and outside of AID, to be a principal strength of the bilateral U.S. assistance program.'

However, two years after that cable was sent, investigations began to uncover high levels of corruption in AID. A retired AID country director listed three investigations, one by the GAO, one by an Office of Management and Budget 'swat team', and one by AID's own Inspector General. He alleged that the corruption reached as high as Bush's administrator, Ronald Roskens, and that as a result, the Clinton administration came to office in 1993 very much 'concerned about the catalogue of ills and problems' in AID. The result was the beginning of a movement in Congress to abolish AID, and its later 'reinventing' under Clinton. In the view of the retired official, the latter had the consequence of shifting 'the center of power' not downwards towards the missions, but upwards into the office of the Assistant Administrator for Management. The termination of the policy, in place since 1963, of using projects as the primary vehicle for implementing AID programmes led, in the view of a contractor, to a great deal of confusion at the mission level about how the goal of sustainability was to be reconciled with the demand for immediate impact.

The Staffing of AID

Throughout the two years of heavy budget cuts the Mission in Tanzania steadily reduced its staff. In 1980 there were 22 US direct hires (USAID, Annual Budget Submission, 1980). Six years later, just prior to the signing of the IMF Standby Agreement in 1986, the Mission was down to five (USAID, Annual Budget Submission, 1986). When the turnaround began the following year, the number of direct hires began to grow. The 1992 budget submission 'anticipated' ten direct hires by fiscal year 1994 (USAID, Annual Budget Submission, 1992). In November 1994 there were eight. The budget that year was $40 million. The Mission was handling 25 per cent money with one-third as many people as it was at the end of the period of reaching the poor majority.

The change towards increasingly exogenous staffing was partly a consequence of the overall shrinking of AID's size. The Administrator appointed by Clinton to save AID, J. Brian Atwood, stated in late 1995 that AID staff had been reduced by 20 per cent in the three years the Clinton administration had been in office, from 11 500 to 9200 (*Orlando Sentinel*, 27 Nov. 1995). A high-ranking official in Washington offered his opinion that the reductions in force were having the positive effect of winnowing out the least competent and improving the quality of personnel. Direct hires were, in his view, the best available people, able to 'live among the people and breathe in the cultures, who can give us accurate information and tell us what's going on'. A contractor with fourteen years' experience disagreed. He thought AID had changed 'from a hands-on, implementation-focused organization doing in-the-dirt development, and became a bank. It attracts different personalities now. The hands-on people wanted to do development work; the "bankers" are bean counters; they're cold, heartless and cynical.'

In addition to its increasing reliance on exogenous personnel for programme design and implementation, AID steadily increased its reliance on NGOs. A cable from the Africa Bureau to all missions on 13 April 1985 referred to 'a growing interest in expanding the role' of NGOs in official development. In the 1960–73 institution-building period in Tanzania 46 per cent of all projects were implemented by NGOs. In the 1974–80 period of reaching the poor majority, the proportion reached 81 per cent, its height, before declining slightly to 71 per cent in the 1981–95 period of forcing political reform.

Feedback

The desire in Washington for missions to quantify 'people-level impact indicators' (or 'benchmarks' as they were also called) was serious. On 13 April 1985 the Africa Bureau cabled its missions that 'benchmarks need to be specific and quantified as much as possible and directly related to changes the program is trying to effect'. On 6 December 1986 it cabled about the 'need for more precise program-level indicators that can help to identify progress more objectively ... quantified to the extent possible'.

It took time for the missions to catch on to what was wanted. On 8 May 1991 the Bureau cabled several missions to say there were 'major gaps in understanding what the Bureau means when it requests reporting on people level impact', and the Tanzania mission was singled out as an example. Its indicators still 'reflected a strong output bias rather than people level impact'. Nine months later the Tanzania mission still was not on top of it. On 14 February 1992 the Bureau complained that the problems with its indicators was making it impossible 'for reviewers to see the progress being made from year to year'. The Bureau made a recommendation: 'If an indicator cannot be quantified, it would be helpful to the reviewer if the means of measurement could be described in a narrative form.'

Eventually the Mission cottoned on. The change in its indicators is apparent in two projects launched three years apart in 1988 and 1990. The first, the $64.2 million Agricultural Transport Assistance Program (ATAP) started in 1988, had no indicators, and so the Mission came under fire from the Bureau. ATAP's objectives were of the old output variety: to inventory and reclassify rural roads; to develop a national road maintenance strategy; to hire and train personnel; to get the government to increase its road maintenance budget; and finally to rely on private Tanzanian contractors to rehabilitate and maintain 500 kilometres of rural roads (USAID, ATAP Project Paper, 1988). In contrast, the $17.7 million Tanzania Family Planning Services Support Project launched in 1990 included the sorts of indicators Washington wanted to see: for example, an increase in the contraceptive prevalence rate and numbers of acceptors who return for resupply; an increase in the number of Tanzanians aware of family planning and knowledgeable about at least one modern method of contraception; and a decrease in the average desired family size reported in regularly conducted surveys (USAID, Tanzania Family Planning Services Support Project Paper, 1990).

Autonomy of AID

On 20 December 1989 the Africa Bureau cabled its missions to communicate its understanding of the difficulties they faced in planning: 'AID missions are challenged to design and manage the country program in such a way that it responds to the foreign policy needs of the U.S. government and implements the assistance policy directives of Congress and agency leadership.' In this single sentence the Africa Bureau listed the three influences to which the Mission in Tanzania had always been most responsive: the foreign policy of the President, the mandates of the Congress, and the directives of AID.

The State Department: State Department influence over AID declined in the 1980s. Embassies played less and less of a role in determining missions' levels of aid. By the 1990s the State Department was being kept out of AID planning as a matter of routine. When AID was deciding in 1994 which missions to close, an official involved in the decision revealed that 'State was not brought in till very late, otherwise they never would have let us close any, because they see a mission closing as reducing their leverage in a country'. As of February 1995 AID had closed 21 of a target 25 missions, nine in Africa.

The Congress: A 1983 GAO study that compared AID with its Canadian, French, Swedish, British, and West German counterparts in Tanzania found that, of the six, AID was the most accountable to legislative controls (US GAO 1983). The 1985 famine in Ethiopia contributed to the passage of the 1987 DFA. This act exempted missions in Africa from many of the restrictions on AID overall, and fixed the annual level of aid to Africa at a nominal $800 million.

The DFA, combined with all the other previous attempts by Congress to legislate altruistic reforms, contributed to the AID 'handbook' that by

1995 was 37 volumes long and could fill a shopping trolley. The agency was 'barnacled over' (as one official in Washington characterized it) by mandates and earmarks. The Mission Director in Tanzania lamented having to try to achieve no fewer than 33 separate objectives and address 77 disparate priorities. As one official in Washington summed it up with a sigh, 'We propose; Congress decides.'

When the Soviet Union broke apart in 1991, AID's enemies in Congress saw an opportunity. Unfortunately for AID, the opening came at a time when corruption in the agency was revealed to be at an all-time high. In June of that year Republican Representative John Kasich provided the House with specific instances of AID corruption: contractors in Rwanda who sold food aid for profit and then used the money to construct tennis courts; a malaria researcher who stole a nominal $144 000; an NGO in Egypt that lent money to fictitious borrowers; and a deputy director who took a nominal $70 000 in kickback. A former AID official indicated that much of the corruption was due to political patronage. He recounted in the press 'being dragged into congressman's offices when I wouldn't approve grants ... They'd say "I don't want the best [contractor]. I want my friend taken care of"' (*Dallas Morning News*, 8 Aug. 1993).

The Democratic Chairman of the Senate Appropriations Subcommittee, Patrick Leahy, suggested the government should 'just get rid of it and start over again' (Reuters, 18 Jan. 1993), later stating that AID had become 'exhausted intellectually, conceptually and politically' (Associated Press, 24 Sept. 1993).

Clinton picked for his AID administrator a long-time Democratic operative named J. Brian Atwood and gave him the mission of saving AID. Congress confirmed him in mid-May 1993. Proclaiming the agency was 'encumbered by excessive red tape and beaten down by poor morale' (*Christian Science Monitor*, 13 May 1993) and announcing that he had 'inherited a mess' (Associated Press, 24 Sept. 1993), Atwood set about cleaning it up. He declared that AID would be a 'reinvention laboratory' for Vice President Al Gore. There would be no sacred cows; the 'entire agency is on the chopping block' (*Dallas Morning News*, 8 Aug. 1993).

On the eve of the 1994 election, Secretary of State Warren Christopher submitted a plan to fold AID into the State Department as a cost-minimizing measure. The proposal was quickly disavowed by the administration, and Christopher was sent to go on record withdrawing it (*Congressional Record*, 31 July 1995).

Then the elections brought the first Republican majority to both houses of Congress since 1948 and gave the chair of the Senate Foreign Relations Committee to Jesse Helms, a long-time opponent of foreign aid. Senator

Helms took up the call to abolish AID with a vengeance. His office began to issue press releases referring to AID as the 'enemy' and to AID material as 'captured enemy documents', denigrating the agency in such hostile language it felt compelled officially to protest (*Washington Post*, 1 Aug. 1995). Helms seized upon Christopher's rescinded proposal, revised it, and introduced it as S. 908 under the disingenuous name of The Foreign Relations Revitalization Act. The bill would abolish AID and turn its functions and budget over to the State Department (*Congressional Record*, 31 July 1995). The House passed a counterpart to the Helms bill, H.R. 1561, in the summer of 1995. President Clinton promised to veto it. This rallied Democratic Senators and key moderate Republicans such as foreign affairs specialist Richard Lugar, who saw it as too radical, and the Helms bill was kept from coming to a vote.

The President: at the start of the 1980 presidential campaign, the Carter administration dismissed Ronald Reagan too lightly as an ideologue who reduced complex issues to simple terms that he was, admittedly, able to communicate very effectively (Jordan 1982:302–3). Likc Johnson and Nixon, Reagan did not have a first-class education, and came from modest origins. Like Johnson, Nixon and Carter, his administration would pronounce a doctrine. Reagan's policy agenda as a whole called for so many significant changes that even conservatives referred to it as a 'crusade' and a 'revolution' (Boaz 1988:1–2). The core change to foreign policy was 'rolling back Soviet power, particularly in the Third World' (Ravenal 1988:138). The Reagan Doctrine pledged assistance to any movement fighting to overthrow a Communist regime. By openly recognizing that politics was important to economic change, the new administration overturned the remnants of the Mann Doctrine and laid the 'Big Lie' of development finally to rest.

In balance, however, the changes Reagan made in US foreign policy were less a revolution than a restoration, a return to earlier principles. Reagan's policy on foreign aid was also something less than revolutionary. In 1983 he appointed a commission chaired by Frank Carlucci (former Chargé d'Affaires in Zanzibar) to review US foreign aid policy. The commission submitted its report in November 1983. Conservatives soon attacked its recommendations as inconsequential, nothing that would not have been supported by any of Reagan's predecessors (Bandow 1988:144–5).

The Mission certainly did not see the changes as a revolution. It reported in 1982 that 'the Administration's emphasis on policy change, private sector growth, technology transfer and institution building has not affected our strategy objectives as much as it has our methodology for achieving those objectives. The most striking difference in approach is the emphasis ... on policy consideration' (USAID, Annual Budget Submission, 1982).

Of Reagan's eight years in office, no new spending was obligated in Tanzania in four. From 1983 to 1986 the Mission was under Brooke. In the two years before and after Brooke, a total of $143.4 million was obligated, an average $18 million per year, the same as the Kennedy administration.

George Bush entered the White House in 1989, promising a kinder and gentler America. Like Kennedy before him, he came from a privileged background, the son of a Senator, educated in an Ivy League school. Like Kennedy, Bush was a Second World War veteran.

Bush made no large changes in African policy other than softening some of its rougher edges.[12] His administration's biggest foreign policy triumph was the Gulf War victory in 1991. Desert Storm also occasioned a serious bump in US–Tanzanian relations. President Mwinyi, a Zanzibari, was sensitive to the interests of Tanzania's Muslim minority. Iran had recently increased its diplomatic presence in the country (Magyar 1993). When Iraq invaded Kuwait in August 1990, the Mwinyi government condemned the aggression. However, it was not sympathetic to Desert Shield. During the build-up of coalition forces in Saudi Arabia, Mwinyi permitted Saddam Hussein to recruit soldiers from among Tanzania's urban unemployed. The Bush administration was outraged, and in response pulled the Peace Corps out of the country, professing concern for the safety of the volunteers. In 1991 no new spending was pledged to Tanzania.

Of the four years Bush was in office, new spending was obligated in three, a total of $95.1 million. The average under Bush of $24 million was less than the $33 million under Nixon but more than the $21 million under Carter.

Bill Clinton won election by a plurality in a three-way race, overcoming severe criticisms about his character to do so. His campaign focused intensely on domestic affairs, particularly the economy and a programme to reinvent government. Like Kennedy and Bush, Clinton had a good education. Like Kennedy, Ford and Bush, he had no real foreign policy agenda. He was a pragmatist, like Bush, and succeeded him as the second president in the post-Cold War era.

Clinton selected two former State Department officials to handle his foreign policy: Warren Christopher as Secretary of State and Anthony Lake as National Security Adviser.[13] The administration took a cautious approach to foreign affairs. Lake declared its intention was 'to be more activist in promoting democracy and human rights ... more interventionist' (*Boston Globe*, 22 Nov. 1993). Unfortunately, the climate resembled the isolationist 1920s, which was going to make it very hard to conduct foreign policy (*Christian Science Monitor*, 1 Aug. 1994).

Upon his confirmation in May 1993, Atwood announced the administration's new objectives for AID: to support sustainable development that protected the environment, to slow the world population explosion, to develop a rapid disaster response capability, and to promote democracy. The political conditions of US assistance were now total. To receive American aid, countries were going to have to show that they were moving towards multiparty democracy. With this announcement Clinton restored the Kennedy ideal of using American foreign aid to support democracy.

As AID became the laboratory for reinventing government that Atwood had promised it would be, the administration began working on a bill to replace the 1961 FAA in its entirety. On 3 February 1994 the Clinton administration introduced the Peace, Prosperity and Democracy Act to replace the antiquated FAA (*Washington Times*, 4 Feb. 1994). The goals laid out in the bill were 'not necessarily what African leaders want. They imply political development' (*Washington Post*, 4 Sept. 1994).

Then the elections of 1994 swept a Republican majority into Congress and stopped the administration's momentum. AID's very existence was suddenly seriously threatened. The administration began sending signals that, although its defence of AID was firm, it recognized the possibility that AID's enemies in Congress might succeed.

Of Clinton's first three years in office, new spending was obligated in Tanzania only in two. In 1995 the struggle between the administration and the Republican majority in Congress over AID's continued existence began. Without an appropriation bill, the Mission could not launch any new projects. Total new spending in Tanzania under the Clinton administration was $32.6 million, an average of $11 million per year, less than all administrations except Johnson.

Interpreting the Behaviour of AID: 1981–95

In the seven-year period of reaching the poor majority, the Mission obligated a total of $118.6 million, an average of $16.9 million per year. In the fifteen-year period of forcing political reform, the mission obligated a total $263.1 million, an average of $17.5 million per year, virtually the same. Not all sectors held even. Two sectors saw an increase, one saw no change, and three sectors saw a decrease.

Average support for infrastructure increased the most, from less than a million dollars annually in 1974–80 to $4.6 million per year in 1981–95. Support for public administration rose from an average of $2.5 million to $5.4 million per year. There was a very slight change in average support for Tanzania's industrial sector, from zero to a quarter of a million dollars. Activities in the agriculture, social services and finance sectors all saw declines. Agriculture declined the most: average spending on food production projects fell from \$4.6 million in 1974–80 to a mere \$200 000 per year in 1981–95. Support for social services fell from \$4.8 million to \$3.5 million, and assistance to the Tanzanian financial sector from an average of \$4.3 million to \$4.0 million per year.

The average for total new spending in the period of forcing political reform was roughly the same as the previous period of reaching the poor majority. The number of projects launched in 1981–95 was, however, halved, from an average of two projects per year to one. The average cost per project thus continued its climb, from \$7.4 million in the period of reaching the poor majority to \$13.9 million in the period of forcing political reform.

The Mission remained as aloof from the other donors in the 1980s and 1990s as it had in the previous two decades. In the Mission's view, coordination among donors seemed to have been viewed as desirable only to the extent that other donors coordinated with AID. The Mission reported in 1990 that it was having success in this regard. 'Another significant turn of events is the much more critical approach of the Nordic countries ... They appear to be aligning their assistance to that of USAID's program systems approach. This represents the most important result of our donor coordination effort thus far' (USAID, Assessment of Program Impact, 1990).

CONCLUSION

In the 35 years of this study the USA provided a total of \$637.6 million in aid to Tanzania in constant 1987 dollars, \$255.9 million in the 1961–73 period of institution building, \$118.6 million in the 1974–80 period of reaching the poor majority, and \$263.1 million in the 1981–95 period of forcing political reform (an average of \$18.2 million in new spending per year). Spending decreased from \$19.7 million in the first period to \$16.9 million in the second period, then rose to \$17.5 million in the third.

The Mission launched 90 projects from 1961 to 1995, 56 in the first 13 years, 16 in the next seven, and 18 in the final 15 years. The average overall cost per project was \$7.1 million: \$4.6 million in the first period, \$7.4 million in the second, and \$14.6 million per project in the third.

Figure 3.1 shows constant dollar new spending obligations over time. The five largest increases in chronological order were in 1970, 1973, 1978–80, 1987–88 and 1992. The increases in 1973 and 1992 represented

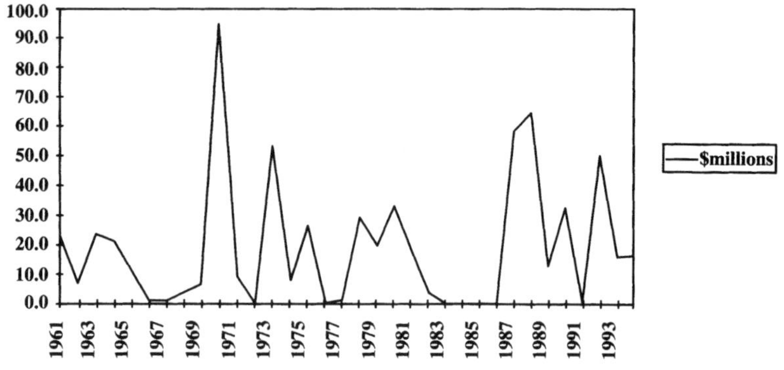

Figure 3.1 New spending obligations, 1961–94 (in constant 1987 dollars)

a return to the status quo after temporary disruptions in relations following disputes over unrelated issues regarding Taiwan and Iraq. The increase in 1975 was a reversal of policy, a humanitarian action taken to save people from famine (America springing to the rescue). The increase in 1978–80 was a result of the convergence of the Carter Doctrine with the New Directions, the period of time when altruism had its strongest influence in US foreign policy.

The biggest increase of the five was in 1970. Part of the increase was just Tanzania's share of the aid given to the front-line states that year to grease the skids for 'Tar Baby'. But part of it certainly was a tit-for-tat reaction to the Chinese decision to build a railway in Tanzania. The second largest increase, 1987–88, was a payoff for Tanzania's abjuration of *Ujamaa*.

The five deepest reductions in US aid came in 1966–67, 1972, 1976–77, 1983–86, and 1991. All were attributable to higher-level realist concerns. The first cut was made by Congress in anger over the Vietnam War. The others were due to Tanzanian opposition to US foreign policy on Taiwan in 1971, on Angola in 1975, on structural adjustment after 1980, and on the Gulf War in 1991.

Average annual spending varied across the eight administrations in office from 1961 to 1995; Table 3.1 ranks them. Interestingly, the top two spenders were Republican administrations – Nixon and Bush – and the bottom two were Democrats – Johnson and Clinton. The Republican presidents used foreign aid to Tanzania as a policy instrument more than the Democrats did. For 35 years the strategies and the behaviour of the AID mission in Tanzania were shaped by the competing propensities of realism and altruism.

Realist considerations determined the level of aid provided. On four occasions no new spending was obligated in Tanzania to punish it for

Table 3.1 Average annual new spending obligations by presidential administration

Administration	*$ millions*
Nixon (R)	32.7
Bush (R)	23.8
Carter (D)	20.7
Kennedy (D)	18.0
Reagan (R)	17.9
Ford (R)	11.9
Clinton (D)	10.9
Johnson (D)	7.7

R = Republican D = Democratic

opposing US policy. Three times it was substantially increased to encourage Tanzanian support of US policies, first in 1970 to make 'Tar Baby' more palatable to Tanzania, second in 1978 to persuade Tanzania to support the Carter Doctrine, and third in 1987 to compensate Tanzania for abandoning *Ujamaa.*

Some of the political interventions AID experienced were inspired by altruism. In 1966, 1973 and 1987, for example, Congress passed mandates requiring AID to concentrate on alleviating African poverty.

Much altruism came from within. The 35 years of plans, reports and analyses produced by the Mission are replete with expressions of humanitarian concerns. AID's officials and the private contractors and consultants who work for the agency do not appear to be driven by narrow self-interest.

An Analysis of the Variables

Source

The source of AID strategies in Tanzania was, as expected, the US government. In the institution-building period and the period of reaching the poor majority AID took pains to show it was being compatible with Tanzania's national development plans. With the election of Ronald Reagan, however, this pretence was ended, and the USA began forcing political reform.

Conditions

AID always provided assistance on a conditional basis. Over time there were three main conditions. The first two were the easiest for Tanzania to meet. From 1960 to 1973 the Nyerere government had only to maintain a form of neutrality that was not pro-Communist to receive American aid. From 1974 to 1980 Tanzania needed only to demonstrate sufficient poverty. The third condition was the hardest. Tanzania had to abandon socialism and then later to convert to multiparty democracy. The trend was towards the extreme, as expected (that is, from comparatively easy to more drastic conditions).

Structure

AID has always been a mix of centralized functions (reporting and accounting) and decentralized functions (planning and implementation). AID's geographical dispersion has made it dependent on its line officers and the private contractors and consultants it engages for the contextual knowledge that is crucial to sustainable development. The uncertainty of AID's task environment requires constant adaptation and adjustment of programmes, making AID a 'bottom-heavy' organization. However, its political vulnerability due to its enduring unpopularity back home and its continual micro-management by Congress has meant that whenever AID attempts to devolve decision-making authority to the field in one area (for example, in project planning), there has almost always been an increased centralization in some other area (for example, new mandates and earmarks). The question of whether AID is centralized or decentralized is difficult to answer.

Staffing

The earliest projects launched in the era of the 'manpower gap' were staffed by a higher proportion of direct hires than is the case today. Over time the overall number of direct hire positions was reduced (direct hire secretaries, for example, were eliminated) and given over to contractors and consultants. This was matched by a trend towards greater reliance on NGOs for project implementation. The trend towards exogenous staffing was as expected.

Feedback

The use of feedback was always high in AID. What changed was the *type* of feedback sought. In the institution-building period, feedback was in the form of 'output' statistics. In the period of reaching the poor majority, AID began to develop 'people-level impact indicators'. These became required of all projects during the period of forcing political reform. Every AID project in Tanzania had a basket of quantified 'benchmarks' to measure success by 1995.

Autonomy

The level of AID's autonomy has always been mixed. In the earliest years the Mission was quite closely tied to the Embassy, but as AID eked out greater overall freedom from the State Department, Congress steadily reduced its autonomy. From time to time the President exerted strong control through his foreign policies. AID's autonomy within the US government can therefore best be described as mixed. The agency successfully reserved for itself a high level of autonomy in the donor community, as always. The Mission remained extremely aloof from the other donor organizations in Tanzania.

The Four Traps of Foreign Aid

In Chapter 1, donor organizations were theorized to be vulnerable to four traps. Of these, AID can be judged to be thoroughly entangled in one, but free of the other three.

Fiscal Accountability

Donor agencies must to a greater or lesser extent account for their activities to their home government. If accountability is the single overriding concern for a donor organization, it becomes a trap. In the American political system of divided government, AID is administered by the President but is accountable to the Congress. Beginning shortly after its creation, and increasingly after 1973, AID became 'barnacled over' with Congressional mandates and earmarks which, by 1995, had accumulated into a 37-volume 'handbook'. The Mission in Tanzania repeatedly complained over the years about the strangling effect Congress had on its ability to do the job. The 1983 GAO report found AID was the most accountable to its home legislature of the six largest donors in Tanzania at that time.

Political Solidarity

If the desire to express solidarity with a country by giving it aid overwhelms all other criteria, such that the recipient learns it can expect the donor to provide it with pretty much whatever it asks, then solidarity is a trap for the donor. The US government never felt much solidarity with Tanzanian socialism. Even in its most tolerant period under Carter in the latter half of the period of reaching the poor majority, AID accepted

Ujamaa with reservations. AID steered clear of the solidarity trap in Tanzania.

Organizational Insularity

If a donor organization does not permit objective evaluations of its activities, it is susceptible to the insularity trap. Insularity was never a problem for AID; Congress made sure of that. AID's extreme unpopularity and political vulnerability made it a favourite target over the years for its enemies in the legislature, both the constantly varying groups opposing US foreign policies of the moment and the steadfast populist proponents of the America-first principle of isolationism. In obedience to the unceasing and cumulative stream of dictates that emanated from its unfriendly political environment over 35 years, the Mission in Tanzania changed from a focus on infrastructure in the 1960s to concentrating on rural development in the 1970s, and then went back to infrastructure in the 1980s, finally moving to a focus on finance and health in the 1990s. It developed people-level impact indicators for all its projects, and steadily increased its reliance on outside consultants, contractors and NGOs to design and implement its programmes and to evaluate its progress. In Tanzania, AID did not fall into the insularity trap.

Coordination

If a donor's paramount concern is to keep in step with the donor community in a recipient country, if its main strategy is just to go along with the majority, it falls into the coordination trap. In the case of AID, the official record makes clear that AID always has held (and continues to hold) itself aloof from the other donors in Tanzania. It saw and sees itself as an opinion maker, a leader, not a follower, and accepts coordination only if that means that other donors bring their policies into conformance with its own. Only once did AID conform to another donor in Tanzania: in 1981, when the Reagan administration ordered the Mission to bring its policy into line with the IMF. With the exception of that single instance, AID did not fall prey to the coordination trap in Tanzania.

The Dialectic of Altruism and Realism in an Agency under Siege

That AID's strategy and behaviour in Tanzania changed over 35 years is not surprising. But measured as new spending obligations per year, the volatility of change is remarkable. Most of the fluctuations shown above in Figure 3.1 can be explained by external factors, changes in the budget or in US foreign policies, or in Tanzania's attitudes towards them. Some of them cannot.

The changes in new spending that cannot be explained by external factors can be explained by the motivation of AID's individual employees and its organizational culture. When the Mission was left free of political interference, as much as it could it conducted its operations in a spirit of altruism. This spirit was both an honest reflection of the intent of AID's authorizing legislation and a common characteristic of its personnel.

The net effect on AID of 35 years of warring propensities, of the dialectic between realism and altruism, has been three basic sets of strategies and differences in the behaviour of its mission in Tanzania. The term 'pragmatic altruism' has been used here to describe the pattern across the three periods of time. In each of these periods, in some years US aid to Tanzania seemed like bribes, but most years it resembled philanthropy.

Notes

1. The first American aid to Tanzania was delivered in 1955, and consisted of $981 000 (in nominal terms) for a single British-run agricultural project.
2. New project spending in Tanzania fell from $53.1 million in 1973 to $8.4 million in 1974, and to $2.3 million in 1975. The amounts are in constant 1987 dollars.
3. This study considers money *obligated* per year, not money actually disbursed. This is done partly because of the complexity of quantifying streams of aid over time (Wood 1986), but also because, once a project is authorized and goes on line, it takes on a life of its own. Ongoing projects are resistant to policy change. The amounts of money disbursed per year thus do not reveal subtle changes in AID strategy and behaviour as well as the amounts of new spending obligated per year. Therefore the full cost of each project in Tanzania is attributed to the year the project was launched.
4. In contrast to Sida, AID's form of country programming never gave planning responsibility to the Tanzanians.
5. One official of long service recalled direct hire poultry breeders. Another remembered American direct hire secretaries.
6. By the Bush administration, AID contract personnel numbered about 55 000 worldwide (*Christian Science Monitor*, 7 Oct. 1993) as compared to 11 500 direct hires (*Orlando Sentinel*, 27 Nov. 1995).
7. The implementing organizations of nine projects launched in 1961–73 are not known.
8. This was the only state visit to the USA that Nyerere ever made.
9. Reagan would reportedly come away from the summit very impressed with the intellect of Julius Nyerere, but unconvinced by his ideas.

10. The Brooke Amendment required AID to close its mission in any country that was simultaneously in arrears on its debt repayments to the USA and not under an agreement with the IMF. Tanzania was one such country.
11. $800 million in nominal dollars (later reduced to $600 million).
12. His administration negotiated peaceful settlements in Namibia and Angola and enforced the existing sanctions on South Africa, which the Reagan administration had never done, in exchange for which Congress dropped proposals for adding more.
13. Christopher had served in the State Department under Carter, and had since been working as an attorney in Los Angeles. He could 'lawyer any issue to death' (Woodward 1993). Lake had been among the advisers to Henry Kissinger who resigned in 1970 to protest about the invasion of Cambodia. He later was Director of Policy Planning at the Sate Department under Carter.

References

Acheson, Dean G. (1969) *Present at the Creation: My Years in the State Department*. New York: Norton.

Attwood, William (1967) *The Reds and the Blacks: A Personal Adventure*. New York: Harper & Row.

Bandow, Doug (1988) 'Making Friends in the Third World', in David Boaz (ed.), *Assessing the Reagan Years*. Washington, DC: The Cato Institute.

Bienen, Henry (1967) *Tanzania: Party Transformation and Economic Development*. Princeton, NJ: Princeton University Press.

Biersteker, Thomas J. (1987) *Multinationals, the State, and Control of the Nigerian Economy*. Princeton, NJ: Princeton University Press.

Blue, Richard, Edmond Hutchinson, Fred Mann and James Weaver (1976) 'Conceptual Framework for USAID Agricultural Assistance in Tanzania'. USAID.
Congressional Presentation (1967–94).
Country Assistance Program (1963–66).
Country Development Strategy Statement (1979–81).
Country Program Strategy Paper (1992).

Blue, Richard and James Weaver (1977) 'Critical Assessment of the Tanzanian Model of Development'. USAID.
Development Assistance Program (1975, 1977).
Field Budget Submission (1972–74).
'History of the U.S.A.I.D. Program in Tanzania' (1985).
Tanzania Overview (1995).

Boaz, David (1988) *Assessing the Reagan Years*. Washington, DC: The Cato Institute.

Brown, Seyom (1984) *On the Front Burner: Issues in U.S. Foreign Policy*. Boston, MA: Little, Brown.

Brzezinski, Zbigniew (1983) *Power and Principle: Memoirs of the National Security Adviser 1977–1981*. New York: Farrar Strauss Giroux.

Campbell, Colin and Bert A. Rockman (eds) (1991) *The Bush Presidency: First Appraisals*. Chatham, NJ: Chatham House.

Chenery, Hollis and Stroudt, A.M. (1966) 'Foreign Assistance and Economic Development', *American Economic Review*, LVI.

Crane, George T. and Abla Amawi (eds) (1991) *The Theoretical Evolution of International Political Economy*. New York: Oxford University Press.

Crouch, C. (1987) *Western Responses to Tanzanian Socialism (1967–1983)*. Brookfield, VT, and Aldershot: Avebury.

Downs, Anthony (1967) *Inside Bureaucracy*. Boston, MA: Little, Brown.

Esman, Milton J. (1967) 'The Institution-Building Concepts – An Interim Appraisal'. Pittsburgh: Graduate School of Public and International Affairs, University of Pittsburgh, cited in Dennis A. Rondienlli, *Development Administration and U.S. Foreign Aid Policy*. Boulder, CO, and London: Lynne Rienner.

Freeland, Richard (1972) *The Truman Doctrine and the Origins of McCarthyism*. New York: Knopf.

Gilpin, Robert (1987) *The Political Economy of International Relations*, Princeton, NJ: Princeton University Press.

Goodsell, Charles T. (1985) *The Case for Bureaucracy: A Public Administration Polemic* (second edition). Chatham, NJ: Chatham House.

Hargrove, Erwin C. (1978) 'Issue Networks and the Executive Establishment', in Anthony King (ed.), *The New American Political System*, Washington, DC: American Enterprise Institute.

Hargrove, Erwin C. (1988) *Jimmy Carter as President: Leadership and the Politics of the Public Good*. Baton Rouge: Louisiana State University Press.

Hayter, Theresa (1971) *Aid as Imperialism*. Harmondsworth, Middlesex: Penguin Books.

Heinrichs, Waldo (1994) 'Lyndon B. Johnson: Change and Continuity' in W.I. Cohen and N.B. Tucker (eds), *Lyndon Johnson Confronts the World: American Foreign Policy 1963–1968*. New York, Cambridge University Press.

Hirschman, Albert (1967) *Development Projects Observed*. Washington, DC: The Brookings Institution.

Hook, Steven W. (1995) *National Interest and Foreign Aid*. Boulder, CO: Lynne Rienner.

Hyde, Albert C. (ed.) (1992) *Government Budgeting: Theory, Process, Politics* (second edition). Pacific Grove, CA: Brooks/Cole.

Hyden, Goran (1980) *Beyond Ujamaa: Underdevelopment and an Uncaptured Peasantry*. Berkeley, CA: University of California Press.

Hyland, William G. (ed.) (1987) *The Reagan Foreign Policy*. New York: New American Library.

Ink, Dwight (1993) 'Administration and Technical Assistance', in Kenneth W. Thompson (ed.), *Foreign Policy in the Reagan Administration: Nine Intimate Perspectives*. New York: University Press of America.

Jordan, Hamilton (1983) *Crisis: The Last Year of the Carter Presidency*. New York: Putnam.

Kemp, Geoffrey (1993) 'Presidential Management of the Federal Bureaucracy', in R.J. Art and S. Brown (eds), *U.S. Foreign Policy: The Search for a New Role*. New York: Macmillan.

Kindleberger, Charles P. (1987) *Marshall Plan Days*. Winchester, MA: Allen & Unwin.

Kingdon, John W. (1984) *Agendas, Alternatives, and Public Policies*. New York: HarperCollins.

Kissinger, Henry (1979) *White House Years*. Boston, MA: Little, Brown.

Krasner, Stephen D. (1985) *Structural Conflict: The Third World Against Global Liberalism*. Berkeley: University of California Press.

Lake, Anthony (1976) *The 'Tar Baby' Option: American Policy Toward Southern Rhodesia*. New York: Columbia University Press.

Lee, Robert D. and Ronald W. Johnson (1989) *Public Budgeting Systems*. Gaithersburg, MD: Aspen Publishers.

Lumsdaine, David H. (1993) *Moral Vision in International Politics: The Foreign Aid Regime 1949–1989*. Princeton, NJ: Princeton University Press.

Lyons, Terrence (1994) 'Keeping Africa off the Agenda', in W.I. Cohen and N.B. Tucker (eds), *Lyndon Johnson Confronts the World: American Foreign Policy, 1963–1968*. New York: Cambridge University Press.

McCullough, David G. (1992) *Truman*. New York: Simon & Schuster.

Mahoney, Richard D. (1983) *JFK: Ordeal in Africa*. New York: Oxford University Press.

Meier, Kenneth (1979) *Politics and the Bureaucracy: Policymaking in the Fourth Branch of Government*. North Scituate, MA: Duxbury Press.

Millikan, M.F. and W.W. Rostow (1957) *A Proposal: Key to an Effective Foreign Policy*. New York: Harper.

Morgenthau, Hans J. (1962) 'Preface to a Political Theory of Foreign Aid', in Robert H. Goldwin (ed.), *Why Foreign Aid*? Chicago: Rand McNally.

Morris, Roger (1977) *Uncertain Greatness: Henry Kissinger and American Foreign Policy*. New York: Harper & Row.

Mudge, J., Michael Crosswell and Kwan Kim (1980) 'Tanzanian Development Performance and Implications for Development Assistance'. USAID.

Noer, Thomas J. (1989) 'New Frontiers and Old Priorities in Africa', in Thomas J. Patterson (ed.), *Kennedy's Quest for Victory: American Foreign Policy, 1961–1963*. New York: Oxford University Press.

Packenham, Robert (1973) *Liberal America and the Third World: Political Development Ideas in Foreign Aid and Social Science*. Princeton NJ, Princeton University Press.

Ravenal, Earl C. (1987) 'Reagan's Failed Restoration: Superpower Relations in the 1980s', in David Boaz (ed.), *Assessing the Reagan Years*. Washington, DC: The Cato Institute.

Reilly, John E. (1988) 'America's State of Mind: Trends in Public Attitudes Toward Foreign Policy', in Charles W. Kegley Jr and Eugene R. Wittkopf (eds), *The Domestic Sources of American Foreign Policy*. New York: St Martin's Press.

Riddell, Roger C. (1987) *Foreign Aid Reconsidered*. Baltimore, MD: Johns Hopkins University Press.

Rogers, Peter (1992) 'Aid, Dependency, and the Tanzanian State in the Ujamaa Period', Master's Thesis, University of Florida.

Rondinelli, Dennis A. (1987) *Development Administration and U.S. Foreign Aid Policy*. Boulder, CO, and London: Lynne Rienner.

Rosenstein-Rodan, P.N. (1961) 'International Aid for Underdeveloped Countries'. *Review of Economics and Statistics*, p. 43.

Rossiter, Clinton (1961) *The Federalist Papers*. New York: New American Library.

Rostow, W.W. (1960) *The Stages of Economic Growth: A Non-Communist Manifesto*. Cambridge: Cambridge University Press.

Schick, Allen (1980) *Congress and Money: Budgeting, Spending and Taxing*. Washington, DC: The Urban Institute.

Schurmann, Franz (1987) *The Foreign Politics of Richard Nixon: The Grand Design*. Berkeley: University of California Press.
Stockwell, John (1978) *In Search of Enemies: A CIA Story*. New York: W.W. Norton.
Strange, Susan (1991) 'Casino Capitalism', in K.W. Stiles and T. Akaha, *International Political Economy: A Reader*. New York: HarperCollins.
Tendler, Judith (1975) *Inside Foreign Aid*. Baltimore, MD: Johns Hopkins University Press.
Tower, John (1988) 'Congress versus the President: the Formulation and Implementation of American Foreign Policy' in W. Hyland (ed.) *The Reagan Foreign Policy*. New York: New American Library.
Tucker, Nancy Bernkopf (1994) 'Lyndon Johnson: A Final Reckoning', in W.I. Cohen and N.B. Tucker (eds), *Lyndon Johnson Confronts the World: American Foreign Policy, 1963–1968*. New York: Cambridge University Press.
Ungar, Sanford J. (1993) 'U.S. Policy Toward Africa', in R.J. Art and S. Brown (eds), *U.S. Foreign Policy: The Search for a New Role*. New York: Macmillan.
USAID (selected bibliography)
Action Plan (1987–94).
Annual Budget Submission (1977–94).
'Appraisal Report of the AID Program in Tanzania' (1978).
Assessment of Program Impact (1990–94).
Background Paper, 'Donor Assistance to Tanzania: Past Trends and Recent Developments', Dirk Dijkerman (1987).
'Concept Paper for AID. Development Assistance to Tanzania' (1987).
Concept Paper (1989).
US Department of State (1981), 'Bulletin', vol. 81 (December).
US Department of State 'Dispatch', 31 May 1993; 26 July 1993.
US GAO (1983) 'Donor Approaches to Development Assistance: Implications for the United States'.
Wallerstein, Immanuel (1979) *The Capitalist World-Economy*. New York: Cambridge University Press.
Wildavsky, Aaron (1988) *The New Politics of the Budgetary Process*. Glenview: Scott Foresman.
Wilson, James Q. (1989) *American Government* (fourth edition). Lexington, MA and Toronto: Heath.
Wood, Robert E. (1970) 'When Government Works', *The Public Interest*, Winter.
Wood, Robert E. (1986) *From Marshall Plan to Debt Crisis: Foreign Aid and Development Choices*. Berkeley, CA: University of California Press.
Woodward, Bob (1994) *The Agenda: Inside the Clinton White House*. New York: Simon & Schuster.
Zimmerman, Robert (1993) *Dollars, Diplomacy, and Dependency: Dilemmas of U.S. Foreign Aid*. Boulder, CO: Lynne Rienner.

4 Giving Aid on the Recipient's Terms: The Swedish Experience in Tanzania

Ole Elgström

INTRODUCTION

The purpose of this introductory section is to describe the Swedish–Tanzanian aid relationship in more general terms. The first official Swedish aid to Tanzania was initiated in 1964. Tanzania has ever since been one of Sweden's main aid recipients. In the 1980s, Tanzania received between 10 and 15 per cent of Swedish bilateral ODA. At the same time, Sweden is Tanzania's largest bilateral donor, contributing approximately 10–15 per cent of the total DAC assistance (SASDA, Secretariat for Analysis of Swedish Development Assistance, 1994:20). Over the years, Tanzania has received over 18 billion Swedish kronor (SEK, in 1993 prices; approximately US$3 billion). The flow of Swedish assistance increased rapidly in the early 1970s, in line with the steep increase in the general aid budget (SASDA 1994:22). In current prices, aid expanded from SEK 50 million in 1970 to 250 in 1975. In fixed prices it then remained on about the same level for almost two decades, from 1974/75 until 1992/93, when there was a rather dramatic cut in the aid allocation.

Tanzania was for a long time considered the favourite country of Swedish donors. A perceived ideological kinship, with socialist regimes in both countries for many years, was perhaps the main factor behind this close relationship. The initial reason for including Tanzania among Sweden's main recipients (six altogether in 1965, when Sida was created) was, however, also due to close personal links between key persons in both countries. Swedish missionaries had worked for many years in East Africa. Particularly close connections existed between Tage Erlander, the Prime Minister, Ulla Lindström, the Minister with responsibility for foreign aid, and Barbro Johansson, a leading missionary who took up Tanzanian citizenship and later became a Member of Parliament in Tanzania.

When Nyerere's *Ujamaa* programme was launched, the Swedish Social Democratic government leaders found it natural to support this endeavour to create an African form of socialism, officially based on values such as equity and self-reliance (goals prominent in Swedish aid rhetoric at that time). Tanzanian ideology, stressing an egalitarian non-exploitative society and welfare policies via the public sector, held a very strong appeal for these Social Democrats.

The large-scale aid programme has perpetuated itself over the years in the sense that this massive flow of money and personnel has tended to create vested interests in a continued close relationship. Many Swedes have developed extremely warm feelings for Tanzania, having spent several years there and having found close personal friends among Tanzanians. A 'Tanzania lobby' slowly developed, defending the aid programme and its components.

The economic crisis affecting Tanzania as well as most other African countries from the late 1970s challenged this rosy picture of Tanzania. Although many observers attributed the economic down-turn to external events, others saw the causes in Nyerere's socialist policies. In general, the confidence in the ability of the Tanzanian government to handle the crisis diminished dramatically. The result was major changes in aid policy and also, under the non-socialist Swedish government that came to power in 1991, a sharp decrease in aid allocations to the country. In the 1990s, Sweden's policy is basically tied to existing IMF and IBRD adjustment programmes, with an emphasis on market conditions and good governance, meaning a democratic development in Tanzania.

Almost all Swedish assistance has come in the form of grants. In general, Swedish aid has had the reputation of being 'soft', with few conditions. The level of tied aid has, for example, been relatively low and political conditionality was absent until the mid-1980s. This obviously contributed to a feeling in Tanzania that Sweden was a friendly, benevolent donor. The positive feelings between the countries have thus been reciprocal for most of the period, even though developments during the last decade have sometimes strained good relations.

SIDA AS A SWEDISH ADMINISTRATIVE AGENCY

Sweden is a parliamentary democracy. The government must thus seek the acceptance of the Swedish Parliament, the Riksdag. As long as the political party (or parties) in government enjoys the support of a stable majority in Parliament, it is almost certain to be able to carry through its policies. During the time period under study, the Swedish political scene was dominated by a struggle between the Social Democratic Party and a non-socialist bloc, consisting of four main parties. The Social Democrats ruled until 1976; then different non-socialist coalitions ruled for six years. A new Social Democratic era between 1982 and 1991 was followed by a three-year non-socialist interlude, once more to be followed by a socialist victory in 1994.

In the foreign policy sector, responsibility is shared between Parliament and the government. As regards foreign aid, the Riksdag decides the annual foreign aid budget, and the financial frame for each recipient country. It defines and decides the general foreign aid policy objectives, and which areas are to be prioritized in aid cooperation. The government bears the overall policy responsibility for Swedish aid. The ultimate responsibility rests with the Foreign Ministry, which for most of the period covered here had a special department in charge of the overall planning and coordination of aid activities.

Sweden adheres to a different concept of relations between ministries and central administrative agencies than is found in other European countries. The ministries are rather small, and are supposed to concentrate on policy-making: that is, making fundamental political decisions. The central agencies are independent of the ministries. Their function is to implement the decisions of government and Parliament faithfully, but it is their own responsibility to choose the most effective means to reach the policy goals set up. Ministers are not supposed to intervene in the affairs of an agency, or at least not as regards specific cases.

The Ministry for Foreign Affairs is an atypical Swedish ministry, in that it is also responsible for implementing foreign policy through its embassies. The execution of foreign aid is, however, handled by a separate agency, Sida. The result is a certain ambiguity in the demarcation between the ministry's and Sida's tasks and spheres of competence; this ambiguity has in some instances led to conflict (Elgström 1992:54–7).

Sida is thus the central executive aid agency for planning, administering and evaluating bilateral development cooperation programmes. It replaced the Board for International Assistance, the first agency, in 1965 with the task of implementing the ideas behind the 1962 Government Bill, which stressed moral duty and international solidarity as the main motives for aid-giving. In 1994, Sida's total personnel consisted of 746 persons, out of which 513 were permanent employees. Among the 746, 406 were working in Stockholm, while the rest were stationed at or connected to the Development Cooperation Offices (DCOs) in the recipient countries. Sida's organization has changed over time, but has always been characterized by a competition between two principles of organization: geographical and functional tasks. As will be shown below, this has been a constant source of friction within the organization, as has the division of responsibilities between Stockholm and the field offices.

During the 1970s, a number of new aid agencies were founded. SAREC became responsible for research cooperation with the LDCs. The Import Promotion Office for Products from Developing Countries, the Swedish Agency for International Technical and Economic Cooperation and SWEDFUND (the Swedish Fund for Industrial Cooperation with Developing Countries) became engaged in commercial and industrial activities in a much broader set of recipient countries than did Sida, and were partly created as a response to demands for an increased role for Swedish commercial interests in aid-giving. For similar reasons, the Industry Division of Sida ceased to exist in 1991, and was replaced by a new agency, Swedecorp (Swedish Industrial and Trade Development Corporation). However, the Swedish structure of foreign aid administration was once more reorganized in 1995: at this time, the Social Democratic Government decided to return to a formula with one overarching organization including all the formerly independent agencies. The reasons for this move were related partly to efficiency (the sheer number of agencies had made coordination difficult and double-work frequent), and partly to ideology (the Social Democrats were less enthusiastic about commercial interests in aid than their non-socialist predecessors).

SIDA'S AUTONOMY AND RESPONSIVENESS

The peculiarity of the Swedish political and administrative system has definite implications of interest here. Even though the capacity of Sida to influence goal priorities should not be underestimated, given its role of providing background material to decision-makers, objectives are in the end decided upon by Parliament. Sida thus has to act in a way which is arguably in agreement with Parliamentary guidelines, and hence its autonomy in this area seems very limited.

On the level of strategies, however, Sida's freedom of action seems substantial. Swedish aid objectives are on a high level of abstraction and do not place stringent limitations on strategic choices. Administrative agencies are supposed to decide how to reach the goals set by Parliament independently. As regards strategies, Sida can furthermore rely on its expertise and on its ability to shape the public agenda concerning foreign aid. No one knows better than the donor agency what the situation in a recipient country permits; no one can interpret reigning development ideas better than Sida. The agency has manifold ways to shape both public opinion and elite attitudes. The conclusion is that Sida must be hypothesized to have rather a large degree of autonomy when it comes to decisions about strategy.

According to the literature on the foreign policy of small or weak states, they tend to be reactive rather than proactive actors in world politics. Most often, a small state is supposed to follow a strategy of adaptation. A major reason for such behaviour is their perceived lack of resources, whether military, economic and political (see Vital 1967:3–10; Handel 1981:3–6; Elgström 1982:200–16).

Being a relatively small state, Sweden would in its foreign aid policy have to be an adaptive actor with little external autonomy. The high degree of dependence upon the external environment would predict a high degree of responsiveness to other actors, especially to major powers. It could also be argued that a small state is prone to be more attentive to the sovereignty problems of other small states than are great powers. The result could be high responsiveness to weak recipients. These hypotheses must, however, be tempered by bringing in possible counterarguments: Sweden is a relatively rich country and could, because of its relative generosity in the aid arena, be considered at least a middle-range power in this field, giving Sweden more autonomy there than the country would have in, for example, security policy.

Our general hypothesis is that Sida has a relatively low degree of autonomy, and high responsiveness, *vis-à-vis* the Swedish political authorities as regards goals, but a higher level of autonomy as regards strategy decisions. Its external autonomy is expected to be limited, which would predict a high degree of responsiveness to external actors. In general, Swedish foreign aid is expected to be much more influenced by external environmental events than, for example, the policy of its American counterpart, USAID. For this reason it is important to examine somewhat more closely the determinants of change in foreign aid policy.

EXPLAINING CHANGES IN FOREIGN AID POLICY

Foreign aid is an element of a country's foreign policy. In many relationships between rich and poor states, development cooperation constitutes the most prominent type of interaction. Thus, an interest in developments in aid policy implies a focus on foreign policy change. This topic was largely neglected for a long time by analysts of comparative foreign policy

(Rosati, Hagan and Sampson 1994:4). During the last decade, however, a number of well-known schlolars have turned their attention to policy change (Holsti 1982; Hermann 1990).

In a recent review of the literature, Jerel Rosati, Joe Hagan and Martin Sampson III (1994) find a consensus on the need for multicausal explanations. Furthermore, they identify three 'sets of causal dynamics' that underlie change – and affect continuity – in foreign policy: (1) change in global structures and the state's international position; (2) domestic political realignment; and (3) the policy-making process. The first two are essentially sets of conditions that pressure, or drive, governments towards restructuring. The third set refers to factors which often act to condition foreign policy responses to new international pressures and opportunities. The policy-making process is thus seen as an intervening variable between external and internal driving forces and policy change. Process variables can serve to inhibit change, as pointed out by Goldmann (1988), but can also 'push' a leadership towards change (Hagan and Rosati 1994:273). The simple model shown in Figure 4.1 will be the guideline for the ensuing analysis.

Missing from the picture of driving forces behind shifts in aid policy given in Figure 4.1 are ideas and images. The basic values and core beliefs among decision-makers, and the images of reality they hold, are important ingredients in any theory trying to explain aid policy change. General ideological convictions (which may shift as a result, for example, of regime change in the donor country) may have crucial repercussions on aid policy. Even more obvious is the importance of ideas about development, and whether they stem from development theory or from actor-bound convictions. In general, ideas function as guidelines, as beacons that point out which strategy to select (Goldstein and Keohane 1993:3–30).

Goldstein and Keohane equate ideas with 'beliefs held by individuals', and in this context make a distinction between 'world views', 'principled beliefs' and 'causal beliefs'. World views are ideas on a very high level of abstraction: a religion may entail such fundamental beliefs. Principled beliefs refer to normative ideas about what is right or wrong, while causal beliefs denote beliefs about cause and effect. Kjell Goldmann also contends that policy change is based on 'a change in ideas, on rethinking, on reappraisal' (1988:10), and makes a distinction between changes in actors'

Figure 4.1 A simple model of foreign aid policy change

value systems, in their 'definition of prevailing circumstances' and in their causal beliefs (Goldmann 1988:11).

In this study, we have chosen to use the concepts of ideas and images, and include in these concepts basic values, causal beliefs and beliefs about reality held by decision-makers. Existing beliefs and ideas function as a cognitive filter of incoming information. External stimuli, including new ideas, pass through this screen filter. Some impulses do not reach decision-makers, while others are reinterpreted. Ideas can, however, also be endogenous, resulting from autonomous, creative thought processes within individual actors.

New ideas may thus stem from both external factors, from internal factors (for example, regime change) and from autonomous rethinking. In the following analysis we will give special prominence to the potential role of ideas and images in explaining aid policy change.

CHANGES AND CONTINUITY IN SWEDISH AID POLICY

Since the beginning, in 1964, it has been possible to distinguish four major periods of Swedish aid to Tanzania, each with its own particular policy emphasis. In this section we will introduce the underlying aid philosophy for each period and how it has influenced basic priorities as regards goals and strategies. In doing so, the sources of aid objectives and the bases for the provision of aid will be highlighted. Also, the role of agency-related variables – agency structure and staffing and the uses of feedback within the system – are discussed.

The main *objectives* of Swedish policy have remained essentially the same since the Aid Bill of 1962, the first comprehensive government document on aid policy. Poverty alleviation was from the start the overarching goal, the 'bottom line' of Sida's assistance. Four other basic goals were there from the beginning: Swedish aid should contribute to economic growth, political and economic autonomy, a democratic development in society, and economic and social equity. A fifth objective was added in 1988 (a sustainable use of natural resources and environmental protection), and a sixth in 1996 (gender equality). Priorities have, however, shifted, and the task of the sections below is to describe the effects this has had in the case of aid to Tanzania.

Within the framework of basic images of donor and recipient roles, and general Swedish aid objectives, Sida enjoys considerable freedom of manoeuvre. Even though prevailing images prohibit certain types of strategies (for example, a friendly, trustful relationship does not permit a coercive strategy using threats and sanctions), below this threshold a wide selection of strategies is possible. In this context, strategy stands for long-term considerations of how to attack development problems. In concrete terms, this means here a concentration upon which issue-areas Sida has chosen to support in order to assist Tanzania in its development efforts. Sectoral distribution over time is used as a basic indicator of strategy.

THE FOUR PERIODS OF SWEDISH AID TO TANZANIA

As in the cases of the USA and China, it is quite easy to trace and characterize different periods in Swedish aid policy in relation to Tanzania. During the first years of Sida assistance, economic growth was the primary force. Aid was given either as soft loans or as project assistance, primarily to the social sector. Much hope was placed on the Tanzanian government and its ability to create rapid economic development.

The first turning-point occurred around 1970, when assistance was transformed in a markedly recipient-oriented fashion. 'Aid on the terms of the recipient' became the reigning ideology with equity the dominating goal, and great consideration was paid to Tanzanian desires as regards sector priorities. In the late 1970s, the emerging economic crisis made changes necessary, and from 1979 a transitional phase began characterized by a high degree of uncertainty regarding goals and strategy in combination with growing worries about recipient policy. In 1983 the transition was completed, and aid adjusted to the new crisis environment. Sida accepted IMF/World Bank strategies of building an 'enabling environment' for economic growth, relying on market forces. The conflict between donor control and recipient responsibility became particularly apparent in this last period.

Project Support and Economic Growth, 1965–70

Aid Philosophy

The 1960s were dominated by the so-called 'gap theories'. Underdevelopment was caused by a lack of necessary resources: money, material, and human resources. A massive transfer of foreign assistance was the cure. Once the recipient had passed a 'development threshold', development – equated with economic growth – would be self-generating, and aid was no longer needed.

To formulate and implement the detailed development plans needed for such an enterprise, a strong, development-oriented state structure was viewed as a necessity. The emphasis on a centrally planned, massive development effort gave the recipient state a basic role. Few people questioned the ability of LDCs to manage these grandiose development plans. These ideas were readily accepted in Swedish aid circles. 'Swedish policy-makers and aid administrators adopted the idea of long term planning whole-heartedly' (Anell 1986:240). In the case of Tanzania, the early Swedish interest in the social sector also implied a strong state, able to promote large-scale educational and health programmes. In brief, foreign aid quickly became highly government-to-government oriented.

Swedish aid to Tanzania in these first years can be said to have consisted of two parts: first, a programme of technical assistance, including a large number of small projects, primarily in the social sector; second, a programme for financial credits, dominated by a 'banker's approach' (*Lär sig Sida*, 1988:56). Tanzania had in 1965 produced its first five-year plan, which was considered 'ambitious but not unrealistic' (Sida 1966:3). Tanzania was counted as a creditworthy and competent bank customer, and support was extended to a range of government projects.

In both instances, aid was directed to the Tanzanian central administration. Ideology was not the prime reason behind Swedish aid at this time. Instead, Tanzania's long-term planning was accepted as reliable and realistic. As regards projects, donor influence was considered natural and essential. Swedish aid during this period was relatively unconditional, not so much because of ideological considerations as the conviction that the recipient had the ability to reach the desired goals. Conditions were thus not necessary.

Aid Objectives

Aid to Tanzania during these first years closely followed the general trend of Swedish development assistance. In line with basic tenets in gap theory, the goal of economic growth was heavily emphasized. Growth was considered a prerequisite for reaching other goals, not least the poverty alleviation objective, which was foremost in the minds of decision-makers when writing the 1962 Aid Bill (interviews). For many Swedes, including the first Director General of Sida, Ernst Michanek, foreign aid was a way of transferring the domestic notion of social welfare on to the international scene.

The goal of income redistribution was believed to follow almost automatically from general growth. With a strong, developmentally-inclined recipient government in charge, no big problems with goal inconsistencies were perceived. Independence was in a vague sense also important during this phase; Tanzania had recently gained political sovereignty, and the task of strengthening the newly-won independence was high in the minds of Swedish decision-makers (interviews). The democracy goal, on the other hand, was seldom mentioned during this phase, and seems to have played a very limited role for concrete aid policy.

In these first years of aid to Tanzania, the source of aid objectives was undoubtedly the Swedish Government and the Riksdag. The priority put on economic growth was established by the Government Bill of 1962. There is no indication that Sida disagreed with this emphasis, but the priority originated from political sources.

Strategy

During the first years of Sida assistance, there was no clear overarching strategy. Aid policy was in its infancy, and officials were groping for definite solutions to upcoming problems. Direct support was given to a multitude of individual projects. There was, however, a marked concentration on the social sector (interviews; SASDA 1994:31). As much as 85 per cent of Swedish disbursements went to this sector. Adult education and public health were two main beneficiaries. These areas were selected both as a response to recipient wishes and as an acknowledgement of special Swedish competence (interviews).

Social sector support corresponded well to the fundamental Swedish objective of poverty alleviation. This type of project support had, however, certain problematic features: progress was often exceedingly slow, which made it hard to defend expenditures to politicians who wanted quick results. Moreover, recipient capacity was often lacking, a fact that necessitated a heavy reliance on Swedish experts. During these early years, Swedish policy models were usually directly transferred to the Tanzanian reality, without adaptation to the local context. It must be remembered, though, that the social sectors were prioritized by Tanzanian authorities at this time, and that substantial improvements did occur; it was not until much later that the above-mentioned difficulties became obvious.

Structure and Staffing

In these early days of foreign assistance, the aid apparatus was heavily centralized. The office in Skockholm became more and more organized, and from the late 1960s, when aid allocations increased rapidly, the number of employees there also expanded, to reach 290 in 1971 (Bistånd genom Sida 1970/71). Sida had no established field organization in these early days. Projects were managed by officials at the functional sector bureaus in Stockholm acting as project secretaries, with close supervision over; 'their' projects. Still, Sida in 1971 employed almost 300 field-workers, placed in specific projects or programmes (Bistånd genom Sida 1970/71).

In the 1960s, Sida's organization was characterized by a division between 'technical' and 'financial' assistance. This administrative division was accompanied also by a cultural split. Two schools of thought existed, each with its own conception of the proper role of an aid organization, and of the most effective ways of transferring development assistance. The 'bankers' were situated in one of the two line departments, in charge of financial assistance. This task had earlier been handled by the Ministry of Finance, and the attitudes and values from that organization were 'inherited' by the officials at the new department. Economic efficiency was the guiding norm, and the transfer of resources was considered the main business of aid.

The foreign aid 'missionaries' or 'project people' (as they were often referred to), on the other hand, were generalists, often with a deep interest and involvement in development affairs. The importance of specific projects was stressed. Officials of this persuasion wanted Sida to take an active part in project development and advocated a strong Swedish involvement in the day-to-day business of aid. The existence of these different schools of thought – which in various shapes have continued to exist within the organization – created favourable conditions for a lively debate within Sida about the correct way of handling assistance. Nonetheless, at a practical level Sida's organization in those days was essentially attuned to project administration (DsUD 1984:1, 6).

A number of Swedish technical assistance experts were hired to occupy important positions in the Tanzanian administration. In full accordance with the reigning aid philosophy, Swedish personnel during this period were supplied as 'gap-fillers' (Sida 1992:2): 'Swedish/experts ... fill vacancies within the agencies and institutions of the recipient country, and perform their duties as if they were officials of the recipient country' (P1968:100).

Aid on the Terms of the Recipient, 1970–79

Aid Philosophy

From 1970, there was a marked politicization of Swedish aid policy. In the Government Aid Bill of 1970, the Social Democratic Government stated that

> it is natural for Sweden first and foremost to seek to cooperate with countries, the governments of which in their economic and social policies

> strive to accomplish such structural changes as create the conditions for development characterized by economic and social equality. When our direct aid is expanded, we should therefore ensure that new projects will be launched primarily in such countries. (P1970:17)

Tanzania was one of the definite beneficiaries of this new policy because, from the ideological perspective of the day, in Swedish aid policy circles it was an almost ideal recipient. Furthermore, it was also easy to justify substantial increases in aid from a more general foreign policy perspective: Tanzania was counted as one of the front-line states, suffering because of its opposition to the South African apartheid policy (Palmlund 1986:119). As a result, the amount of assistance started to grow dramatically in the early 1970s.

This enormous increase in resources transferred was a clear sign of the confidence the Swedish aid community had in President Nyerere. He was a prominent spokesman for the Third World, and his writings and speeches were studied with interest within Sida, and frequently quoted. In the words of one interviewee: 'I read Nyerere's book as a Bible, as did many of my generation.'

The trust in Tanzania's authorities made it comparatively easy to introduce the novel idea of 'country programming' to Sweden. This principle was introduced in the 1972 Government Aid Bill. In concrete terms, country programming meant that aid was to be given for a period of several years, instead of for just one year at a time. After a 'policy dialogue' between donor and recipient, which in principle was to be a candid but friendly dialogue between equal partners, a three-year frame was decided upon. Within this framework, the recipient authorities were expected to be able to use the aid as they themselves wished. For example, they could choose sectors as well as projects (P1974:43). Country programming was a clear indication from the Swedish side that it considered it the responsibility of the recipient to plan and manage aid. From Sida's own perspective, country programming made it much easier to administer the steadily and quickly increasing aid appropriations.

In brief, the introduction of country programming was one main ingredient in the ideology of giving aid 'on the terms of the recipient'. The high level of confidence Sida had in Tanzania's authorities made it possible for the agency to allow them to decide their own priorities. In practice, however, the Tanzanians continued to listen to, and try to detect, Swedish wishes and priorities (interviews). As the Tanzanian bureaucracy never really had the capacity to handle all the planning and performance, Sida was needed as a partner, and Swedish officials in the field retained a significant degree of influence regarding strategic decisions (interviews).

The principle of unconditional aid was also a sign of the strong belief in recipient state capacity that existed at this time. The state machinery was considered the main engine of development. The Tanzanian government was a shining example which, according to foreign aid supporters, proved that it was realistic to expect a recipient government to play such a role.

Aid Objectives

By 1970, some of the optimism of the mid-1960s had disappeared. Even though many newly independent states showed impressive growth rates, inequality within showed no tendency to decline. The automatic linkage between growth and equity (the trickle-down effect) was now being questioned.

This new trend coincided in Sweden with the politicization of the aid debate. The Social Democratic Government stressed the importance of cooperating with countries that shared Swedish priorities concerning, for example, social welfare. The equity goal was heavily emphasized. As the basic objective was to eradicate poverty, growth in itself could not have priority if the ensuing wealth was not redistributed to create more of equality. The non-socialist opposition, in contrast, preferred countries where the chances for efficient use of the projects were the greatest.

Following government policy, Sida describes in the country programme document of 1971 how Tanzania has followed a policy 'which to a larger extent than many other developing countries has stressed the importance of countryside development and the danger that development efforts will only reach a smaller part of the population ... The national development objectives correspond well with the values behind Swedish aid policy' (Sida Länder program 1971:1).

The massive increases in aid flows to Tanzania can thus be explained largely by the extent to which official priorities in the two countries were politically and ideologically compatible. This was also evident in regard to the autonomy objective. In the Arusha Declaration of 1967, Nyerere had underlined the importance he attached to the concept of self-reliance. To achieve 'real' development, a developing country had to rely on its own resources and free itself from the bounds of colonialism and capitalism. These thoughts found practical expression in the efforts to create an import substituting industry. The Swedish government applauded this policy, which was very much in line with the active foreign policy of Sweden (Elgström 1982); among other things, this policy championed the cause of small state autonomy.

Strategy

The amount of aid to Tanzania grew rapidly in the early 1970s. It increased to almost all sectors. A noteworthy development was the concentration on infrastructure. Such investments swallowed large amounts of resources, which made it easier for Sida to transfer its aid to Tanzania.

One infrastructural concentration was water projects. Tanzania had decided to make rural development a priority area, but declined offers of aid to the agricultural sector, which the Tanzanian government believed the country could handle itself. Swedish support for the new national goal of 'free water for all' – that is, the opportunity for every household to have 'safe water within 400 metres' (Elgström 1992:109) – was very warmly welcomed. Between 1965 and 1975, Sweden financed around 80 per cent of all new rural water schemes on mainland Tanzania (Therkildsen 1988:104).

In the mid-1970s, industry became a prioritized area. During a seminar with donors in the early 1970s, President Nyerere had made it plain that Tanzania wanted donor governments to concentrate on helping the country in the two areas of education and industrial development. Sweden listened, and complied. This was, after all, the decade of 'aid on the term of the recipient'. Although these Tanzanian priorities were important for Sida's decision to support Tanzania's Basic Industry Strategy, it was also justified with reference to the domestic Swedish base for such assistance. Voices had been raised in support of an increased use of Swedish industrial competence in foreign aid (Elgström 1992:83). In the second half of the 1970s support for the industry sector came to occupy between 15 and 25 per cent of total Swedish aid allocations, a level maintained also through most of the 1980s.

'Concentration of Swedish aid efforts' became a prominent goal in the latter part of the decade. Sida took a decision to concentrate its aid to the industrial and educational sectors and to cut the overall number of projects; officials and politicians alike saluted this move. It was soon evident, however, that most sectors were heavily defended by strong interests, both within and outside Sida. That it is easier to include new areas than to delete existing ones was also proved by the decision by the agency's Board to add new aid programmes in spite of the concentration policy.

Structure and Staffing

In the first half of the 1970s, Sida was a rapidly growing organization. The enormous increases in aid expenditures were followed by a massive increase in personnel. In 1975, 792 officials were employed by Sida, of whom 312 worked in Stockholm (Sida's petita 1975/76). The substantial annual inflow of new employees also had the consequence of creating large cohorts of officials of about the same age and with a similar ideological orientation, typically characterized by a strong interest in Third World development and a deep sympathy for the plight of the recipient countries. This generation of officials came to dominate the organization for many years, as they grew in rank and experience.

This period was also an era of decentralization. The introduction of country programming created a need for country coordination. This task was soon taken over by the DCOs, the field units of Sida, which were created in 1969 and established in Dar es Salaam in 1970. The principle of 'field-orientation' meant new tasks and responsibilities for the DCOs, which at the end of the decade occupied an important place in aid management. Country programmes were written primarily at the field level. This meant that the priorities of the officials at the DCO in Dar es Salaam had a large influence on Sida policy towards Tanzania. As these officials were inclined to listen closely to the signals sent from Tanzanian authorities, decentralization tended to reinforce the policy of recipient-based priority-setting.

Furthermore, the use of contract employees (*kontraktsanställda*) – individuals employed by Sida for specific tasks, but acting as officials within the recipient country's administration – became common. Towards the end of the decade, almost 500 Swedes were employed in this way (Sida, 1992:4). These people were no longer seen as filling particular gaps, but as important links in a process of transferring knowledge. In the case of Tanzania, some of these officials exerted considerable influence because of their strategic positions in the Tanzanian bureaucracy and their simultaneous good contacts with Swedish aid officials.

In Stockholm, in the early 1970s, Sida became primarily sector-oriented. Four sectoral divisions were created with the responsibility for sector analysis, as well as preparation and administration of aid projects. Besides these main units, special desk offices for each programme country were established with responsibility for integrating and coordinating the aid programme. This meant an organization devoted to two competing principles, a functional and a geographical, which provided fertile ground for internal conflicts.

Another organizational development, as indicated above, was the establishment of new aid agencies independent of Sida. The result was a more homogeneous Sida, even more dominated by like-minded individuals, attached to the ideological tenets of 'aid on the terms of the recipient'. Officials with a more business-like attitude to development cooperation moved to the other newly created agencies.

Uncertainty and Confusion 1979–83

Aid Philosophy

These years constituted a transitional period during which Swedish aid policy to Tanzania was subject to very powerful incentives for change. Before 1979, Sweden had complete trust in the Tanzanian capacity to promote development. It was a favourite country for both ideological and practical reasons. The heavy emphasis on the social sector during the 1970s had ameliorated the living conditions of most citizens and most indicators of social development showed substantial improvements, far better than most other African countries. This appreciation, however, would begin to wane in the early 1980s as the government's incapacity to manage national development became increasingly apparent.

In the late 1970s, Tanzania had – as had most other African states – plunged into a grave economic crisis. In the beginning of this economic down-turn, many observers, both in Tanzania and in donor countries, either did not acknowledge that it really was a crisis or just saw it as a temporary phenomenon. It soon became clear, however, that the type of aid given before did not work anymore. The time was ripe for reconsideration.

The IMF, together with most bilateral donors, considered the measures taken by Tanzania to fight the crisis completely insufficient, and even inappropriate. In the early 1980s, the Fund – acting on its neo-liberal strategy for financial stabilization – demanded changes in macro-economic policy, including drastic devaluation and cuts in the public sector. For the Tanzanian government, and even more for the ruling party, an acceptance would have meant a painful reconsideration of fundamental ideological tenets. The Tanzanian leadership also firmly believed that the policy measures required by the IMF would not lead to the intended objectives. Tanzania thus refused to follow the IMF recommendations. The result was a decrease in foreign aid, which lasted until 1986.

In Swedish–Tanzanian relations, the first response to the economic problems was a realization – on both sides – that a deeper Swedish involvement in the planning procedure was necessary. 'Concerned participation', coined by the then Foreign Minister of Tanzania, Ibrahim Kaduma, was the phrase used to describe this development. 'The long-lasting cooperation and the good relations between Sweden and Tanzania which have developed in the path of foreign aid has led to wishes for a more active Swedish participation in many areas', as was stated in a document from Sida (Sida 1979:6). Many of the signals sent from the field about grave problems with different aid programmes were initially also ignored (Elgström 1992:111). Sweden was slow to realize that existing modes of assistance were inappropriate in the new environment.

When the IMF started to propose a far-reaching structural adjustment programme in 1979–80, Sweden was one of the few countries not to support these demands. Within Sida a certain scepticism existed towards the Fund and the World Bank. Both organizations were seen as being far too insensitive to Third World realities and to the social implications of their programmes. Furthermore, the internal Sida norms stressed the immorality of imposing policy conditions on weak countries. It was only when Sida belatedly realized, like others had already, that the crisis was really deep and structural in nature, that Sweden accepted the macro-economic changes as necessary. 'In the end we realized that things couldn't go on; we had support the policy of the IMF', remembers one interviewee. A rather intense internal debate within Sida and the Foreign Ministry's aid office took place (Elgström 1992:80). The outcome was a change in policy in 1983–84.

It has been claimed that the Swedish reluctance to support IMF policy postponed necessary reforms for several years and in that way aggravated the results of the crisis. On the other hand, this period of deliberation can also be seen as useful, in the sense that the policy debate which took place, in both countries as well as between them, prepared Tanzania for the inevitable change in policy and in that way paved the way for better programme implementation.

Aid Objectives and Strategies

By the end of the 1970s, the early development optimism waned. At the turn of the decade, most observers agreed that foreign aid policy was in urgent need of a basic change of direction. The economic crisis had irrevocably demonstrated that existing policies did not work. Bit by bit, the firm conviction that equity was the undisputed overarching goal of Swedish foreign aid was being eroded. At a time of fundamental crisis, this goal was being downplayed. 'How could redistribution of the fruits of successful development be a priority, when development did not produce any gains to distribute?' (Palmquist 1995:17). And how could self-reliance be a major goal in a situation when aid dependency only kept increasing?

During this phase, uncertainty reigned. 'You could say that this was a period of goal vacuum. We didn't know exactly what goals to pursue – it was obvious, however, that the existing assistance didn't work' (interview). To cling to the old top objectives was no longer realistic, but what were the alternatives? Old ideals lingered, while reality demanded shifts in priorities.

Much the same can be said about sector strategy. The sectors that had been selected for special attention in the 1970s remained prioritized. Thus water and industry continued to be major areas for assistance. Some initiatives to change the type and focus of projects, however, were taken. For example, efforts were made to gradually shift to small-scale programmes using adapted technology and emphasizing popular participation in planning and implementation. The creation of the HESAWA, a combined health, sanitation and water programme with a stress on rural development, is a case in point (Elgström 1992:116–17).

The Structure and Staffing

Tanzania's dismal economic performance reinforced existing differences within Sida regarding what strategy to adopt. Many individuals defended the approach of the 1970s with its insistence on recipient influence and autonomy. These officials blamed the economic disarray on external events, and continued to believe in the Tanzanian socialist way. People who had spent many years in the country and who had followed the successes of the early years were more likely to resist dramatic changes in Sida policy.

Those officials, on the other hand, who for a long time had harboured doubts about the reigning Tanzanian ideology now found plenty of ammunition for their attacks on the dominant policies. The 'bankers', promoters of economic efficiency and financial control, raised their voices in a way unheard of in the 1970s. The result was a very heated debate within the Swedish aid community. It is probably fair to conclude that the dominance of officials with strong feelings for Tanzania, fostered in the ideological climate of 'aid on the terms of the recipient', prolonged existing strategies and postponed the change from development policy to crisis management.

Another notable feature of this period, and even more so in later periods, was sector resistance to budget cuts. Officials in the sector divisions have always tended to defend the interests of their particular sector. Now, when the threat of decreasing aid allocations became reality, such defence mechanisms were activated. With the support of corresponding interests within the Tanzanian administration, sector officials managed in many instances to postpone or prevent changes in aid allocations. In Tanzania, the clearest example is resistance to cuts in aid to the industrial sector (see Elgström 1992).

Saving the Tanzanian Economy, 1983 to 1995

Aid Philosophy

In 1983, Sweden decided to start arguing with Tanzania about the inevitability of bowing to IMF pressures. Initial efforts bilaterally to persuade Tanzania into adopting more far-reaching adjustment measures failed: the results were 'too little, too late', and did not impress IMF officials.

In 1984, a high-level symposium was arranged where the Nordic countries jointly discussed macro-economic policies with Tanzania. The Nordic countries declared

> that they would continue to provide assistance at the same level as before even if the Government did not manage to reach an agreement with the IMF. If Tanzania wanted to attract *additional* resources from other sources, however, the Nordic countries saw no other way out than a settlement with the IMF. (Ėdgren 1986:56)

Some observers have called this meeting a watershed, claiming that this concerted effort by the Nordic states finally convinced the Tanzanian leadership of the necessity of making a deal with the IMF. When Tanzania's most devoted friends spoke unequivocally in favour of an agreement, there was no alternative. It must be remembered, however, that there were also increasingly powerful forces in the Tanzanian political system in support of reform. In 1986, after President Nyerere had stepped down, Tanzania finally accepted IMF's conditions and signed the ERP.

This shift in policy towards Tanzania marks the most significant change in Swedish aid policy since the 1980s. Acceptance of the necessity of economic policy conditionality as a basis for the provision of aid was going to be standard practice from now on. Individual aid projects were to be seen as meaningless unless the government could provide an enabling macro-economic environment. 'Correct' economic policies became a *sine qua non* for effective assistance. The initial support for Tanzania against the demands from the IMF was abandoned in favour of the one-note choir of donor voices.

Donors began treating the Tanzanian government as weak and without capacity to carry out difficult policy decisions, As a consequence, the donors had engaged in formulating guidelines for the road to recovery. The Swedish assumption of project and programme responsibility created several problems. There was a discernible tendency on the part of different donor agencies to set up separate project organizations with few links to the ordinary Tanzanian administration. In order to get hold of indispensable equipment, it was considered necessary to circumvent – or to 'by-pass' as aid jargon puts it – the ordinary bureaucratic processes. The motive was higher effectiveness and better donor control over resource utilization. The result was isolated project islands, relatively autonomous, but also totally dependent on aid, and thus almost impossible to conclude as foreign aid projects (Odén and Sedin 1988:6).

The support of IMF's stabilization programmes, however, was not unequivocal. Sida officials were anxious from the beginning about the possible social consequences of these programmes. Many new policy measures were perceived to have negative effects for weak groups in society. Sida thus set out to combine its support with special efforts targeted on groups at risk: 'Earlier than other countries we realized the problems with the structural adjustment programmes, and introduced the ideas of "aid with a human face" and "the social dimension"' (interview). Swedish government officials were instrumental in persuading the World Bank to include social components in its aid packages (interviews).

In the late 1980s, the degree of confidence in Tanzanian authorities had reached its nadir. 'An experience of the 1980s has been the defective capacity and competence of African bureaucracies, not least in the economic-political area' (P1988/89:55). This lack of confidence in the recipient administration was accompanied by an ideological shift. The earlier widespread emphasis on 'the strong, developmental state' had in the 1990s generally given way to a world-view where the state is assigned a much less prominent role in bringing about development. In Sweden, this change became pronounced because of the advent of a non-socialist government in 1991. In its first Aid Bill, the government stated: 'There is a steadily growing understanding of the need to clearly delimit the role of the state to creating the physical, legal and social infrastructure, which is so important for a well functioning market economy' (P1991/92:51).

Swedish aid in the 1990s has a marked emphasis on market economy and economic growth. The state apparatus has been given the limited and well-defined task of facilitating the functioning of the market. 'Good governance' has become the buzzword of the day. In practice, this means that Sida has followed the USA and other Western donors in their insistence on a democratic political development as a prerequisite for increased aid allocations. Economic conditionality is now being supplemented by demands of a political nature.

One of the paradoxes during this period has been that officials in Sida still persist in the hope that recipient governments can take on a greater role in administering aid. In an internal agency review – *rollutredningen* – finished in 1988, it was argued that the recipient should be given more responsibility for its own development. This belief is still very strong in Sida. In 1995, Sida started an internal programme review with a view to the future titled 'Vision 2015' in which (again) the main challenge is how to find ways of making sure that aid does not become permanent and that recipient institutions can adopt a greater responsibility for Swedish aid funds.

Aid Objectives

When Sida eventually accepted that the gravity and structural nature of the crisis necessitated a far-reaching reconsideration, economic growth as aid objective once again gained prominence. Without economic restructuring, leading to economic progress, it was in fact futile to discuss other goals (for example, equity). 'The most important goal for Swedish aid during recent years has been to participate in laying the ground for economic recovery', Sida proclaimed in 1985 (Sida 1985:4).

At the same time, Sida wanted to preserve the gains made by Tanzania in the social sectors. In fact, all indicators of school enrolment and health care began to show signs of decline in the late 1980s. Thus social development concerns were incorporated into the aid agenda in more explicit terms on the premise that it was essential to stop the deterioration of social services. Economic growth, however, remained the highest priority (Sida 1987II:7).

Concern for the environment was introduced in 1988 as a new policy objective. It was expected that 'green' ideas would permeate all aid planning. This was, of course, a long-term objective, especially as recipient countries do not always share such preferences. It also seems to have played a relatively minor role in Tanzania (interviews). These last few years have also witnessed intensified efforts to improve the situations of Tanzanian women. Gender equality had been a sub-goal of Sida for some years but, towards the end of the 1980s, gender issues became more pronounced. This support was claimed to be positive for growth, as most of the burden of agricultural work rested on the female population. In 1996, gender equality was introduced as a separate, sixth policy objective in Swedish foreign aid.

During recent years, the democracy objective, including concern for human rights, has also become increasingly crucial. Following global trends, 'good governance' is more and more perceived as a *sine qua non* for a sustainable development. In official Sida rhetoric, democratic developments, together with economic growth, have top priority (Sida 1993:9). In practical terms, despite increasing funds for democracy projects, the impact of the goal seems to have been much less penetrating. 'I have the feeling that the democracy and environmental goals may increase the number of projects with such labels. But I do not think they play much of a role for programmes that are not specifically labelled "democracy projects"' (interview).

In summary, aid objectives in this period have been largely agency-derived in the sense that Sida has reserved to itself the responsibility of judging what is the best type of aid for Tanzania. These choices, however, were also heavily influenced by inputs from the donor community, not least the IMF and the World Bank. The role of domestic Swedish political actors seems to have diminished: both the government and Riksdag accept Sida's interpretation of necessary aid policy measures. The shift towards a more neo-liberal aid policy was, however, strongly applauded, particularly by the Moderate Party, the largest non-socialist party in Sweden.

Strategy

In the early 1980s, there was growing realization that continued new investments would only lead to an ever-increasing import need, and to more demands for foreign currency (a scarce resource). Tanzania would suffer rather than benefit. In the industrial as well as in the water sector, Sida now turned to an emphasis on maintenance and rehabilitation. Existing plants had to be made viable and existing water schemes made to function before any new investments were to occur. This major shift in policy took place even in the face of resistance from Tanzanian sectorial interests (Elgström 1992).

On the strategic level, the crisis necessitated a large programme of import support. Tanzania was in dire need of imports and had no possibility of financing them. The Swedish contribution thus aimed at relieving the foreign exchange shortage. Import support has gained a very prominent place in the Swedish aid programme. More than 30 per cent of aid to Tanzania has been allocated to import support since the advent of the crisis. In this early period, import support was given to individual enterprises directly. A large part (74 per cent of Swedish support) of these were parastatals, the efficiency of which was very low. Commodity import support 'was not used to foster structural change in the industrial sector, but rather simply to preserve that heavily protected sector' (SASDA 1994:56).

Towards the end of the decade, import support underwent changes: a market-based system replaced the earlier commodity programme (SASDA 1994:57). Sida, however, has not demanded privatization as a necessary measure to receive assistance as other donors have. As long as firms can demonstrate that they operate according to commercial principles, the type of ownership does not matter to Sweden.

At the beginning of the 1990s, Sweden concentrated its efforts more and more on balance of payment and budget support. After several years of debate, aid to the industrial sector was drastically cut. On the other hand, assistance to the social sector has once again come into focus, following Sida's anxiety over the social consequences of the adjustment programmes. An interesting development is the initiation of a new programme in public administration based on the premise that civil service reform is important and potentially likely to produce a more efficient and effective government. 'Good governance' is supposed to demand an effective bureaucracy, with the capacity to create a favourable environment for market forces. Programmes to increase quality (in the Tanzanian Ministry of Finance, the Tanzania Revenue Authority and the Institute of Tax and Administration, among others) have been initiated.

Structure and Staffing

In 1986, Sida went through a major reorganization. In order to strengthen country coordination, three powerful regional departments were created, and sector divisions were given a more supportive role. One consequence was much more realistic possibilities for the head of a regional department to implement a change in sector allocation in a certain recipient country. In spite of opposition from sectoral interests in both countries, such reallocations were also made in the Tanzanian programme.

The introduction of strong regional departments may be interpreted as part of a trend of centralization. The power of the DCOs was curtailed and, following a heated debate on the role of field missions, the DCO was in 1994 placed under the supervision of the Swedish Embassy in the country. Nonetheless, the number of Sida's employees in the field offices continues to be high. In 1994, 340 out of Sida's total of 746 employees (all categories) – 45 per cent – worked in the field (Sida, Bistånd i siffror och diagram, 1993/94:31). Ten people were permanently employed at the DCO in Dar es Salaam.

Another distinct development has been the increasing use of consultants, emphasized by most interviewees as a mixed blessing. Sida has been forced by the Swedish government to cut its number of employees (in order to save money) whilst the total aid budget has continued to increase. In the early 1990s, 400 long-term consultants worked for Sida, while the number of contract employees had decreased down to around one hundred. Even though there are obvious advantages with using consultants – for example, regarding efficiency – many of our interviewees stressed the disadvantages. Consultants may hesitate to terminate their profitable relationship with Sida, and this could lead to a tendency to invent ever new projects, often in collaboration with their Tanzanian partners. While consultancy firms do not seem to have any real influence over Sida policy, they may have a big impact in the field. 'They are very important and may even have too much influence. They control us much more than we control them', complained one of our respondents. Furthermore, by being a step removed from the operative arena, Sida officials complain that the agency does not learn as well.

The difference between the 'project people' and the 'bankers' still exists and has come to the fore again because of the reintegration of all aid agencies under one umbrella organization. The former emphasize today concrete projects or programmes, and put a premium on understanding and empathizing with the recipient. A strong moral commitment to a more equitable world order is still discernible, even though the impact of reality has led to an often cynical outward attitude. The 'bankers' prefer the transfer of resources, and advocate an emphasis on infrastructure and macro-economic stability. They perceive themselves as 'brokers', linking resources and competence in donor and recipient. Thus they also advocate the use of consultants of plan and implement projects. Development assistance is perceived as a fundamentally cooperative endeavour, where all parties – including the donor – have to receive benefits. The officials of this persuasion seem to have been strengthened by Swedish membership of the European Union, and by the prevailing aid climate in the world today.

Summary

Swedish aid objectives have remained relatively constant during the period under study. Six main goals, decided upon by Parliament, have guided Sida's aid strategies for over three decades. We have, however, observed rather dramatic shifts in priorities among these goals over time: from an emphasis on economic growth, via a strong commitment to equity and self-reliance, to a renewed interest in economic growth and in democracy as prerequisites for development.

In general, the main source of aid priorities has been the Swedish Riksdag and the government. Objectives have thus been primarily donor-country derived. The partial exception was the period covering the 1970s when the philosophy applauding 'aid on the terms of the recipient' prevailed. In those days, objectives were also to a certain extent recipient country-derived. It should be remembered, however, that Tanzania's development goals were shared by the Swedish aid elite. Few hard choices had to be made between Tanzanian and Swedish priorities. Sida's influence over the aid objectives seems to have been minor. Because the overarching goals have remained quite stable, and because of compatibility between Swedish and Tanzanian views for much of the period covered in this study, Sida has been able to exercise a relatively high degree of discretion with regard to both strategy and behaviour. It has no doubt been the single most important Swedish actor in the aid policy arena.

Sida's assistance was for a long time characterized by its low level of conditionality. The general faith in the capacity of recipient governments to implement development policies in the 1960s made conditions unnecessary, except on the project level, where Swedish concerns came to the fore. In the following decade, the principle of recipient autonomy prevailed. With the advent of the economic crisis in the late 1970s, Sida's aid tended more and more to follow in the footsteps of the donor community at large. After a few years of indecision, macro-economic conditionality was accepted, and in the 1990s political conditionality in terms of good governance was added to the portfolio of aid conditionalies.

As hypothesized, Sida has been 'in between' as regards the degree of centralization. To begin with, Sida was a rather centralized organization without any field level units. The evolution towards a more decentralized organization, which started when the DCOs were introduced in the early 1970s, became more accentuated over time. In the second half of the decade, the DCOs played a very influential role in both the planning and implementation of aid. This trend, however, was reversed in the 1980s, culminating in the decision to place the DCOs under the supervision of the embassies. With growing emphasis on political conditionality, it is almost inevitable that direction has again become more centralized. It is worth stressing, however, that in 1995, it was Sida rather than the Foreign Office which provided the intellectual and operational leadership in deciding the issues of political conditionality.

For a long time Sida relied mostly on contract employees, hired in their individual capacity by the agency itself for carrying out projects in Tanzania. Some of these contract employees eventually became permanent Sida employees. Since the early 1980s, Sida has been more or less forced, by budgetary necessities, to switch to using consultancy firms for project preparations and implementation. These consultants have not been absorbed by Sida, but have typically retained a working relationship with Sida for a long time. They have become part of an 'old-boy network' of actors engaged in the foreign aid business. The Swedish Audit Bureau has criticized the way Sida has been hiring its consultants, and the practice more recently has been to use a system of open tender.

EXPLAINING DISCONTINUITIES IN SWEDISH AID POLICY

Ideology as a Driving Force

Although there has been a definite degree of continuity in Swedish aid policy, particularly with regard to choice of recipient countries, there have also been important breaks. How far have these discontinuities been the result of factors on the domestic Swedish scene? How far do they stem from external factors? What role have Sida's own decision-making structures played in shaping aid policy? And what importance should be attached to ideas, images and theories about development? These are the questions that will be addressed in this section.

There is little doubt that developments in Tanzania, more than any other single country, influenced the evolution of the Swedish aid policy. Tanzania was from a very early point a 'favourite' recipient of Swedish aid. The trust and friendship that existed between President Nyerere and some of his ministers, on the one hand, and Prime Minister Tage Erlander and his advisers, not least Olof Palme, on the other, made Tanzania special in Swedish aid circles. President Nyerere's decision to emphasize poverty eradication and national self-reliance were received with enthusiasm among Swedish Social Democrats. By becoming a spokesperson for an NIEO in the early 1970s he further enhanced his reputation as a true champion of the poor of the world. In the late 1960s and the 1970s, our interviewees confirm, the driving force behind Swedish aid policy was ideological and, in particular, influenced by what took place in Tanzania. In that sense, there was a distinct external, ideological influence.

How much did Swedish aid administrators learn from their experience in Tanzania? Sweden was one donor country that had wholeheartedly adopted the strategy of country programming on the assumption that it would enhance recipient input into the aid administration process and provide a means for more effective feedback. Apart from learning the lesson that 'trickle-down' effects of economic growth are very minute or non-existent, a factor that reinforced Swedish beliefs in the importance of the equity objective in foreign aid, there is little evidence throughout the 1970s that any real feed-back lessons were incorporated into Swedish aid policy. The latter remained constant throughout the 1970s and criticisms which were starting to be voiced about Tanzania's policies, notably the effects of the enforced villagization between 1973 and 1976, did not influence Swedish aid policy in general or even specifically in relation to Tanzania.

The orientation of Swedish aid policy was also influenced by what happened on the domestic political scene. As in so many other countries around the world, 1968 marked a radicalization of policy. It reinforced already existing inklings in leading Swedish Social Democratic circles that the world was moving to the left. Not surprisingly, the Swedish left, led by the Social Democrats, had its best election result ever in 1968. Aid to Tanzania became a way of demonstrating Swedish commitments to socialist developments around the world (Elgström 1992:42).

Within Sida, these ideological currents translated into a very strong orientation that 'aid on the conditions of the recipient' was the right way to go forward. If recipient governments had a commitment to poverty eradication and national self-reliance – like Tanzania – there was no reason to apply particular conditions to the aid given. Administratively, this conviction was reinforced by the country programming approach and the departure of the 'bankers' to the newly established aid agencies catering more directly for Swedish commercial interests. Sida, still the 'flagship' organization in the Swedish aid policy process, continued to have much more influence than the others. Hence it is not surprising that leftist ideas continued to shape Swedish aid policy during the 1970s.

It should be stressed here also that general development theory in those days favoured the role of a strong state. Foreign aid was influenced by Keynesian ideas that development could be accelerated and managed by proper public sector interventions. Comprehensive development planning had become institutionalized in the 1960s and served as yet another rationale for concentrating resource allocation to the state. Donors and recipients were in basic agreement on this issue during much of the 1970s.

Our interviews confirm that many of the officials hired by Sida were influenced by the leftist ideas that prevailed in the late 1960s and early 1970s (see also Wohlgemuth 1977). Their cognitive patterns served as accelerators, reinforcing the policy orientation presented above.

Thus, this study confirms the importance of beliefs and ideas in foreign relations. The Social Democratic welfare ideology, which had been very successful in Sweden, made a deep impression on Swedish aid policy from the start (Stokke 1989:19, 279). Altruism prevailed both at the official and operative level. If anything, critics of the Swedish policy were found among the foreign aid workers who had an opportunity to experience the problems in implementing specific projects or programmes 'on the terms of the recipient'. In spite of a growing choir of complaints from this category in the 1970s, Swedish aid policy stayed firm, especially in the case of Tanzania. These complaints never penetrated the cognitive shield of the aid officials in the Swedish political establishment (Elgström 1992:111).

Economic Change Factors and Cognitive Stabilizers

The serious economic downturn in many African economies in the latter part of the 1970s was an external factor that influenced donor outlook and policy. These changing economic conditions, caused largely by the hike in oil prices, meant that several existing development programmes and projects got into trouble. Particularly serious was the shortage of foreign currency for the import of necessary inputs and spare parts. This problem was noticed by the donors and it is clear that this kind of negative feedback served as an intervening variable between economic crisis and policy change.

Change, however, was not immediate, particularly in the Swedish case. By 1980, most donors had accepted the need for a policy change in the direction of a greater reliance on the market to solve problems of growth and resource allocation. The state was increasingly being viewed as a hindrance to development, an albatross around Africa's neck. Unlike other donors, Sweden was quite slow in approving the neo-liberal formula advocated by the IMF and the World Bank. Existing cognitive patterns among Sida officials precluded a rapid policy change. They were so deeply convinced that the old development formula would still work that they felt threatened and unwilling to modify their position. Signals about project failures, as indicated above, in spite of becoming increasingly massive, seemed to have little effect on the policy outlook in Sida (Elgström 1992:111).

On the domestic Swedish scene, a regime change took place in 1976. This was the first time since 1932 that Sweden had had a non-socialist government. While these new circumstances made politicians more anxious to demonstrate that foreign aid was cost-effective and worth the taxpayers' support, the more remarkable thing about this interlude (1976–82) was how little it changed Sweden domestically and how little its foreign aid policy was affected.

One reason for this is that not only was the foreign aid portfolio being controlled by the most pro-aid party in the governing non-socialist coalition, but this group lacked a real core of strong foreign aid analysts who could play a leading role in the Foreign Office. As a result, the government was very much in the hands of Sida. The leftist views prevailing in the agency were difficult to dislodge or modify. Furthermore, Sida's own sectoral divisions worked closely with their counterparts in Tanzania to maintain ongoing programmes and projects (interviews).

Sida had for a long time considered itself a pace-setter in the field of foreign aid and it was perhaps particularly hard for the Swedes to ponder a more radical shift in policy. In the case of Tanzania, it was particularly painful because the Swedes had been in the forefront of presenting the country as a model recipient. With the benefit of hindsight, it is now easy to say that there existed a policy vacuum during much of the critical period of 1979–83. The foreign aid sector seemed insulated from critical review. There were no signals or measures taken to identify how the Swedish aid programme to Tanzania (or other countries) might be modified to cope with the new economic situation. What this does confirm is that the cognitive stabilizers (Goldmann 1988) were very strongly institutionalized within Sida and that the agency did carry considerable influence in the foreign aid policy circles. The motto seems to have been that it is safer to continue the same old road than to diverge and choose a new path.

Crisis and Ideological Shift

The single biggest change in Swedish aid policy towards Tanzania came only grudgingly in 1983–84. Our interviews with Swedish officials indicate that this step was not an easy one. There was a definite degree of discomfort in having to make this announcement. It has sometimes been presented as if the Nordic countries threatened Tanzania with a total cessation of aid if the government did not sign an IMF agreement. This gives the wrong impression. According to our sources, the message conveyed to Tanzania was a rather soft one with no explicit conditionality attached to it. Sweden and the other Nordic countries fell back on their trustful relations with Tanzania and expected that the government would fully respond to the request made to sign and IMF agreement. It subsequently did so, although it took until 1986 before it was signed.

We argue here that the trigger behind this policy change in Swedish aid policy was the downturn in the Tanzanian economy and its inability to respond to *ad hoc* policy measures taken independently of IMF. It finally dawned on Swedish policy-makers that Tanzania was moving down a blind alley. The dramatic nature of the Tanzanian economic recession sent impulses that finally penetrated their cognitive barriers. In this sense, external factors were decisive for the policy shift. As difficult as to inform Tanzania about the new Swedish policy stand was the idea of accommodating Swedish aid policy to that of the other donors, notably the IMF/World Bank. Sweden had always taken pride in having an aid policy that was pro-recipient. For many, it was viewed as particularly progressive. What happened in 1983–84, therefore, marked a major retreat. Economists within the agency, however, realized that Swedish aid would not be of much use at all as long as the economy of Tanzania remained so out of balance. As Sweden joined the rest of the donor community in insisting on macro-economic reforms, it let itself be extensively guided by the World Bank and the OECD/Development Assistance Committee, a donor forum for coordination of aid policies. Although Sweden's initial signal to Tanzania in 1983–84 had been that it would continue giving unconditional aid, economic and financial conditionalities were increasingly being included in Swedish aid policy as the 1980s proceeded. To compensate for this hardening stand, Sida began pushing for more consideration of the social costs of the SAPs in African countries. In this way, it tried to regain some of its lost reputation as a leading donor agency.

In the 1990s, the questions of 'good governance' and democratization have become increasingly prominent in the aid debate. Again, it is the OECD/DAC that has played a leading role in coordinating donor policy in this area. The trigger behind this politicization of foreign aid was the fall of the Soviet empire. In the mid-1990s Sida was actively engaged in defining its own position in regard to democratization.

Compared to the external influences, including the impact of predominant neo-liberal development ideas, on Swedish aid policy since the early 1980s, domestic Swedish factors appear rather unimportant. Swedish public opinion accepted the policy shift in 1983–84. The economic difficulties facing Sweden in the 1980s gave rise to a new ideological climate in which a tougher and much stricter Swedish policy, stressing recipient responsibility, was replacing the old policy of 'aid on the terms of the recipient'. For the first time, Tanzanian obligations were closely monitored and sanctions imposed if officials in charge of specific programmes or projects could not account for money received. This, for example, happened in November 1994 when balance of payment support was temporarily suspended after the Nordic donors found that the Tanzanian Ministry of Finance was acting contrary to policy guidelines in exempting importers from duties. It is important to note, however, that although Swedes were becoming more concerned with issues of financial propriety and management, they retained their belief that giving foreign aid is morally right. Swedish public support for foreign aid – in terms of 'strong support' or just 'support' – never dropped below two-thirds.

The foreign aid debate in the 1990s came to focus on which countries to prioritize. When a non-socialist coalition came to power in 1991, it was the much stronger and assertive Moderate Party that took the lead. Greater emphasis was being placed on countries with neo-liberal policies and a climate for private sector growth. Tanzania was not considered one such country and therefore suffered a significant decrease in Swedish aid from 1992. There was much less change, however, at the operative level. For example, sector allocation and project selection remained much the same as before (interviews). Because the influence of Swedish public opinion on foreign aid has been rather minimal and the media have focused mainly on exposing the shortcomings of Swedish project aid in various countries, not least Tanzania, Sida kept its prominent position in aid policy circles throughout the 1980s. By the end of the decade, the adjustment to the neo-liberal ingredients in Swedish aid policy had been completed. The ideological divisions that had characterized the transition period between 1979 and 1983 were now an echo from the past. The reorganization that took place in 1985 gave more power to the regional divisions. Sectoral interests were now more effectively contained and a greater focus on country programming achieved. A deliberate attempt to cut Sida's influence was taken by the non-socialist government in the early 1990s, but its efforts were not very successful.

Sida thus remained the principal source of ideas about what to do with the new political dimensions of foreign aid. The Foreign Office remained relatively passive, even after the Social Democrats regained control of government in 1990. Sida was clearly the 'power-house' for new ideas about how to operationalize such concepts as democracy and governance in specific aid contexts, although some of these ideas were obtained from consultants and contacts with other donors.

Summary

Our review of changes in Swedish aid policy confirms that ideas and beliefs have played a significant role in determining policy. In the Swedish case, foreign aid policy has officially been part of the regular foreign policy establishment, but it has retained quite a distinct profile and throughout the whole period has been headed by a special cabinet minister. In this respect, foreign aid has been a visible and prominent part of Swedish foreign policy. The latter has never been very extensively influenced by the realist argument that only national security and interest count in foreign policy. Being a small power with no ambitions to control any other country or region of the world, Sweden had often acted quite altruistically in the global arena. More specifically, Sweden has always been a strong advocate for North–South dialogue and a sharing of resources with the poorer countries of the world. These concerns have taken their inspiration both from within Sweden itself, notably its long-standing social welfare legacy, and from the international arena where ideas about development have seeped into Swedish circles and helped shape aid policy. In more recent years, the predominant neo-liberal development ideology has exerted considerable influence on Swedish officials and decision-makers.

Ideas have played both a progressive and conservative role. Progressive notions of aid, determined by recipient needs and interests, prevailed in the 1970s and helped drive the foreign aid budget to a level where 1 per cent of GDP was accepted as the *minimum* level of aid disbursement from rich to poor countries. Although Swedish aid never got much beyond this minimal level, Sweden conscientiously tried to maintain it as long as its economy could afford it. With the problems emerging in the Swedish economy in the 1980s, however, compromises were made and eventually the level crept below the official minimum level. In the mid-1990s, it stayed on average at a level of 0.85 per cent of GDP, still much higher than most international donors.

While ideological structures have been the major force in determining *what direction* aid policy has taken in the face of change-producing stimuli, the main trigger behind such policy change has been external events and developments, most notably changes in the international economic context. The transformation of Swedish aid during the 1980s due to the economic crisis in Africa is the most illustrative example. Domestic factors have been much less influential. The regime change in 1976 did not produce any major effects; the changes in the 1990s had only a partial and limited impact.

Swedish policy-makers and aid administrators in the 1970s took for granted that aid should be given without any particular conditionalities. They did not accept that something might be fundamentally wrong with the recipient government administration; that aid, in fact, did not really help the intended target groups, notably the poor, but ended up in the pockets of the elite or was mismanaged in other ways. There were strong ideological blinders or cognitive stabilizers in Swedish aid policy preventing a rapid adjustment to the new circumstances that both Sweden and Tanzania faced in the late 1970s. Swedish aid policy in general, and in relation to Tanzania in particular, remained constant for a much longer time than in most other donor countries because of the strong influence of those officials who had come to accept the 'Swedish way' of giving aid, which implied no conditions. Negative feedback from Tanzania – and other countries – did not really shake the policy-makers into adopting new positions. It was only after a long time that Swedish officials began to realize that Swedish support for Tanzanian objections to the IMF and the World Bank was counterproductive. We find, therefore, in line with Hagan and Rosati (1994), that decision-making processes serve as intervening variables, in this case Sida's own structures contributing initially to an acceleration of the growth of Swedish aid to Tanzania and subsequently serving as a brake on policy changes.

AUTONOMY AND RESPONSIVENESS: THE CASE OF SIDA

Our analysis above leads us to the conclusion that agency behaviour is contained by overall policy goals, but because these are relatively general and have been stable, Sida has been able to enjoy a certain degree of autonomy. Policy shifts have been induced more by external than by domestic factors. Even so, Sida has demonstrated that it has a definite freedom of action when it comes to choosing its strategies and the means to realize these. Thus, these issues call for a little more analysis.

The concept of autonomy is tied to control of resources. The more an organization has control of resources, the more autonomous it is likely to be in its relation with other actors. Autonomy, however, is also determined by rules. Official or unofficial, these set the limits for what an organization can do or provide guidelines for strategy and behaviour.

Like other bureaucratic agencies, Sida's control of financial resources is virtually nil. It does not collect its own revenue, nor is it engaged in income-generating activities. Thus, it is dependent on what amounts the Riksdag is ready to set aside for the agency. Formally, Swedish legislators not only set the general objectives for foreign aid but also decide the allocation between the recipient countries. The fact that Sida does not control its own financial resources, however, does not seem to restrict its autonomy. To understand this apparent paradox, it is necessary to recognize that other resources – political and informational – are also important. In the Swedish case, Sida has been able to rely on three factors that have helped sustain its relative autonomy. The first is the rule that members of the Riksdag are anxious to demonstrate an outward unity on foreign policy issues. This seems to have spilled over also to the area of foreign aid. There have been remarkably few disagreements in the Swedish foreign aid debate except concerning choice of priority countries. The second factor is that there has always been a considerable voting majority in the Riksdag in favour of continued foreign aid at the highest possible level. Even during the period when the non-socialist coalitions ruled the country, this majority was there, because the coalition included at least one or two parties that were strongly pro-foreign aid. The third is that Swedish public opinion has continued to support the idea that the country should provide foreign aid. Sida, therefore, has been able to rely on (or, if necessary, help to mobilize) political resources for itself. These have often outweighed the lack of financial autonomy in that the Riksdag has continued from one year to the other to allocate considerable amounts of money for foreign aid. Cutbacks in the Swedish budget in the mid-1990s have not hit foreign aid any harder than other sectors. The fact that foreign aid has enjoyed stable public and legislative support over all these years has definitely helped Sida in obtaining and maintaining its autonomy.

Sida has also been able to uphold its autonomous status by control over informational resources. Although for much of this period there have existed three or four other aid agencies, it is Sida that has occupied centre-stage. Although these other organizations have been part of the official Riksdag system of consulting relevant agencies and interest groups ('remiss'), Sida's voice has always weighed most heavily. It has possessed the informational resources to provide a much broader perspective on particular issues than any of the other agencies.

Sida's autonomy, however, is not fully appreciated without reference to the official autonomy that Swedish administrative agencies enjoy according to constitutional law. Because a cabinet minister, even if he or she has formal responsibility for a particular bureaucratic agency, cannot interfere in its day-to-day affairs, Swedish administrative agencies are freer from political interferences than their counterparts in other countries.

To find out how Sida officials themselves view the relative power of relevant actors in the field of foreign aid, we asked seventeen knowledgeable officials to assess on a scale of 1 to 5 (with five being high and one low) the influence that these actors have on decisions about aid to Tanzania. Their answers confirm much of what has been argued above. It is interesting, however, that they see cabinet ministers (2.58 on average) and the Foreign Office (2.77) as more influential than the Riksdag (1.87). When asked more specifically, however, which role the Foreign Office plays *vis-à-vis* Sida when it comes to aid to Tanzania, our respondents almost without exception answered 'largely uninfluential'. They did inform us of attempts by the Foreign Office in the early 1970s and then again in 1992 to gain more control over Sida, but none of these attempts was portrayed as particularly successful.

The increased reliance on consultants was noted by many of our respondents as a potential threat to Sida's autonomy. It tends to undercut Sida's position as the centre of all expertise on aid and development issues. The effect has been that the remaining staff in Sida became generalists with knowledge only of specific countries and more broadly defined development issues. Furthermore, consultants may not always be ready to follow the same normative preferences as Sida in their dealings with institutions in recipient countries. In short, our interviewees indicate that Sida's own autonomy – and credibility – may be threatened by the delegation of programme or project responsibilities to consultants.

Responsiveness is related to autonomy in the sense that the latter is a prerequisite for being responsive. Dependency reduces or eliminates the prospect of responsiveness. Thus autonomy is an important aspect of understanding responsiveness. We do not suggest that Sida in the formal sense has been unresponsive to impulses from the Swedish government. As suggested above, as a bureaucratic agency, it is under supervision by the Foreign Office. All the same, what really strikes the analyst here is the degree of autonomy it has been able to sustain. It is this autonomy that has enabled Sida's own staff to feel confident about being responsive to recipient countries. In the specific case of Tanzania, there is plenty of evidence to suggest that Swedish aid policy has been very much influenced by policies and events in that country. Particularly during the days when the principle of 'aid on the terms of the recipient' was followed almost literally, responsibility for strategy and policy orientation was in the hands of Tanzanian officials. This unusually high degree of responsiveness to the Tanzanian authorities seems to have had at least two major effects on Swedish aid policy.

The first is the rather paradoxical finding that Sida is not learning very much from the field (*Lär sig Sida?* 1988). Although Sida has commissioned a large number of evaluations, it is not particularly open to influences from outside, including from recipient countries. It could be argued that this finding contradicts our argument that Sida is highly responsive to recipient country events. A more plausible explanation, however, is that Sida has not only delegated, but almost abrogated, its responsibility for administering the aid programmes and projects once the money reaches Tanzania. In short, it has not considered the feedback as particularly significant. It has been more important for Sida to prove that the money has been pumped into Tanzania than to incorporate the lessons from how the funds were used. The extent to which there has been a feedback seems confined to attempts by Tanzanian officials, working in cohort with sector representatives in Sida, to protect and prolong ongoing projects or programmes. These coalitions have occasionally also included interest groups and politicians in either Sweden or Tanzania. Although a concerted effort was begun in 1995 to concentrate programming and have fewer projects, the lessons before had clearly been that Sida was better at adding new assignments – and keeping them going – than at subtracting programmes or projects.

Much of the above characterization fits the situation after 1984 less well. Sida's responsiveness has declined in recent years as Sweden has tightened its demands for reporting. While there is still an ambition to have the Tanzanians take responsibility for Swedish aid, the lack of trust in what they do with the money, fuelled by growing evidence in the early 1990s of official corruption, has forced Sida to become increasingly restrictive. Sida officials in Dar es Salaam found this new approach unfortunate but necessary. Some found it difficult to convey these new stricter guidelines to their Tanzanian counterparts. It was not the language that they had learnt in Sida in the past. It is also worth mentioning that this change in Swedish aid policy has not gone unnoticed in Tanzania. In interviews we had with Tanzanian officials, the general way of describing the Swedish aid was to characterize it as given on 'humanitarian' grounds. A few, however, suggested that 'Swedish aid had become more like the American aid' (that is, tied to political conditionalities).

This may be an oversimplification in that Sweden still retains the objective of being as responsive as possible. The reason for its restrictiveness has not been on the Swedish but on the Tanzanian side: the cavalier and careless attitude towards Swedish aid that certain officials in the Tanzanian establishment had adopted in the 1980s. All the same, the perception that Swedish aid has become increasingly similar to that of the USA is not completely inaccurate. As we have noted above, Swedish aid policy after 1984 shifted towards acceptance of the mainstream structural adjustment approach approved and adopted by the rest of the donor community. To the extent, therefore, that Swedish responsiveness to Tanzania declined after 1984, it was driven more by adherence to other donor demands than pressures from domestic Swedish sources. In this respect, the relative autonomy from Swedish direction has continued. What has happened is that Sida's responsiveness has shifted from the recipient to the rest of the donor community. Even if Sida has lost its ability to speak as champion of the recipient, however, the old philosophy lingers on and makes many Sida officials uneasy about the strict conditionalities, economic as well as political, that are now being imposed on recipient countries by the combined weight of the whole donor community.

Our hypothesis was that Sida would have a relatively low degree of autonomy, and high degree of responsiveness, *vis-à-vis* the political authorities in Sweden. It is confirmed only at the level of general policy. The broader framework for aid policy is set not by Sida but by the Riksdag, with inputs from the Foreign Office. The significance of this finding, however, is qualified by the fact that, because of the stability of Swedish aid policy, the scope for autonomy at the strategic and operative levels has been very high. The hypothesis that Sida would demonstrate only a low level of autonomy *vis-à-vis* external actors is also only partially confirmed. The assumption in the literature on how small states behave in the international arena is that, due to limited resources and external dependence, they tend to adapt to external, more powerful actors. This is not borne out by the findings of this study. Sida has often taken a leading role in the international donor community and, although its influence was probably higher in the 1970s than it has been since, Sida is considered a respected actor to whose voice others (both donors and recipients) listen. The most striking thing about Sida in this study, however, is its high degree of responsiveness to Tanzania. Until very recently, it was as if the country could do no wrong. Mistakes committed on the Tanzanian side were overlooked for a very long time. Negative feedback did not penetrate the cognitive stabilizers in the minds of Sida officials. Instead, business continued as usual. It is only in the 1990s, after a long series of incidents of misappropriation and mismanagement of Swedish funds, that things have begun to change.

CONCLUSIONS

In the first chapter, Hyden and Mukandala argued that because donors tend to overemphasize a particular aspect of the foreign aid process, they are prone to fall into traps that place constraints on the overall effectiveness of their operations. They identified four such traps: (1) *fiscal accountability*, (2) *political solidarity*, (3) *coordination*, and (4) *organizational insularity*.

In pulling together the various arguments of this chapter, it seems that Sida has largely avoided two traps but has fallen into two others, one quite deeply. For virtually the whole period, Sida has avoided the fiscal accountability trap. Some have argued, like the Swedish National Audit Board, that Sida has been irresponsible towards Swedish taxpayers by not insisting on better fiscal accountability. It is only in the 1990s that Sida has become more insistent on adherence to fiscal regulations and to the need for greater efficiency in the use of Swedish aid money. This shift in policy notwithstanding, pressures from Swedish sources to account for the money have been at best modest. The most significant thing that has happened is that Sida has tightened its own internal regulations.

Sida has occasionally tried to take advantage of its relative autonomy to become inward-looking. Officials have sometimes dismissed opinions from outside, even though many observers would agree that these views could assist the agency. Similarly, many evaluations have been carried out by Sida officials themselves. The tendency towards insulation has clearly been there. All the same, this insular propensity has never survived for any length of time. Pressures from other sources, notably the donor community or the recipient country, have eventually taken over. Thus Sida has really never fallen into the organizational insularity trap.

The agency, however, definitely fell into the political solidarity trap. For the whole of the 1970s – and into the 1980s – Sida was mesmerized by the idea that aid must be given on the terms set by the recipient, and that Swedish aid was an act of solidarity. The full depth of this sentiment can only be understood if reference is made again to the connection between Swedish views of foreign aid and domestic social welfare. The idea of sharing through heavy taxation was something that Swedes generally accepted during those years and it was only natural that this solidarity be extended to include poor people also in other parts of the world. This belief clouded other considerations, particularly in the case of Swedish aid to Tanzania. Thus programme failures, as in the case of the rural water scheme, never led to closure but only redefinition. The assumption all the time was that the recipient should have the right to take responsibility for correcting its mistakes and that Swedish funds should be ready to support such changes. Little did Sida officials question the capacity, let alone integrity, of the officials on the recipient side. Consequently it is not surprising that there is very little on the ground in Tanzania today which may be called a project or programme success created with Swedish money. Those projects, such as adult education, which looked very good in the early phases, proved unsustainable and gradually turned into failures.

Since 1984, Sida has slowly tried to get itself out of the political solidarity trap, but it appears as if it has partly landed in the coordination one instead. The need to restructure African economies in the 1980s paved the way for closer donor collaboration on macro-economic issues. Not only did the World Bank and the IMF provide a technical lead, but their neo-liberal ideology also became the dominant view of what needed to be done. Donors closed ranks behind this ideology. Although donors such as Sweden have insisted on modifications of the original programmes, the technical and political consensus in the donor community has been so massive that recipient governments have had little choice but to comply.

Finally, it should be pointed out that while Sweden was perceived in the first chapter as occupying a middle position between the USA and China, this chapter suggests that Sida behaviour and strategy have tilted: initially to the left, more recently to the right. In that sense, Swedish aid policy, while remaining quite stable over the years, has provided scope for shifts in strategy and behaviour. Because Sida largely failed to ask the hard questions of Tanzania, these shifts in strategy and behaviour did not seem to have produced any real improvement in the use of Swedish aid funds nor any betterment for the many Tanzanians they were supposed to assist.

In the mid-1990s, presenting Swedish aid as an integral part of an international undertaking led by the World Bank and its 'Global Coalition for Africa' provided a convenient way of escaping the disappointments suffered when Tanzania was the prima donna in Swedish bilateral aid policy.

References

Anell, L. (1986) 'Images of Distant Countries', in P. Fruhling (ed.), *Swedish Development Aid in Perspective*. Stockholm: Almqvist & Wicksell International, pp. 233–47.

DsUD 1984:1 (1984) *Effektivare biståndsadministration*. Stockholm: Utrikesdepartementet.

Edgren, G. (1982) 'Changing Terms', in P. Fruhling (ed.), *Swedish Development Aid in Perspective*. Stockholm: Almqvist & Wicksell International, pp. 47–63.

Elgström, O. (1982) *Aktiv utrikespolitik*. Lund: Studentlitteratur.

Elgström, O. (1992) *Foreign Aid Negotiations. The Swedish–Tanzanian Aid Dialogue*. Aldershot: Avebury.

Elgström, O. (1996) *Miljömålet för svenskt bistånd – beslut och genomförande*. Lund: Department of Political Science, University of Lund.

Goldmann, K. (1988) *Change and Stability in Foreign Policy. The Problems and Possibilities of Détente*. Hemel Hempstead: Harvester Wheatsheaf.

Goldstein, J. and R.O. Keohane (eds) (1993) *Ideas and Foreign Policy. Beliefs, Institutions, and Political Change*. Ithaca and London: Cornell University Press.

Government Aid Bills. Proposition (P): 1968, 1970, 1972, 1974, 1982/83, 1988/89, 1991/92.

Hagan, J.D. and J.A. Rosati (1994) 'Emerging Issues in Research on Foreign Policy Restructuring', in Rosati *et al.* (1994), *Foreign Policy Restructuring*. Columbia, SC: University of South Carolina Press, pp. 265–79.

Hermann, C. (1990) 'Changing Course: When Governments Choose to Redirect Foreign Policy', *International Studies Quarterly*, 34:3–21.

Holsti, K. (ed.) (1982) *Why Nations Realign. Foreign Policy Restructuring in the Postwar World*. London: Allen & Unwin.

Lär sig SIDA? En granskning av SIDAs förmåga att lära sig av erfarenheterna (1988). Stockholm: Riksrevisionsverket.

Odén, B. and B. Sedin (1988) 'På biståndets bakgård', *Debatt SIDA*, no. 3.

Palmlund, T. (1986) 'Altruism and Other Motives', in P. Fruhling (ed.), *Swedish Development Aid in Perspective*. Stockholm: Almqvist & Wicksell International, pp. 109–25.

Palmquist, N. (1995) 'Förändringar i det svenska biståndet till Tanzania: vilka och varför?' (mimeo) Department of Political Science, University of Lund.

Rosati, J.A., Hagan, J.D. and M.W. Sampson III (eds) (1994) *Foreign Policy Restructuring: How Governments Respond to Global Change*. Columbia, SC: University of South Carolina Press.

SASDA (1994), *Evaluation of Swedish Development Cooperation with Tanzania*. DsUD 1994:113. Stockholm: SASDA.

Sida (1992) *Utveckling är människor. Om Sidas personalbistånd.* Stockholm: SIDA.

Sida Official Documents:
1971: Länderprogram, Tanzania.
1977: Regeringsskrivelse: Samarbetsprogrammet med Tanzania 1977/78–1979/80.
1979: Regeringsskrivelse: Utvecklingssamarbetet med Tanzania 1979/80–1981/82.
1985: Regeringsskrivelse: Utvecklingssamarbetet med Tanzania 1985/86–1986/87.
1987: PM om utvecklingssamarbete med Tanzania 1987/88–1988/89.
1993: Utkast regeringsskrivelse: Utvecklingssamarbetet med Tanzania 1994/95–1996/97.
Bistånd i siffror och diagram 1993/94. Stockholm. Sida 1995.
Bistånd genom Sida 1970/71.
Sida's petita 1975/76.

Stokke, O. (ed.) (1989) *Western Middle Powers and Global Poverty.* Uppsala: The Scandinavian Institute of African Studies.

Therkildsen, O. (1988) *Watering White Elephants.* Uppsala: The Scandinavian Institute of African Studies.

Wohlgemuth, L. (ed.) (1976) *Bistånd på mottagarens villkor.* Stockholm: SIDA.

5 From Proletarian Internationalism to Mutual Development: China's Cooperation with Tanzania, 1965–95

Ai Ping

INTRODUCTION

In this chapter, we will take the PRC's economic and technical cooperation with Tanzania as an example in order to study the PRC's foreign aid in general and its meso level – the agencies in charge of its implementation – in particular.

The reason for doing this lies, first of all, in the fact that China's foreign aid has yet to be thoroughly analysed. The PRC has been one of the most important aid providers to Tanzania. In addition to the famous TAZARA, linking Zambia's Copperbelt with the Tanzanian port of Dar es Salaam, China's aid to agricultural development of the country is equally impressive. The Chinese-built Mbarali Farm once met one-quarter of the rice demand of the country's domestic market. Farm implements manufactured by UFI (built with Chinese aid) made up 85 per cent of the total hand farm tools produced in Tanzania for many years. China's extensive aid to Tanzania raises some interesting questions. For example, China had never been a colonizer or a developed country itself; why then should it provide aid to Tanzania, and to many other countries with a much higher per capita GNP?

Second, China itself, being a developing country with a relatively backward economy, could not provide its aid in the same way as the developed countries. It faces the heavy task of modernizing its own economy, and is badly in need of large amounts of investment funds. Its own currency has been inconvertible. So, unlike Sida, the aid agencies in China could not simply write cheque and give them to the recipient countries. At the same time, during the first half of the period that we are studying (1965–80), the political and economic system that prevailed in China was a highly centralized one. In the economic field, the state sector was predominant and the institution was characterized by the so-called 'product and planned economy'. The government was not only the organizer of the macro-economy but to a very large extent also the manager of the productive activities. Compatible with this, China's foreign aid, even the concrete matters concerning the actual projects and their implementation, was undertaken either directly by a government department or under its close organization and supervision. So the aid agencies in China could not, like the USAID, pass on the job to some private enterprise and pay the bill. Actually, the major form of China's aid was to ship tons of Chinese-made equipment, many more Chinese goods and large groups of 'experts' to the recipient countries to build 'complete plant projects' or, to use a term more familiar outside the country, 'turnkey' projects such as the Mbarali Farm and UFI. To accomplish all this work, a sophisticated mechanism was established in the country and, through a series of negotiations and signing of diplomatic documents, put in place abroad.

Third, China's aid strategy and behaviour, again unlike USAID and Sida, was not very much influenced by the fad of development economics but mainly by its own experience and philosophy. China, in its recent history, had been weak and beaten many times and, after the founding of the people's Republic, it had been threatened, blockaded, contained and isolated by the Western powers. These experiences had made China value its national independence highly, and regard economic independence as a necessary condition for political independence. In the field of economic development, China has, out of necessity, all along persisted in the principle of relying mainly on its own efforts while seeking external help only as a last resort. Its fundamental aim in the provision of aid has been to improve the recipient countries' ability to develop on their own. Thus the PRC's government has laid special emphasis on the construction of productive projects needed by the recipient countries. At the same time, the Chinese leaders, informed by the Marxist philosophy of historical materialism and the socialist economic strategy of 'product and planned economy', believed that economic development had its own 'objective laws'. They further believed that a country with a relatively backward economy should first develop its agriculture and solve the problem of feeding and clothing its people and then, on this basis, develop its industry and gradually establish a relatively independent economy. This belief made the Chinese government pay particular attention to agricultural projects in its foreign aid.

Another reason for China to favour aid to agricultural development of the recipient country is that this is the sector where its own strength lies. China has over many centuries developed a traditional agricultural system and techniques that stressed intensified farming. After the founding of the People's Republic, China built a number of large-scale state farms. So one may say that China had a fairly complete grasp of agricultural knowledge for different levels of economic and technical development. Taking its aid to Tanzania's agriculture as an example, there are large-scale state farms with relatively high levels of mechanization and modern techniques, and also extension service stations aimed at popularizing suitable techniques that can raise per-unit yield of crops without large amounts of capital input. In addition, there are manufacturing plants specializing in farm implements. As the reader will find in later sections, Chinese aid efforts have been quite persistent. For example, the Chinese have been working on the Mbarali Farm under conditions similar to their Tanzanian counterparts for more than 20 years now.

Fourth, China's foreign aid has undergone less frequent, but more fundamental changes in its strategy, behaviour and mechanisms. According to the authors of the *Contemporary China's Foreign Economic Cooperation* (1989), China's foreign aid efforts can be divided into four periods: (1) the initial period from 1950 to 1963; (2) the developing period between 1964 and 1970; (3) the fast expansion period from 1971 to 1978; and (4) the new stage of development through readjustment and reform since 1979. But, so far as the strategy, behaviour, and mechanism are concerned, the most significant dividing line is the year 1979. Before 1979, China's foreign aid was based more on the notion of 'proletarian internationalism' and had a strong element of 'idealism'. Its efforts since the 1980s have become more realistic, with stress on 'equality and mutual benefit, emphasizing actual results, with different forms and aimed at mutual development'. At the same time, the relevant department of the Chinese government has all along been exploring ways to readjust the principle, form, structure, implementation and management mechanisms of China's foreign aid in accordance with the changed domestic and international conditions.

Compared with Western countries, China has been influenced relatively little by the 'donor community', yet it could not ignore the major changes in the recipient countries. Later on, we will see that when privatization became the trend, China sped up its exploration for new forms of aid rather than continuing the construction of more turnkey projects.

To sum up, the untold story of Chinese economic and technical cooperation with Tanzania is not only interesting in and of itself, but also offers much food for thought. Some of the efforts China made to aid Tanzania happened a long time ago. Yet Chinese foreign aid should not be of interest only to the historians; it is an unfinished story. It has left a number of legacies which might serve as trail marks pointing to the future. It is at least a good testing ground for the model set up by this project to pioneer the comparative study of the donor agencies. This, the author believes, is the fifth point of interest in studying Chinese aid.

This chapter is structured to explore the above-mentioned points one by one. The second section describes the formation of PRC's principles in its foreign relations which forms the rationale of the Chinese foreign aid. The third section provides a general survey of China's foreign aid and explains the major form and implementation mechanism of China's external economic and technical aid between 1965 and 1985. The fourth section gives a general picture of China's aid to Tanzania with some detailed cases, particularly projects aimed at promoting Tanzania's agricultural development. The fifth section provides a description of China's readjustment of its external economic cooperation sector. The sixth section sums up some characteristics of China's economic aid according to the general framework of this project, and the final section draws some conclusions regarding the legacies of China's economic aid to Tanzania.

THE EIGHT PRINCIPLES

In 1964, during his trip to Africa, Zhou Enlai, the PRC's Premier, made public China's Eight Principles on Foreign Economic and Technical Aid. Since then, these eight points have remained the fundamental principles guiding China's efforts to provide economic aid to many Third World countries, including Tanzania. In order to understand their origin it is necessary to look briefly into the foreign policy of the new People's Republic, particularly those parts that were connected with its external economic relations.

The foreign policy of the People's Republic was determined by the specific historic conditions as well as domestic and international conjuncture at the time of its formation in 1949. China was a power with thousands of years of civilized history. However, as the world entered the modern era, particularly after the mid-nineteenth century, it had become a poverty-stricken and weak country that was semi-colonial in nature. The major reason behind China's sad position as an old and out-of-date state lay inside the country, but the expansion and the aggression by the imperialists from both the west and the east had made the national contradictions even sharper and the historical task to revitalize the Chinese nation more urgent. The ancient imperial court of the Qing Dynasty (1644–1911) was defeated many times by the Western powers and unequal treaties were imposed on China one after another. During this period, progressive Chinese, who were few in number at the beginning, believed that they should open their eyes to the world. Some of them came to see the feudal dynasty as the root cause of China's problem. The latter was overthrown by the Republican Revolution in 1911 but was followed only by civil wars, first among different sects of warlords, and frequent changes of governments. During all this turmoil, the Western powers insisted that the unequal treaties they had imposed on China must be 'honoured'. Only the Soviet Union under Lenin openly announced abrogation of the unequal treaties between the imperial Russia and feudalist China. That was the starting point of close relations between the Soviet Union and China, not only with the Communist Party of China (CPC) but with the Kuomintang as well (Lui Dexi 1995). Several generations braved the dangers and sacrifices and finally managed to establish the People's Republic in 1949.

The Communists decided to break away from traditional Chinese diplomacy, although many argued that China had no diplomatic policies. Unlike the Qing court and the later warlords ('governments' who 'always conducted diplomatic affairs on their knees', as Zhou Enlai was fond of putting it), the PRC sought the historical opportunity to guard its hard won independence and sovereignty in earnest (Zhou Enlai 1990).

In the modern world, however, independence and sovereignty do not mean one does not need friends, particularly for a country that had just experienced decades of war. The government came to power only to find a bankrupt national economy, extreme poverty among hundreds of millions of its people, and a very heavy financial burden as a result of the war. This coincided with the beginning of the Cold War and all governments were asked, or forced, to choose among two camps.

At the end of the 1940s there was a debate among American foreign policy-makers about who 'lost' China, and for a short while hesitation about what to do with the situation in China. When the CPC-led People's Liberation Army captured Nanjing, the capital of the Kuomintang government, the American ambassador did not move to Guangzhou like many other foreign diplomats, including the Soviet ambassador. He even thought about making a trip to Communist-occupied Beiping, as Beijing was called before it became the national capital, perhaps not as the US ambassador but as the formal president of an American-funded university there. Unfortunately, his plan was not approved and he was called back very soon (Lui Dexi 1995). President Truman's hesitation did not last long as the Korean War broke out on 25 June 1950. He announced the decision to send the Seventh Fleet to the Taiwan Strait. The first one or two months of the war in Korea led to the situation in which troops under American command advanced towards the Sino-Korean border. The northeastern part of China, one of the few industrial bases of the new-born People's Republic, faced an immediate threat from air bombardment. Mao Zedong personally made the very difficult decision to send Chinese volunteers to Korea, as he believed that it would not be possible to start the reconstruction of the country with the strongest army in the world right outside China's door (Mao Zedong 1994).

In the context of the specific international and historical conditions, the first task that New China faced in the field of international relations was to establish a safe footing and strive for a peaceful environment conducive to its efforts to cure the wounds of the war and to rehabilitate and develop the national economy (Contemporary China's Foreign Affairs 1985).

During the early period of the People's Republic, China decided on six major items of its foreign policy for peace. They were: 'set up a separate kitchen'; 'lean to one side'; 'invite guests only after cleaning up the house first'; 'treat others as others would do you'; 'exchange for what each other needs'; and 'be united with the people the world over' (Contemporary China's Foreign Affairs 1985). These principles were laid out in a typical Chinese figurative way, and thus a bit of explanation is necessary.

'To set up a separate kitchen' meant that, unlike what previous governments in China had done when they came to power (that is, seek foreign support by accepting the existing unequal treaties), the PRC would not recognize these treaties and the old diplomatic relations established by the Kuomintang government. PRC's diplomatic relations with other countries would be established through negotiations on a new basis.

'To lean to one side' meant a clear announcement that China would stand with the socialist camp headed by the Soviet Union. The CPC's direct contact with the Americans started during the Second World War. In the beginning relations were quite positive, as they both belonged to the Allied countries and China hoped that the Americans might provide some badly needed materials to help CPC's efforts to fight the Japanese. However, relations greatly deteriorated as Americans sent in arms and military advisers to help Chiang Kai-shek fight the civil war after the end of China's war against the Japanese. As Chiang was defeated and America lost face, the CPC saw no hope of being recognized by the USA. So, as the Cold War had already fermented, the only realistic way for them to have some international support was to side with the Soviet Union.

The literal meaning of 'inviting guests only after cleaning up the house first' was actually not to rush to have dealings with the Western powers, but first to have a chance to eliminate the influence of the West that had accumulated through decades of political, economic and cultural 'invasions'. So, to translate that into foreign policy meant that the treaties and agreements entered into by the Kuomintang government and foreign governments would be closely examined first and then recognized, abolished, changed, or renegotiated according to the contents of each.

'To treat others as they would do you' was a principle targeted at the Western powers. It meant that China would adopt an attitude towards each Western country acccording to its attitude. Not all the Western countries had adopted the same policy as the USA. Great Britain, for example, with its interests in China in mind, was quick to express its recognition of PRC and to establish diplomatic relations. But it refused to sever relations with Kuomintang and, on some occasions, sided with that regime. So, a kind of 'semi-diplomatic relationship' was established between the PRC and the UK.

'To exchange for what each other needs' expressed the CPC's desire to go into commercial business on the basis of equality and mutual benefit, even if the state-to-state relation could not be normalized in the near future.

'To unite with the people the world over' was a continuation of the CPC's previous practice of adopting a friendly attitude towards people even if their governments were hostile to the New China. Even though PRC might not have diplomatic relations with Western countries, some of which happened to be colonial powers at the same time, China could reach out its friendly hands to the people of these countries (Zhou Enlai 1990).

For the new PRC, 'foreign affairs' was high on the priority list, as it involved survival. Only after the armistice of the Korean War was the PRC freed from the immediate threat of war. After the Afro-Asian Conference held in Bandung, Indonesia, in 1955, the national liberation movements of the colonies surged ahead and the colonial system gradually collapsed. For China this meant it could come directly into contact with African countries and develop relations with them.

The PRC's foreign policy, however, was not simply a product of expediency. It was guided by the philosophy and the world outlook of the top leaders of the CPC. Premier Zhou Enlai pointed out as early as 1951 that after the victory of the October Revolution in Russia, there appeared in the world two camps antagonistic towards each other. Ever since then, the national liberation struggles by the colonial and semi-colonial countries were no longer part of the capitalist revolution but a part of socialist revolution. Zhou went on, 'our task is to support and promote the development of the national liberation movement' (Zhou Enlai 1990). This 'support and promotion' can be, and actually very often is, a moral one, so it would not contradict China's declaration of non-interference of other's internal affairs.

Due to the isolation and containment the PRC suffered, it was during the Bandung Conference that top Chinese leaders had an opportunity for the first time to explain their foreign policy face-to-face – including the philosophy and the world outlook guiding it – to leaders of many Asian and African countries. During the Bandung Conference, Premier Zhou said, 'we Asian and African countries need to cooperate in the economic and cultural fields so as to facilitate our efforts to eliminate the economic and cultural backwardness that resulted from the long time plunder and oppression by colonialism' (Zhou Enlai 1990). Here, for the first time without the proverbs for which the Chinese language is known and the exaggerations that usually characterize Chinese rhetoric, Zhou was explaining 'revolution'. What's more, we also get a hint of the Chinese leader's logic of 'development economics': the economic and cultural backwardness was the result of extended plunder and oppression. Once the people had their fate in their own hands, the economy would be on a fast track of economic development.

At the Bandung Conference there were only scores of Africans representing half a dozen African countries, some of which had not yet won their independence. The first time Zhou could speak not only to leaders, but also to large groups of ordinary African people and to the world was through the mass media during his trip to ten African countries in 1963 and 1964. Premier Zhou pointed out during this trip that

> one of the major contents of the People's Republic of China's foreign policy is to actively support the national liberation movements in Asia, Africa and Latin America. China itself is a country that has been liberated from the shackles of imperialism and colonialism ... It is her duty to support those countries that are winning and will win their victories. (Long Live the Asian–African People Anti-Imperialist Solidarity 1964)

We may say then that before the African countries gained their independence, China's support to them was mainly moral. Independence made it possible for the two sides to come into direct contact and allowed China to offer some more tangible assistance.

China is called a donor only for the sake of convenience. From the very start, its efforts were the result of completely different historical circumstances from those of the West and were guided by a totally different philosophy and world outlook. As Zhou put it during his trip to Africa:

> the newly independent Asian and African countries need, on the one hand, to rely on themselves to develop an independent national economy, and, on the other hand, also to conduct friendly cooperation on the basis of equality and mutual benefit. It is particularly necessary for

> Asian and African countries, in their respective process of developing an independent national economy, to exchange for what each other is short of, complement each other's weak points and strong points and help each other. All the help is a mutual one and should be in total conformity with the principle of equality and mutual benefit and non-interference in each other's internal affairs. It will never be allowed to engage in control, plunder, interference or subversion in the name of aid. (Zhou Enlai 1990)

Zhou explained during his trip the eight principles that would govern the future economic relations between China and African countries:

1. The Chinese government has always been based on the principle of equality and mutual benefit in providing external assistance. It never regards such assistance as unilateral. The assistance is considered to be mutual.
2. The Chinese government strictly respects the sovereignty of the recipient country in providing external assistance, and never attaches any conditions or asks for any privilege.
3. The Chinese government provides economic assistance in the form of interest-free or low-interest loans. If necessary, the repayment date might be extended to lighten the burden of the recipient country as much as possible.
4. The purpose of the Chinese government in providing external assistance is not to create dependency of the recipient country on China, but to help the recipient country gradually embark on the road of self-reliance and independent economic development.
5. The Chinese government always tries its best to help recipient countries build projects with minimum investment while yielding quick results so that governments of the recipient countries can increase their revenue and accumulate funds.
6. The Chinese government provides equipment and materials of the best quality it can produce and negotiates prices according to the international market. If the equipment and materials provided by the Chinese government are not up to the agreed specifications and quality, the Chinese government guarantees to replace them.
7. The Chinese government shall see to it that, in providing any kind of technology to other countries, the personnel of the recipient country should fully master the technology.
8. The experts dispatched by the Chinese government to help construction in the recipient country should enjoy the same living conditions as the

> experts of the recipient country. The Chinese experts are not allowed to make any special demands and ask for any special amenities. (Brilliant Achievements 1985)

It is now easy to see that the Eight Principles on External Economic and Technical Assistance were a logical extension of the above-mentioned foreign policy of the People's Republic in the field of economic assistance. Determined by the specific historical conditions, the PRC's foreign aid was an internationalist effort of 'the poor helping the poor'.

THE EVOLUTION OF CHINESE AID STRUCTURE

This section provides a general survey of China's foreign aid so that the readers will be able to put the PRC's economic and technical cooperation with Tanzania into perspective. In doing so, we will follow the periodization mentioned in the introduction of this chapter.

The Initial Phase

During the first period, the major recipients of Chinese aid were other socialist countries, particularly North Korea and Vietnam, but also Mongolia and Albania. At the very beginning, the major form was material aid. During the Korean War, in addition to war materials, China provided large quantities of material free of charge, such as grain, cotton, medicine and medical equipment, industrial raw and semi-processed material, building material, machinery and daily necessities, altogether valued at 730 million Chinese yuan ($280 million). After the war, the PRC government made grants worth 800 million yuan ($305 million) to North Korea for the four years between 1954 and 1957. Between 1958 and 1963, China provided three interest-free loans to North Korea. At this time, the major form of the aid had changed to 'complete sets of projects'. During this initial period, China provided 29 such projects. China's aid to Vietnam was a similar story. During the Indo-Chinese War between 1950 and 1954, the major form of aid was material, valued at 176 million yuan ($67 million). After the war, PRC also provided 800 million yuan ($305 million) grants to North Vietnam, and the significance of complete sets of projects gradually increased. For both North Korea and Vietnam, China had also offered help to restore their transportation system, rebuild their cities, and receive their students and trainees to learn professional skills (Contemporary China's Foreign Economic Cooperation 1989).

After the Bandung Conference, the PRC's aid expanded to other Asian and African countries. For Asian nationalist countries, China's aid started with Cambodia in 1956, followed by Nepal and Burma. The first African country to receive Chinese aid was Egypt. In November 1956, China provided a grant of 20 million Swiss francs ($4.6 million) to the Egyptian government. During their armed struggle for independence, the Algerians also received some material aid and cash grants, valued at 70 million yuan ($28.4 million). The Guinean President, Sekou Touré, was the first African head of state to visit China. During his visit in September 1960, an economic and technical cooperation agreement was signed. It stipulated that China would offer an interest-free loan of 22.5 million roubles so as to provide complete sets of equipment and technical aid to Guinea. Before the end of 1963, China had also signed similar agreements with Ghana, Mali, and Somalia. During the initial stage, China offered aid to 21 Asian, African, and European countries and built 101 projects for seven of them (Contemporary China's Foreign Economic Cooperation 1989).

At the very beginning, Chinese assistance mainly took the form of material aid. Some small cash grants and technical assistance were also given. The instruction to deliver aid came directly from the central government to the relevant department, which would then carry it out. On 7 August 1952, the Central People's Government made the decision to set up a Ministry of Foreign Trade (MFT). From this point on, material aid was under the unified management of this ministry and carried out by import and export corporations under it.

In 1954, China started to provide aid in the form of complete sets of equipment. The negotiation and signing of agreement was the responsibility of MFT. The instruction to build the aid project would be issued by the State Planning Commission (SPC) to the sector ministries.

On 21 January 1960 the Standing Committee of the Second National People's Congress (NPC), or Chinese Parliament, made the decision to set up the Administration of Foreign Economic Relations (AFER) as an organ directly under the State Council (as the central government was then called) to be in charge of the administration of the country's foreign aid. Foreign aid in the form of complete sets of plants, previously under the control of the SPC and MFT, and aid in the form of cash, previously directly handled by the Ministry of Finance, came under the discretion of this Administration.

The Developing Phase

Premier Zhou's 'Eight Principles on External Economic and Technical Assistance' marked the beginning of the second phase. During this phase, the recipient countries increased to 31. Among the eleven new partners were eight African countries. It was during this stage that the PRC began aid to Tanzania. Between 1964 and 1970, China's expenditure on foreign aid was 144 per cent more than the previous 14 years, and new commitments increased by 116 per cent. As for the structure of the aid programme, the relative importance of complete sets of plants further increased. In these seven years, 313 projects were built for 20 countries. Some of the projects were quite sophisticated in terms of technology. During this stage, the central government's organ in charge of foreign aid gained further prominence. In June 1964, the Standing Committee of the NPC made the decision to set up the Commission for Foreign Economic Relations (CFER) (Contemporary China's Foreign Economic Cooperation 1989).

The Fast Expansion Period

As Henry Kissinger came to China and the PRC's seat in the UN was restored in 1971, China's external relations witnessed rapid developments. The same was also true for the country's foreign aid. While continuing its aid to 31 previously mentioned recipient countries, China provided aid in various forms for an additional 36 other countries during this period. In Africa in particular, as the PRC established diplomatic relations with many more countries, agricultural teams were sent to replace teams that had been sent by Taiwan.

Another reason for the fast expansion of Chinese aid during this period was the Vietnam War, which had now entered its decisive stage. During the years between 1971 and 1975, China's expenditure for aid to Vietnam, Laos and Cambodia comprised 43 per cent of China's total aid. Approximately 93 per cent of that 43 per cent went to Vietnam alone.

The implementation of aid projects during this period was a particularly difficult task. Many projects formulated at the end of the 1960s and early 1970s were all under construction at this time. In all, between 1971 and 1978, 470 projects were built for 37 countries, more than the total for the previous 16 years. Owing to all these factors, the PRC's expenditure on foreign aid during this period was 59 per cent than the total of the previous 21 years.

The greatest expansion occurred in the first five years (1971–75). During these years, expenditure on foreign aid averaged 5.88 per cent of the total central government expenditure. In 1973, it peaked at 6.92 per cent. It soon became clear that China could not afford to continue giving aid at such high level (Contemporary China's Foreign Economic Cooperation 1989). During this period, CFER was changed into the Ministry of Foreign Economic Relations (MFER) through a decision made by the

Central Committee of the CPC (CCCPC) and the State Council on 17 January 1975.

The New Stage of Readjustment and Development

The year 1978 was a turning point in China's foreign aid efforts. As Vietnam and Albania, two major beneficiaries of Chinese aid, turned against China, the PRC was forced to stop its assistance and withdraw its experts from both countries in July that year. The behaviour of the Vietnamese and the Albanians certainly hurt the feelings of both the Chinese leaders and the broad masses of the people. There was a serious debate as how to evaluate the aid effort and whether China should continue it. In July 1980, the State Council held a meeting to discuss the report of MFER. On 8 November the same year, the CCCPC and the State Council issued a document entitled 'Opinions on Conscientiously Doing a Good Job in Foreign Aid'. The document concluded that it should be noted that while China had assisted others, China itself had also been supported. The PRC's present international position in the world was inseparable from the support of the friendly countries, particularly the Third World countries. To put it in a nutshell, China's external assistance had yielded outstanding results and was of great significance for the country's role in the international arena. But there had also been quite a few shortcomings and problems in the work, some of which had been recognized; relevant measures had been adopted to correct them. The document also restated that China was in need of a peaceful and stable international environment as the country was engaged in its own modernization drive. It was a general principle of its external work as a whole to oppose 'hegemonism' and safeguard world peace. And foreign aid, as part of China's external efforts, must serve these general principles (Contemporary China's Foreign Economic Cooperation 1989).

During the four years between 1979 and 1982, expenditures, both new and continuing, were under strict control, as the country was (financially and economically) in a period of readjustment. On 8 March 1982, MFER, MFT and some other state organs were put together to form the new Ministry of Foreign Economic Relations and Trade (MOFERT) in a major effort to streamline the state apparatus.

Starting in 1983, as the economic and financial situation improved, the scale of foreign aid once again expanded. Between 20 December 1982 and 17 January 1983, Chinese Premier Zhao Ziyang visited 11 African countries. During this trip he announced four principles guiding China's economic and technical cooperation with African countries in the new era. The concrete contents of these principles (which built on the original Eight Principles) are as outlined below:

1. The principle of unity and friendship, equality and mutual benefit shall be followed. The sovereignty of the other side shall be respected without any interference in its internal affairs, any political conditions attached or any privilege demanded.
2. Proceeding from the actual needs and available conditions, efforts shall be made to bring the advantages and potential of both sides into full play to minimize the investment, shorten the construction period and produce quicker results so that sound economic returns may be attained.
3. Forms of cooperation and operation may, depending on the actual conditions of individual cases, vary from providing technical service, technical and management personnel training, scientific and technological exchange, project construction to cooperative production and joint venture operation. The Chinese side assumes responsibility, abides by the agreement, guarantees quality and stresses the sense of obligation to the project it undertakes. The experts and technical personnel sent by the Chinese side do not ask for any special treatment.
4. The purpose of the above-mentioned cooperation and operation lies in learning from each other to make up deficiencies so as to promote the ability of self-reliance and development of the national economy on both sides. (Wu Zhaoqi 1990)

In the seven years between 1979 and 1985, China , while continuing its aid to 64 original recipients, provided aid to 19 new partners. During this period the ratio of project and technical aid as a percentage of the total amount spent on aid increased from the previous period's 37 per cent to 78 per cent of the total. Construction of 242 projects for 62 countries was completed, while technical assistance and management cooperation were conducted for 119 Chinese-aided projects in 43 countries.

To sum up, from 1950 to 1985, China provided economic and technical aid to 87 countries (20 in Asia, 46 in Africa, 16 in Latin America and the South Pacific and five in Europe). The actual expenditure of foreign aid added up to 41.2 billion yuan ($16.7 billion), or 1.7 per cent of the total budgetary expenditure of the central government. Among the total, 15.9 billion yuan ($6.5 billion), or 38.5 per cent, was in the form of project and technical aid; 22.6 billion yuan ($9.2 billion), or 54.8 per cent, was material aid; and 2.7 billion yuan ($1.2 billion), or 6.6 per cent, was assistance in cash. All together 1126 projects were built for 68 countries (Contemporary China's Foreign Economic Cooperation 1989).

Among four forms of foreign aid – cash, material aid, project building and technical cooperation – we are mostly interested in the project building, plus the one most closely linked with it: technical cooperation. This is not only because its importance gradually and steadily increased, but also because it best represents Chinese characteristics of foreign aid. In reality, the implementation of aid in the form of complete sets of projects constitutes the heaviest work load of the Chinese aid agencies.

China's economic and technical assistance to the developing countries not only had a different historical background and a number of unique guiding principles, but it also created a whole set of mechanisms to carry it out. The negotiation and implementation of Chinese-aided projects would go through the following steps. First the leaders of the two countries would, through state visits, decide on the scale of the aid, and then sign an agreement on economic and technical cooperation. The agreement would stipulate the scale of the loan, the time period of use, and the terms of repayment. Then the departments in the two governments concerned with the project would meet. The recipient side would first express how it intended to use the loan (the projects they had in mind) and then the Chinese side would choose among the listed projects for investigation and initial feasibility studies. After this, the two sides would sign a protocol of economic and technical cooperation on the mutually agreed projects. Following this, the ministry in charge of foreign aid in the Chinese central government would assign the task of design and implementation to a ministry or a region (a province, an autonomous region or a municipality) which would in turn form and dispatch an 'expert group' to do further feasibility studies. After these studies were complete the two sides would write the minutes of the talks. These negotiations would be followed by actual designing, construction and installation. The project would be handed over to the recipient country after completion. If technical assistance was still necessary, the two sides would sign another protocol and agree to make it a 'technical cooperation project' funded with the loan provided by the agreement.

Within the Chinese government, the department in charge of foreign aid is currently the Ministry of Foreign Trade and Economic Cooperation (MOFTEC). As mentioned above, the Ministry of Foreign Economic Relations was merged with the Ministry of Foreign Trade, the State Administrative Committee on Import and Export and the State Administrative Committee on Foreign Investment and formed MOFERT in 1982. The new ministry received its present name in 1993.

Its responsibility and functions related to foreign aid include: to prepare and organize inter-governmental economic negotiations and meetings of the mixed commissions and to sign multilateral and bilateral economic agreements on behalf of the government according to the authorization of the State Council; to administer foreign aid, formulate aid plans for each recipient country, and organize the implementation of aid projects and technical cooperation; and to direct the work of Economic Councillor's Office in the Embassies. Within the Ministry, the Department in charge of these jobs is that of Foreign Aid. The department has under it comprehensive sector divisions that are responsible for formulating aid plans, collecting relevant statistics, forming budgets and final accounting, administering the foreign aid fund, and organizing bidding for the aid projects. The department also has geographic divisions that are responsible for formulating aid policy and plans for each country, preparing for bilateral negotiation and drafting agreements, and supervising and dealing with relevant intergovernmental matters.

In the period between 1965 and 1980, the organ in charge of the actual implementation of the construction of the aid projects was the Ministry's Complete Plant Department (once called the Implementation of Aid Projects Department). Outside the country, it was more often referred to as China Complete Plant Export Corporation, or COMPLANT for short. The corporation was formed in 1959 in accordance with Premier Zhou's instructions, and started to conduct large-scale aid to Africa in the mid-1960s. It was responsible for liaising with the Chinese undertakers of the aid projects and guaranteeing the supply of the equipment and parts.

The general Chinese undertakers of the aid projects (for example, the Ministries of Agriculture, Railways, Textile Industry and Communication, as well as various provinces, municipalities and autonomous regions), all had a 'Foreign Aid Office' which handled the task of organizing the implementation of the aid projects. These 'offices' would not, however, deal directly with the recipient government.

The ministry's agency abroad is the Economic Councillor's Office in the Chinese Embassy. In some rare cases (Tanzania, for example), where the foreign aid task was particularly heavy, a PRC Economic Representative's Office was set up at the request of the government as a separate diplomatic entity, and these have slightly different powers and functions. Usually, the task of the Economic Councillor's Office and/or the Representative's Office includes: implementing the Chinese government's principles, policies and development strategies in the field of foreign economic cooperation on the basis of equality and mutual benefit; and organizing and coordinating agencies of the relevant departments of the Chinese government and Chinese enterprises and institutions (including 'expert teams'). Its concrete tasks are: maintaining contacts with relevant departments of the host country's government and institutions as well as multilateral international organizations; opening, facilitating and expanding channels for bilateral economic relations; negotiating and discussing with the relevant departments of the host country government in accordance with the authorization form the headquarters as to how to implement bilateral economic agreements, and reporting back on their implementation; participating in the relevant meetings of the joint (mixed) commissions; conducting investigations; making policy suggestions concerning the development of bilateral economic relations; safeguarding the lawful rights of the Chinese side; and directing and coordinating the important activities of the Chinese enterprises and institutions (as well as visiting delegations and teams).

The Chinese personnel engaged in foreign aid could be roughly divided into two groups. The first are the 'specialists'; that is, officials of the ministry (including corporations and institutions under it and its agencies abroad). They are mainly graduates of institutions of higher learning who studied international economic relations or foreign languages in depth. Most are graduates of universities and colleges in Beijing, Shanghai, Guangzhou and Tianjin which are affiliated to the ministry. They are assigned to work in the ministry or the Foreign Economic Relations Departments in local governments or other ministries at their graduation and are engaged in the work as a career. The second group are those who work for the projects on a temporary basis. They are usually managers, engineers, technicians from the general undertakers or sub-contractors. Sometimes language teachers or interpreters from universities and other departments of the government have also joined this group.

CHINA'S ECONOMIC AND TECHNICAL ASSISTANCE TO TANZANIA[1]

China and Tanzania have all along maintained good relations. When Tanganyika became independent on 9 December 1961, Premier Zhou Enlai and Foreign Minister Chen Yi sent congratulatory messages, together with China's recognition. The two countries established diplomatic relations on the same day. On 10 December 1963, Zanzibar won its independence. President Liu Shaoqi, Premier Zhou Enlai and Foreign Minister Chen Yi expressed cordial greetings in their separate messages. On the following day, the two countries established diplomatic relations. When Tanganyika and Zanzibar became united in 1964, diplomatic relations with China were extended without further negotiations. The Tanzanian government has consistently supported the restoration of the PRC's legal rights in the

UN and China's cause of national reunification, attached great importance to the development of Sino–Tanzanian relations, and encouraged some African countries to establish foreign relations with China. There have been frequent exchange of delegations in all fields since the two countries set up diplomatic relations. The two countries share many common views in international affairs, and cooperate with and support each other (Chen Yulai and Xiaoke 1987).

The principal matters in Chinese assistance to Tanzania are usually directly decided during the visits paid by the leaders of the two countries. From 10 to 19 June 1964, Vice President Kawawa headed a goodwill and economic delegation from the government of the United Republic of Tanganyika and Zanzibar on a visit to China. On 16 June, the two governments signed an Agreement on Economic and Technical Cooperation. The following February, President Nyerere paid a state visit to China. On 20 February, the two countries signed a 'Sino–Tanzanian Friendship Treaty'. During the visits to China by President Nyerere and President Mwinyi in 1974, 1987 and 1992, on all three occasions the two sides signed agreements on economic and technical cooperation (Chen Yulai and Xiaoke 1987).

The Sino-Tanzanian Agreement on Economic and Technical Cooperation signed on 16 June 1964 stipulated that the Chinese government would provide economic and technical assistance to the Tanzanian government in the form of complete sets of equipment, single unit equipment, general goods and technical assistance that the Chinese government could provide and which were needed by the Tanzanian government. The concrete items would be decided through discussion on other occasions. The total value of this assistance would add up to 10 million pounds sterling ($28 million), and was regarded as an interest-free loan with no conditions attached. The 'loan' would be appropriated in stages as the construction of the projects went on over a period of five years, from 1 July 1964 to 30 June 1969, and would be paid back between 1975 and 1984 in the form of agreed export goods, convertible currencies or other currencies mutually agreed upon. The Chinese side would dispatch experts and technicians to Tanzania to provide technical assistance according to need on the Tanzanian side and availability on the Chinese side. Their treatment and working conditions would be discussed and agreed on separate occasions. As for the accounting matters, they would be discussed and agreed upon by foreign currency dealing banks of the two countries. Here we can see that though the Chinese assistance was counted and treated as a 'loan', what was actually provided would not be funding in the form of convertible currency, but a series of complete sets of projects and general goods. And, as Zhou Enlai had made it clear, if the recipient side could not pay it back on time, the repayment might be postponed (Pei Jianzhang 1989).

On 5 January 1965, the Chinese Ambassador signed a Protocol on the Agreement of Economic and Technical Cooperation with a State Minister of Tanzania, through which the concrete items of Chinese aid were decided. These included a textile mill, the Ruvu Experimental Farm and UFI, amongst others.

After the Agreement and the Protocol, the next step would be more detailed matters such as the treatment of the Chinese going to Tanzania. This would be done through a diplomatic document of still lower ranking: an exchange of letters by representatives of the two governments. On the same day, the two sides exchanged letters on the matters of dispatch of Chinese experts and technicians, including their treatment and working conditions. According to this document, the Chinese side would provide the home wages and travel expenses for the Chinese experts and technicians, while the Tanzanian side would provide housing, allowances, local transportation, necessary conditions for their job, medical treatment, and so on. The expenses of the Tanzanian side would actually be covered by funding under the Chinese loan as part of the 'local cost' of the project. This document also stipulated that the Chinese personnel should abide by the host country's laws and regulations and follow the instructions of the Tanzanian government. About a week later, the representatives of the two governments exchanged letters to confirm the amount of allowances that the Chinese experts would receive. There would be four levels, the highest being 615 shillings per month, and the lowest 500 shillings per month. These were the equivalent of roughly $116 and $90 respectively. In 1970, the allowances for the Chinese experts were unified and lowered to 400 shillings a month (or $75).

In May, 1969, the two sides exchanged letters, through which the time period for the loan was prolonged for five years and its repayment was also extended. At the same time, the nominal value of the loan was changed into Chinese currency (RMB 68 965 520 yuan).

From the above we can see that the two countries, through bilateral diplomatic negotiations, created a mechanism to overcome the inconvenience caused by lack of convertible currencies and made it possible for China, a developing country itself, to provide economic and technical assistance to another developing country. This, however, was only the legal aspect of the matter. The real job was much more complicated. Just to mention one example, a joint shipping venture between the two countries was formed to transport Chinese equipment, material and general goods to Tanzania. Detailed regulations on accounting were laid out to keep on record the large influx of goods and human beings.

The major form of Chinese aid to Tanzania is complete sets of projects. Since 1964, China has provided altogether 154 assistance projects of all kinds, the total value being RMB 1.9 billion yuan (at current prices). Of this sum, loans amounted to RMB 1.3 billion yuan and the rest was in the form of grants. China has undertaken 91 complete sets of projects and completed 85. In addition to this, China has also undertaken 31 technical assistance projects, 25 of which have been completed and six are still ongoing. In 1996, there were eight Chinese teams in Tanzania with 111 members.

The most famous project that China has completed in Tanzania is the TAZARA. It is also the biggest project abroad built with Chinese aid. It starts from Dar es Salaam, the capital of Tanzania in the east and ends at Kapiri Mposhi in Zambia in the west, where it joins an existing line. The main line is 1860 km in length and the Tanzanian section is 977 km long. In order to build this line, China sent almost one million tons of equipment, material and goods to Africa and dispatched nearly 50 000 Chinese engineers and technicians to work on site at different times. The 'Freedom Railway', completed in July 1976, became a trunk line connecting the two countries, thus providing both a reliable outlet to the sea for Zambia's important export material – copper – and conducive conditions for the two countries' economic development. In order to build this railway, China provided a loan of almost 500 million yuan ($286 million) and a grant of nearly 50 million yuan ($28.6 million). After the completion of the line China also provided loans or grants to build some necessary complementary installations, including a training centre with a capacity of 200 people and necessary facilities.

As regards Tanzania's industry, China has offered aid to build a textile mill, a saw mill, a leather and shoe factory, a cigarette factory, a sugar refinery and a clothing factory, amongst others. In the field of mining, China has assisted in the prospecting of iron ore and the exploration and construction of a coal mine with an annual productive capacity of 150 000 tons.

As for agriculture, the major projects built with Chinese assistance include the Ruvu State Farm, the Mbarali Farm, UFI, three extension service stations on the mainland and a farm tool repair shop, Ubanga Farm, a sugar cane farm, and some extension service centres on the Zanzibar Islands. The total investment of all these projects amount to nearly 100 million yuan ($ 56 million).

In the field of social welfare, China has offered loans and built water supply projects in the south, in Dodoma and on the Zanzibar islands, a hospital in Pemba and a number of schools. It also donated facilities to produce medicines and vaccines. Starting from 1968, China has dispatched medical teams to Tanzania usually for two years at a time, with 40–50 people each, among whom around 20 work in Zanzibar. To support their efforts, each year China provides 300 000 yuan ($180 000) for medical facilities and medicines to Tanzania.

Three typical examples among many Chinese-built projects aimed at promoting agricultural development deserve further comment.

Ubungo Farm Implement Factory

After Tazania won its independence, Nyerere stressed the importance of agricultural development. One way to achieve this was through improvement of farm tools. After the two countries signed the Agreement of Economic and Technical Cooperation in 1964, the Tanzanian side proposed that a farm tool plant be built with the loan provided by China. On 8 January 1965, minutes of the talks concerning the construction of a farm implement factory were signed between a Chinese expert team and the Industry, Mining Resources and Power Ministry of the Tanzanian government, through which the two sides made a decision on the scale of the factory, its proposed product mix, location, operation system, raw material supply and the division of responsibility of the two sides. On the Chinese side, the general undertaker of the project was the Eighth Machine-Building Industry Ministry, whose major function at home was to guarantee the supply of agricultural machinery. The assistant undertaker was the Ministry of Construction Industry, whose job in the project was to build the factory. The actual job was done by the Machine Building Industry Department of the Beijing Municipal Government. Construction started in February 1968 and finished in September 1969. After a few months of trial production, the factory was handed over to the Tanzanian side in March 1970 and was named UFI. With a total investment of 2.9 million yuan ($1.2 million), the factory had a production capacity of 1000 tons of farm tools, or roughly 180 000 hoes and 10 000 ploughs. After the handover of the factory, the two sides exchanged letters to start technical cooperation. It was decided that China would send engineers and technicians to offer two years of 'technical guidance'. Before the end of the term, the agreement was extended until it was finally ended more than twenty years later in1993. In July 1975, the chief of the Chinese expert team exchanged letters with the Permanent Secretary of the Ministry of Industry to expand the production capacity of the factory from 1000 tons to 2000 tons. The expansion project started in June 1978 and was completed in June 1980. The newly expanded factory was handed over to Tanzania on 30 July.

The expansion project cost 8.7 million yuan ($5.8 million). During the 'technical cooperation' period, China also provided several loans, totalling more than 10 million yuan ($6.7 million) to replace some worn-out equipment and import spare parts and even raw material from China.

Agricultural production in Tanzania, except for a few large scale state farms, relies mainly on hand tools. For most of the time, UFI provided around 85 per cent of the hand tools such as hoes, ploughs, ploughshares, and machetes) needed in the country. Since the products were of good quality and reasonably priced, UFI very often could not meet the demand. It is easy to see its importance in the agricultural development of Tanzania.

Mbarali Farm

On 8 May 1970, the Chief of a Water Conservancy and Agricultural Survey Team of the PRC signed the Minutes of Talks on Construction of Mbarali State Farm (MSF) with his Tanzanian counterpart. The Chinese general undertaker was the Ministry of Agriculture and Forestry, whose supporting partners were the State Commission of Construction and the Ministry of Water Conservancy and Power Industry. The actual implementation of the project was carried out by the Department of Agriculture and Forestry of Jiangsu Province. The construction started during the first quarter of 1971 and was completed in September 1977. The actual investment was 24.9 million yuan ($13.4 million). This time, what the Chinese handed over to the Tanzanian side was a large-scale mechanized state farm with more than 3200 hectares of rice field, a rice-processing shop with an annual capacity of 8000–10000 tons of rice, a poultry farm that could produce 50 000 chickens and a dairy farm that could hold 100 cows. The farm also had its own hydro-power station, water conservancy and irrigation system and living quarters. The quality of the construction was satisfactory and the farm achieved brilliant results during the period between 1978 and 1984. The newly cultivated land was very fertile and per hectare yield once reached as high as 8 tons. That was a record for Africa and could be compared with high yielding areas anywhere in the world. The average annual output of rice during the period was 20 000 tons, amounting to one-quarter of the domestic demand. The investment was recovered in six years. The shining example of the farm had also promoted rice production in the surrounding area. Small farmers in the area grew more than 2000 hectares of paddy rice with annual output of more than 6000 tons. President Nyerere and many other high-ranking officials visited the farm and spoke highly of the contribution made by the Chinese.

After the farm was handed over to the Tanzanians, the two sides continued technical cooperation. Every two years, 20 Chinese experts would come to the farm. Since then, the Chinese government has also provided loans of more than 10.5 million yuan for farm machinery and spare parts, and 6 million yuan to send experts there.

Mbeya Technical Extension Service Station

The Chinese government has provided loans to build three agricultural technical extension service stations on the mainland part of Tanzania. They are located in Dodoma, Mbeya and Morogoro region. We will look at the one in Mbeya as an example.

The predecessor of the station in Mbeya was a Chinese agricultural expert team who first went there in 1976, trying to popularize cultivation skills for maize and vegetables. Later on, the temporary team was supplanted by a permanent station through a series of bilateral protocols in April and May 1978 and minutes of talks in January 1980. The completed station included a demonstration field of 7 hectares and housing totalling more than 900 square metres. The agricultural teams were dispatched by the Agricultural Department of the Shanxi Provincial Government and the construction of the station was done by a team that came to Tanzania mainly for maintenance of the TAZARA. The project was completed and handed over to the Tanzanian side in December 1982. The total investment was 920 000 yuan ($486 000).

Mbeya is one of the major maize-producing areas in Tanzania. The small farmers there were accustomed to a traditional way of extensive cultivation, resulting in a very low per unit yield. The chief aim of the Chinese agriculture team was to popularize an intensive way of cultivation without large amounts of cash input. This included timely sowing, ploughing and levelling the land as soon as the first rain came. To achieve this, the Chinese team also taught local farmers to use cattle in ploughing. It also involved strict sowing, which required rational, closer sowing and changing the old habit of putting several maize seeds into the same pit, thus actually saving seeds. Third, it meant intensive care during the growing season. This mainly referred to hoeing the weeds and thinning the seedlings but also to irrigating the land when the crop was in the ground. Finally, it included timely harvesting. The traditional way was to leave the ripe maize on the stalk to dry itself. Thus the crop was often harmed by birds, ants and wild animals, leading to a decrease of output by as much as 30 per cent. Besides, the Chinese team also spread the knowledge of using natural fertilizer, such as cattle dropping and how to make some simple wood-and-iron farm tools.

The work of the Chinese team was highly valued by the national and regional governments. Dozens of government officials at ministerial level visited the station. Premier Sokoine, in one of his broadcast speeches, commended their work. The station built with Chinese aid is still a permanent base in the region for the popularization of appropriate agricultural techniques.

Technical Cooperation

The following is a more detailed description and analysis of the bilateral technical cooperation after the Chinese-assisted projects were handed over to the Tanzanian side. After the construction of major projects was completed in the 1960s and 1970s, the emphasis and the major form of Chinese aid moved to 'consolidating' existing projects through technical cooperation in the early 1980s. By analysing the bilateral technical cooperation we can see how the Chinese-built projects operated under the specific context prevailing in Tanzania at the time. The empirical material is again from UFI and MSF.

Under its traditional foreign aid system, China, through construction of its 'turnkey' projects, helped Tanzania establish a batch of enterprises and enhance its productive capacity. But, to bring this productive capacity into full play, some technical, institutional and social conditions are necessary. The most direct and basic condition is the skill to man the equipment and facilities. Though the Chinese project builders started to pass on skills and knowledge during the stages of construction and trial production, it was very often necessary for both sides to continue such cooperation after the hand-over. In fact, for both UFI and MSF, the two sides signed agreements on this matter. During the first five terms of technical cooperation (ten years altogether), with their minds shackled by their strong belief in 'non-interference in others' internal affairs', the Chinese experts concentrated on 'technical guidance' and did not participate in management.

However, 'technical guidance' was not enough to bring the new productive capacity into full play. Also involved is the micro-management system of the enterprise: take MSF, for example. Before 1987, MSF was only a 'project' under the wing of National Agricultural and Food Corporation (NAFCO), which in turn was looked after by the Ministry of Agriculture, and it did not even keep its own separate accounts. All the rice (its major product) was handed over to NAFCO and all the chemical fertilizer and insecticide it needed were provided by NAFCO. The top officials at the farm, as well as those in charge of sections there, were appointed by NAFCO, which also decided the total number of employees and their scale of wages. The distribution system in the farm was characterized by a system of low wages and high welfare (according to Tanzanian standards). All this was very similar to what the Chinese then would term 'eating from the same big pot', a practice they had cast off after reforms in 1978.

After 1987, MSF had its own separate accounting but all other aspects changed very little. The farm failed to accumulate the necessary capital to replace worn-out equipment and it lacked an incentive mechanism to mobilize the initiative of the staff and the workers. Production and finances, therefore, went downhill. The acreage shrank, and yield per unit declined (at the lowest point it was 3 tons/hectare as compared to a peak of over 8 tons/hectare). Very often, the farm had no money to buy its gasoline and spare parts. Huge farm machines became paralysed.

Since the mid-1980s, and particularly in the 1990s, Tanzania has adjusted its economic policies. The country adopted trade liberalization and reduced government involvement in the economy. This, ironically, made the position of MSF even worse. NAFCO no longer guaranteed the sale of its rice. The state even allowed the importation of rice with some preferential treatments such as low tax rates. Gravely threatened by small farmers and imported rice, MSF sometimes was forced to sell at a price lower than the cost. The natural condition of the farm was very favourable to rice production, but the location was far from its major market. The farm was too heavily reliant on a single low-price product: 85 per cent of the sale income came from selling rice. All this made it very vulnerable with the newly emerging market economy.

The UFI experience was not very different. After the hand-over, UFI was put under the National Development Corporation (NDC), a parastatal organization operating under the Ministry of Industry. Its management was appointed by the NDC and changed fairly frequently. All the raw material (pig iron and steel) it needed had to be imported. Under the highly centralized and rigid management system of the state-owned enterprises, the factory, from the very beginning, did not have enough working capital; all its expenditures had to be approved by the NDC and ultimately the Ministry of Industry. Since the country as a whole was almost always short of funds and foreign currency, every step of this complicated process took a long time, greatly affecting the smooth operation of the enterprise. Very often the factory could operate only at 20–30 per cent of its full capacity. This in turn led to loss, and a further deterioration in UFI's financial position. Thus, lack of working capital, a rigid management system, low level of operation, loss-making, and a heavy debt burden contributed to a vicious circle.

Under such circumstances, the Chinese team coming to the enterprise in accordance with the technical cooperation agreement faced a difficult task. Following the principle of 'respect, understanding', support and persuasion through reasoning', they established a good working relationship with their Tanzanian counterparts. Not being in a position to change the external conditions of the enterprise, they concentrated on the internal aspects, particularly technical questions. Problems caused by the macro- and micro-economic system were typically expressed in a technical way. For example, in MSF, wild rice, weeds and degeneration of seeds became 'three evils' that greatly affected rice production, and lack of a responsible attitude led to disrepair of a water-conservancy system and the fact that few pieces of equipment were in a good condition. To solve these problems the Chinese team was sub-divided according to their specialty such as rice-growing, machine repairs, water-conservancy, and so on; they then offered suggestions and advice to their Tanzanian counterparts for decision, and implementation, and jointly made production plans. This way technical guidance was provided throughout the whole process of production. In UFI, the Chinese team also paid particular attention to the maintenance of the equipment so that production would go smoothly when there was a sufficient supply of raw material.

At the same time, through the Chinese Economic Representative's Office, the Chinese team also reported back home on the condition of the project, and applied for loans to replace the worn-out or out-dated machines, and supply spare parts. In UFI they even bought raw material from China. These efforts helped the Chinese-built projects to survive.

Through technical cooperation, the Chinese projects were 'consolidated', but the problem caused by both the traditional way of Chinese aid and the economic management system in Tanzania could not be solved. Chinese teams could not withdraw even more than ten years after the transfer of the enterprise, not because of the need to pass on the skills but due to the inability of the Tanzanian enterprises to survive and develop on their own. Chinese-built projects became a burden on the backs of the two governments. Once the Chinese side stopped 'blood transfusion', the projects could not operate properly. Efficiency declined, machines became wornout, and finally the whole project became paralysed.

The Chinese organ in charge of the economic aid, and those Chinese in the field in particular, wanted to see the projects they built continue to make contributions to Tanzania's economic development as well as to the Sino–Tanzanian friendship, and did not want to see them collapse. So while fulfilling the specific task of technical cooperation, they also made careful and detailed investigations into both the internal management and external environment, and put forward some concrete suggestions as how to improve the situation. Even as Tanzania started to explore ways to read just its economic structure, there appeared in the 1990s some more encouraging signs of efforts to overcome the difficulties that the Chinese-aided projects encountered.

Let us take MSF as an example again. During the first five terms of technical cooperation (1977–87), the task of the Chinese expert team was to conduct 'agro-technical guidance'; starting from the sixth term, their task changed to 'conduct technical guidance on the production and management of Mbarali Rice Farm'. This slight change of wording showed that both sides gradually realized that the Chinese side's participation in management was a necessary condition to run the farm properly. The Chinese experts, while continuing to urge their Tanzanian counterparts to lay stress on levelling the land, solve the problem of the 'three evils', conduct timely maintenance of the equipment, and repair irrigation facilities, made greater efforts to help the management team of the farm to formulate a plan to diversify activities so as to improve the economic results of the farm. In an impressive spirit of self-criticism, the seventh Chinese team who arrived in 1991 wrote in its report back home that the team did not have very clear guidelines and objectives, and suffered from short-term behaviour. The team, which was engaged mainly in general technical guidance and labour management, failed to study systematically the problems the farm encountered, and thus was not in a position to offer more relevant suggestions for the decision-making back home. Mr Zhang, the chief of the team, noted that the Tanzanian government had adopted a new policy towards the state sector, including the foreign-funded projects. According to this new policy of differential treatment, technical cooperation would continue in the better-run state-owned enterprises, while in others the state would explore the possibility of changing them into joint ventures or selling them off. So he put forward a suggestion regarding 'comprehensive treatment' of MSF, meaning a systemic review of the farm's problems. He hoped that the Tanzanian side would enlarge the decision-making power of the farm, provide some badly needed foreign currency and deduct part of the taxes to form a special 'treatment fund'. He also wished that the Chinese government department concerned would organize a more stable expert team, improve its supporting efforts at home and overcome bureaucracy. In addition, he made a series of concrete suggestions concerning the production and management of the farm.

The eighth team that arrived in 1993 tried to actually change the management system. They prepared Swahili memos on state-farm reform in China through which they introduced the Tanzanians to such practices as readjustment of the structural set-up, division of big farms into many smaller accounting units, output-related contracting systems, diversification of activities, and so on. During the harvesting season of 1993, they overcame strong opposing views and persuaded the management team of the farm to adopt a 'quota management' system on a trial basis: every combine had a quota of 7 acres per day, and for each acre above that there would be a bonus of 700 shillings, 70 per cent of which would go to the operator, 20 per cent to maintenance and 10 per cent to the management. This practice showed its effectiveness in five ways: (1) markedly higher quality (because of timely harvesting); (2) faster speed (the harvesting period was shortened by 6 days); (3) lower cost (less overtime pay, extra meals and gas); (4) better attitudes towards the job; and (5) fewer breakdowns and accidents. The Chinese team suggested that the same system should be adopted in an all-round way on the farm.

The Chinese experts were not always lucky enough to have their suggestions accepted. In the fundamental interest of Sino–Tanzanian friendship, they believed that the old ideas should be cast aside so that MSF could continue its contribution to the economic development of the country and to the Sino–Tanzanian friendship through good economic returns. In October 1993, the Agricultural and Forestry Department of Jiangsu Province (which had dispatched the team) approved the team's suggestions to explore with the Tanzanian side the possibility of setting up joint ventures. At the end of the same month, the newly appointed general manager arrived at the farm. In the following months both sides exchanged ideas on this subject many times. In March 1994, the Chinese Economic Representative had a talk with the Permanent Secretary of the Ministry of Agriculture on the subject of changing the form of cooperation and setting up joint ventures on an experimental basis. In June, Jiangsu Province sent a visiting team to Tanzania to examine on the spot the new cooperation. Yet when we visited the farm in August 1994, the Tanzanian side still believed that management power involved 'sovereignty' and could not be changed. As for joint ventures, the Chinese side could only have minority shares. Since then, the Tanzanian position has softened on this issue. Thus, for example, in 1997 the Friendship Textile Mill was reviewed as a joint Chinese–Tanzanian venture.

REFORMING CHINA'S FOREIGN AID SYSTEM

In this section we will first describe briefly China's foreign aid administration system before the reform started in the early 1980s, and then explain the efforts since.

Previous Practice

Before the reform, China had a 'plan and product' economic system. The allocation of the resources was carried out through state plans. The state plans involved not only the state budget, but also the production targets, financing, material supply and product purchasing of the state sectors, which were predominant in the national economy. Unlike what is usually found in a market economy, the plans were mandatory in nature and their fulfilment was guaranteed by a whole set of state (government) organs. Thus, Chinese scholars would describe these practices as managing the economy through administrative measures rather than economic means. Foreign economists would call it a 'command economy'.

Under this system foreign aid, as part of the economic activities of the state sectors, could be implemented only through its incorporation into the unified state plans. Financial, material and personnel requirements would be guaranteed and properly arranged through such plans. At the same time, the implementation involved many different departments and regions. This also required organization, coordination and supervision through a particular management system (Contemporary China's Foreign Economic Cooperation 1989).

The foreign aid plan system included long-term, five-year and annual plans. The long-term and five-year plans, formulated by the aid agency, were macro-plans to fix the general scale of the aid in accordance with the general trend of the country's external relations, foreign aid policy, agreements entered into and the national economic development plans. These plans would be sent to the SPC for examination and 'comprehensive balancing'. The annual plans included the new commitments, expenditure on aid, foreign aid projects, material aid and aid in cash. The new commitment plan would be formulated jointly by the Ministry of Foreign Affairs and the aid agency and sent to the State Council. Others would be formulated by the aid agency in accordance with the agreement signed and the year's state budget and sent to the SPC for examination. The expenditure plan stipulated the value of foreign aid in different forms and reflected its scale and structure. This plan, once checked and approved by Ministry of Finance, would provide an important base for project aid, material aid and cash aid and become part of the state budget and, at the end of the year, final accounting. The project aid plan consisted of a separate implementation progress plan, equipment and material supply plan, construction plan, international transport plan and personnel dispatch plan (Contemporary China's Foreign Economic Cooperation 1989).

Planning was the chief item of the foreign aid management and the Planning Department; a special organ in charge if it was first set up in the agency (AFER) in 1963, when it started to formulate annual foreign economic and technical aid expenditure plans and foreign aid project plans. In the 1960s and early 1970s, the major content of a project plan was the complete equipment and material delivery plan. In 1972, the budgetary estimate approval system was established. Starting in 1973, 'investment' was listed in the plan, and then the foreign aid project plan, after examination by the SPC, became part of the annual national economic plan (Contemporary China's Foreign Economic Cooperation 1989).

Another aspect of foreign aid management was financial management. This included budget and final accounting, cash-flow, fixed assets, material, cost and expenses, settlement and local costs abroad. Financial management before the reform was very different from 'financing' in the West. The actual practice was mainly the system of budget and accounting. Before 1963, the ministries in charge of project building, and MFT (which was in charge of material aid) would, at the beginning of each year, formulate a budget and present it to the Ministry of Finance for approval and, at the end of the year, send in the final accounts. After 1963, AFER, CFER and MFER were in turn responsible for pooling all the expenditure on foreign aid, and preparing the budget and final accounts for Finance. During the implementation of a foreign aid project, the aid agency would sub-appropriate the funding to the undertaker of the project who would in turn be responsible for its financial management. The project expenditure would be settled with the recipient country according to the contracted price (with a reference to the international market price). The actual expenses within China would be reimbursed by the aid agency to the undertaker.

One unique aspect of China's foreign aid management before the reform was the material management. Here, foreign aid material referred mainly to those needed for project building, such as building material, general mechanical and electrical products, special equipment, industrial equipment, machines, instruments and tools for exploration, construction, installation and adjusting of the facilities. Their collection and supply involved almost all the sectors and regions in the country and thousands of enterprises. Without the aid of a market economy, material supply at that time was realized through planning, organizing, supervising and regulating of application, distribution, ordering, production and supply.

The Administration of Foreign Aid

In the mid-1950s, as China had just started foreign aid in the form of provision of complete sets of equipment, the administration of foreign aid was characterized by a system of 'the ministry of general deliverer' (MOGD) that was very similar to the Soviet system in its aid to China. Under this system, the SPC would assign a central government ministry to be the general deliverer according to the sector nature of the project. This ministry would be in charge of the selection of the personnel, collection of relevant data, exploration of the site, formulation of budget and designing instruction, supply of material and equipment, installation and adjustment of the equipment. The MOGD might directly organize the implementation of the project, but more frequently it would entrust an enterprise under it or a sector department in a regional government to do the job, and this unit would be called the 'preparatory unit' (PU). In such cases, MOGD's task would be approval of the construction plan, the design and the implementation plan, the organization, coordination, supervision of and guidance to the survey and expert teams. If the project included civil engineering, special skills such as broadcasting, telecommunication and power generating, the MOGD would entrust the job to a special sector ministry, and this ministry would be called 'the ministry of assisting deliverer' (MOAD). This ministry would in turn entrust the task to an enterprise or a regional department, called the assisting unit (AU). The management structure of the MOGD system is shown in Figure 5.1.

In the early 1970s, China's foreign aid experienced a rapid expansion both in terms of the recipients and the projects to build. And within the country, there had been a trend of decentralization in the state sector: that is, many large and medium sized factories that once were directly managed by the sector ministries were put under government at a lower level (provincial, autonomous regional or municipal). Under such circumstances, the MOGD system could no longer handle the task. So a new administrative system, that of the responsibility of the undertaking ministry (RUM), was put in place.

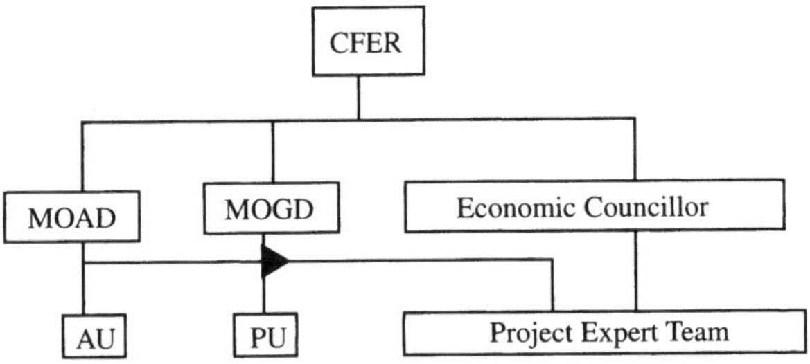

Figure 5.1 Chinese foreign aid management system in the 1960s (MOGD)

The aim of the change was to bring the initiatives of the regional governments (RGs) as well as the ministries of the central government into full play, as there were many more aid commitments to fulfil and the management discretion of the overwhelming majority of the state-owned enterprises was decentralized to the RGs. The concrete arrangement was as follows. The task to fulfil and aid commitment (a project to build) would be assigned to a sector ministry (called the undertaking ministry, UM) according to the nature of the project. An assisting ministry (AM), if necessary, would be chosen as in the previous system. Then, the UM would consult with an RG and, with its agreement, decide on the PU, the design unit (DU) and the AU from the region. These units were usually sector departments, industrial corporations with administrative functions or enterprises which would later carry out the real job. After all this, the MFER, on behalf of the State Council, would issue the formal task instruction to the RG, requiring it to 'strengthen the leadership' of the relevant units and assist the UM to guarantee the fulfilment of the task. Thus, the system, though called 'undertaking ministry's responsibility', actually had two organizers, the UM and the RG. The RG was responsible for all the foreign aid projects undertaken by the units from the region and the UM for all the projects in the sector. The actual implementer of the projects, the PU, would receive 'dual leadership' from both the sector ministry and the RG. But the final responsibility, as the name of the system shows, was in the UM. The administration structure of the RUM system is shown in Figure 5.2.

Reform Efforts

As the world entered the 1980s, against the backdrop of the changing domestic and international situation, increasing problems emerged in China's foreign aid system which had evolved under the product and planned economy. It gradually became unable to keep abreast of the times. As a result, relevant departments of the Chinese government began to make exploratory efforts in a 'step by step' manner in order to adopt the reform measures necessary to render economic assistance to other countries.

Major problems in the original foreign aid system included, first of all, the lack of flexibility in the practice of provision of economic assistance, mainly in the form of complete projects. Sometimes the two sides might fail to agree on the use of the Chinese loan (the project to be built in the recipient country) long after the bilateral economic and technical cooperative agreement was signed, which made it difficult to put the loan into practical use. In the implementation of China's economic assistance to

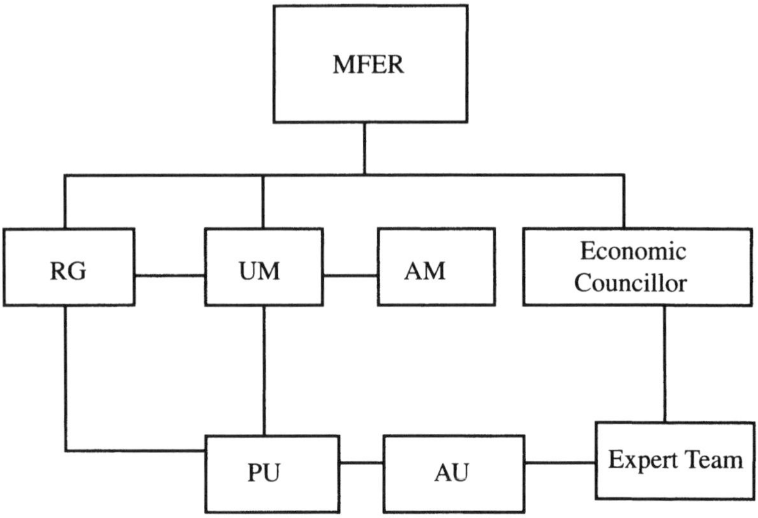

Figure 5.2 Chinese foreign aid management system in the 1970s (RUM)

Tanzania, there had been cases where the term of the Chinese loan had to be extended through an exchange of letters. Second, the Chinese-aided projects, due to their comparatively long building period, could hardly provide a timely solution to the more urgent problems in the recipient countries. Third, after the transfer of the completed projects to the recipient side and the withdrawal of Chinese expert teams, a considerable number of Chinese-aided projects began to operate with inadequate capacity and normal production could not continue, resulting in poor economic returns, losses or even semi-paralysis and paralysis in a few cases. Such phenomena may be attributed to the socio-economic conditions, the technical level and managerial system prevailing in the recipient country, as well as the specific forms through which the Chinese assistance was provided. These forms included, among others, the practice that certain spare parts had to be imported from China. Without further support from China, the Chinese equipment would gradually wear out and the productivity of the project would drop.

Now, with the advantage of hindsight, we can see that these problems had resulted mainly from three factors. First, the fact that China was a developing country itself had restricted its ability to provide aid to other countries. Second, with a closed economy and an inconvertible currency, China's flexibility as regards foreign aid was limited. Third, with a single planned and product economy which enabled China to concentrate its national resources to achieve some great accomplishments, the efficiency and the economic returns of all its economic activities, including foreign aid project building, were also seriously affected. It will take a long time for China to change fundamentally the first factor, and the policy of opening to the ouside world and reform that China had adopted in late 1970s was aimed exactly at addressing the last two factors so as to speed up the process of its development. In this sense, the aid agency's efforts to reform has been part of a much bigger endeavour.

For the administration of the newly committed aid projects, the previous 'undertaking ministry's responsibility system' was replaced in 1980 by a 'general contractual system' (GCS). The real change this time, unlike the earlier one, was not the 'line of command', but the nature of the relations between different actors in foreign aid implementation. Foreign aid projects were no longer mainly 'political tasks' but contracts. Of course, there was still 'political' content in the contract, but it was now basically a contract between two sides and not an instruction from the superior to the inferior along a hierarchical administrative structure. In order to realize this fundamental change, the original 'External Assistance Offices' in the 'UMS', which had been in charge of the implementation of the foreign aid projects, were transformed from government departments into 'International Economic and Technical Cooperation Corporations' (IETCOs), business entities; among the most famous ones have been China National Construction Company, China Civil Engineering and Construction Company and China International Highways and Bridges Construction Company. Many of the provinces that once shouldered heavy tasks of project building also formed their own IETCOs, such as SIECTO (Sichuan International Economic and Technical Cooperation Company) and JIETCO (Jiangsu International Economic and Technical Cooperation Company). The foreign aid ministry, MOFERT, would, through COMPLANT, sign a general contract with these IETCOs, now called 'contracting units' (CUs) and refrain from any direct involvement in the projects. The general contractual system encouraged positive competition, accelerated construction, saved funds and improved the management in project construction (Contemporary China's Foreign Economic Cooperation 1989). The structure of GCS is shown in Figure 5.3, in which dotted lines represent new relations different from the previous administrative one.

In 1984, as China had adopted the general principle of 'separating the function of the government from that of the enterprises' in an effort to undergo economic restructuring, the Ministry redefined explicitly the tasks of the External Assistance Department and that of COMPLANT. The Department, according to the new definition, held responsibility for

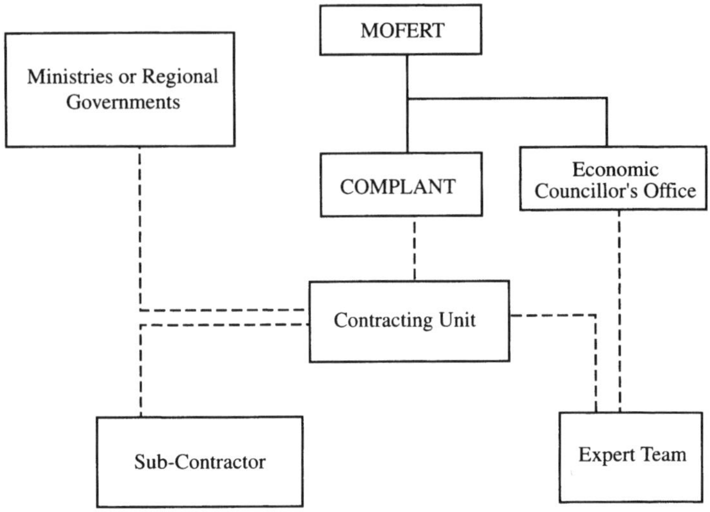

Figure 5.3 Chinese foreign aid management system after the reform (GCS)

preparing bilateral agreements, handling other inter-governmental affairs and coordinating the implementation of the agreements (Yearbook of China's Foreign Economic Relations and Trade 1995).

At the same time, starting from the early 1980s, the emphasis in China's aid to long-term cooperative partners such as Tanzania was shifted to 'consolidating' the existing projects. In addition to supplementing new loans, securing spare parts and upgrading equipment, this shift also put an end to the original practice of concentrating on construction only without any participation in management, and the practice of holding itself responsible only for technical guidance after the transfer of the project. In practice, it chose several 'experimental enterprises' to rescue projects through participation and/or cooperation in management, making the Chinese team responsible for the management by transforming it into a joint venture, leased or commissioned enterprise, and providing spare parts in the form of compensation trade. Experiences gained through the above-mentioned efforts positively facilitated further reforms along these lines (Yearbook of China's Foreign Economic Relations and Trade 1995).

As for the mix of the foreign aid projects, for a fairly long period of time China preferred 'productive' projects. Since the mid-1980s, at the request of recipient countries, China has built a number of 'monumental' projects such as sports stadiums and auditoriums. Such projects seemed to be more attractive during that period and shortly afterwards, since they did not involve the complicated problems of raw material and marketing which were posed by industrial projects. However, the maintenance afterwards became extremely costly and some were rarely utilized. Also, the construction of too many such projects was not feasible. In view of this, China again shifted the emphasis in the early 1990s to the construction of small and medium productive projects that had a ready market and relied on raw materials locally available in the recipient countries (MOFERT 1994).

In the 1990s, China's foreign aid system went through more profound reforms. In recent years, many developing countries, including Tanzania, have accelerated the process of economic liberalization and privatization. Therefore, pure bilateral inter-governmental economic and technical cooperation in the traditional form of project construction could no longer meet the needs of the time. In an effort to better orient economic aid to the needs of the recipient countries, China began to actively explore new ways of providing foreign aid with the emphasis on more flexible use of Chinese loans. In practice, loans could be utilized by the recipient government either as direct state investments or as a re-granted loan to an indigenous enterprise so that the capital could be used to establish a joint venture with a Chinese enterprise. In this way, the amount of funding actually flowing into the recipient country would increase because the Chinese partner could also make its own investment through which it could then become responsible for management and operation. Technical and management know-how would be imparted to the local partner in the process of the operation of the joint venture. It would be a more proper economic entity than a 'political project' that weighed heavily on the back of the two governments.

Administrative rules and regulations promulgated in 1993 concerning foreign aid took the new principle of external assistance as a guideline. They adopted the general-contractor system in the implementation of aid projects and established a project supervision system to assign projects, so as to bring in the competitive mechanism in the choice of the general contractor. In the price-fixation, the aided project would be priced according to the international market price in an attempt to dovetail with international norms. As for the supply of the materials, some transitional measures were adopted to guarantee a smooth transition from the previous system to the new one.

Starting in 1995, high level visits from China to Africa have become more frequent. In that year alone, three vice premiers, Zhu Rongji, Li Lanqing and Qian Qichen, visited Africa. Then, from 8 to 22 May 1996, President Jiang Zemin visited six African countries. This trip is historical as it is the first time that the top leader of the PRC has visited the continent.

During all these visits, one repeated theme was how to improve Sino–African economic cooperation under the changed conditions.

Upon the conclusion of his visit, Vice Premier Zhu said that with greater political stability the Southern African region offered a new opportunity for economic development (*People's Daily*, 28 March 1995). President Jiang was more specific. In his five-point proposal made in a speech to the Organization of African Unity, the third one was to 'seek common development on the basis of mutual benefit'. He said that China would continue to provide, within its own means, government assistance to African countries with no political strings attached. He mentioned in particular that the two sides should work together to revitalize the assistance projects which China had sponsored in the past through establishing joint ventures and other forms of cooperation. Chinese enterprises and companies with considerable economic strength would be encouraged to conduct mutually beneficial cooperation on different scales, in extensive areas and various forms in Africa, and, in accordance with the principle of honouring contracts, guaranteeing quality and valuing credibility (*Beijing Review*, June 1996).

CHINA'S FOREIGN AID STRATEGY AND BEHAVIOUR

In this section, we will use the empirical material presented above to test the model introduced in Chapter 1 so as to bring out some features of the strategy and behaviour of Chinese aid. Our general finding about the model so far as the hypotheses of the Chinese aid agencies are concerned is that they are basically correct, but there must be some important modifications.

The nature of the inter- and intra-organizational relations of the aid agencies in China is highly bureaucratic because of the political and administrative set-up in the country. In spite of the recent reforms, these relations are fragmented. Many of them simply do not meet anywhere, not only because their responsibilities do not overlap, but also because they have different bosses to report to. For example, the Foreign Affairs Committee of the NPC may not directly meet the Foreign Aid Department of MOFERT. In a sense, this is the 'insulation trap' in the extreme: the agencies are not only insulated from the public but also from other arms of the government, and even departments in other ministries.

Then, within the organization, the nature of the relation is one between superior and inferior rather than among equals. This is particularly true for the 'foreign affairs sector' in China. A popular saying that has been known to all in China's government and NGO foreign-related organizations suggests that 'authorization in foreign affairs is always limited'.

Premier Zhou Enlai pointed out at a meeting of the Foreign Ministry that

> diplomacy concerns state-to-state relations. Therefore, everyone should keep in mind that in doing any work in the diplomatic field he must ask for instructions beforehand and submit reports afterwards. In handling state-to-state relations, words must be honoured ... There can be a limited range of flexibility under a set principle; in other words, adaptation according to the circumstances. However, it may not necessarily be a mistake to act a bit slowly when handling new issues. It is better to act a bit slowly when there is not sufficient experience. (Zhou Enlai 1990)

Thus, we must be more careful when applying the model of 'resource exchange'. In comparison with Sweden and the USA, China had, in the first half of the period under study in particular, a highly centralized political system. The CCCPC and the executive arm of the government have always occupied the leading position in the state political apparatus. Foreign economic aid and other major issues are all decided by the CCCPC and the State Council. This differs remarkably from the situation in Sweden and the USA, where the legislature exerts influence on the decision-making through examining and reviewing the budget of aid institutions. In China, even at the present, the NPC (the supreme legislature) only ratifies general policy and budget decisions at the central government level; it does not get involved in budgets for each and every department.

This does not mean, however, that the system is autocratic. It is better to be described as highly centralized in that all the major decisions are made at the top. All the same, closer examination shows that the final decision is made in the form of an 'approval' (or adoption) of the suggested solutions made by the lower ranks. The whole process, in fact, starts from the lowest level of the bureaucratic hierarchy.

The compartmentalization is not yet complete; some matters involve more than one ministry. For example, both the Ministry of Foreign Affairs and MOFERT are concerned with the scale of a loan to a particular country. For this China has a system of 'joint signatures', meaning two or more organs jointly sign the 'request for instruction' to the higher level. Another practice is called the 'categorical management' system. Whenever there is a task of a certain 'category' (or sector) that cannot be neatly put under one ministry, a particular government organ (for example, MOFERT), as 'categorical administrator', acts on behalf of the central government to preside over and coordinate the joint efforts (foreign economic relations in this case) in accordance with the authorization from the State Council.

Third, if we look into the history of the PRC carefully, especially its experience since reform and opening to the outside world started in the late 1970s, we will notice a general trend of clearer separation of government from economic entities and decentralization of decision-making. One feature of China's system before the reform worthy of our attention was that government ministries were not simply administrative in nature. They might actually organize, direct and manage certain affairs, including (but not limited to) economic activities. Taking foreign aid as a case in point, MOFERT and its predecessor were not only entitled to formulate plans and submit them to the central authority for approval, but held responsibility for undertaking and organizing the implementation. Here, MOFERT, as the 'categorical administrator' of foreign aid, not only involved itself in every detail of the implementation (for example, supply of necessary material and equipment through its subordinate, COMPLANT), but also coordinated other ministries or localities to undertake any part of the project it was incapable of on its own. The agricultural projects in Tanzania mentioned previously serve as a succinct example in this respect where the construction was mainly undertaken by a subordinate corporation of the Ministry of Construction and the planning of the farm was conducted by an expert team dispatched by the Agriculture and Forestry Department of Jiangsu Provincial Government. Obviously, this situation has been progressively changing after the introduction of China's economic reform and opening-up policy.

With these general comments, we can now go to the model. Let us look at the five independent variables first. So far as the objectives of the Chinese aid is concerned, under China's highly-centralized system views of the recipient country were often taken very seriously. This was, on the one hand, determined by China's unique system and, on the other hand, in conformity with the fundamental guiding principle of China's foreign economic aid. In a philosophical (world outlook) perspective, China has always believed that after all, things in one country can only be done by its own people since they alone are familiar with the realities and know what is needed. The fundamental objective of China's foreign aid, in line with the guiding principle of foreign economic assistance, lies in the enhancement of the recipient's self-reliance and economic development. As one looks at China's foreign economic assistance from the perspective of the decision-making and implementation system, more often than not the scale of aid (as in the case of Tanzania) was agreed upon by leaders of the two countries in person. Concrete projects were also first proposed by the recipient side before the Chinese side considered its own ability to implement.

It becomes obvious that the 'decision-making power' of the competent department in charge of economic assistance would be very limited given the highly-centralized system. Apart from the factors mentioned above, it was also attributable to the fact that everyone in the foreign aid department was likely to regard the implementation of foreign economic assistance as a serious political task. It might be meaningful here to quote another popular saying in China's diplomatic circle which says, 'no affair is trifle in foreign affairs since political significance is everywhere'. It is necessary to point out that the implication of the term 'political' in China is completely different from that in the Western World. The former has a far wider extension and is by no means derogatory.

With the general survey and the Tanzanian case study offered in the previous sections, we can see that the answer to the question of where the agency's objectives are derived from is more complicated than the model hypothesizes. The major form of the aid – project building – is determined by the concrete conditions of China (an aid provider that is a developing country itself). As for other decisions, such as the scale of the aid and which projects to build, the agency, at first glance, seems to have little say in their making. A closer examination, however, will show that the agency really has a big role to play. Its opinion will influence the decision of the central government through internal 'request for instruction' and the suggestion offered by the Chinese side will, through negotiation and modification, be accepted by the recipient side. Still the general hypothesis of the model that the Chinese agency allows the objectives to derive from the need of the recipient country is correct, so long as the need does not go beyond China's capability.

As for the second independent variable, the basis of the provision of aid, the model is again basically correct after some modification. The conditions which apply to Chinese aid are different. They are objective ones rather than subjective ones. On the Chinese side, the request should be within its capability. On the recipient side, there should be the necessary conditions to accept the specific Chinese form of aid. Some countries' governments would not like to be deeply involved in the productive sectors, and thus hesitate for a long time when deciding on the project to build. This is just one example to prove the latent objective conditions of China's aid. Tanzania happens to be the biggest beneficiary of Chinese aid in Africa because it has been in a better position to receive Chinese aid than most of the other countries on the continent, not least because of a coincidence of the philosophy of economic development.

The structure of the Chinese aid agency is certainly highly centralized. This is determined first of all by the feature of the country's political structure. But here it is also necessary to make some modifications to the model, for Chinese aid is more often than not based on project rather than sector support funding, and money is only very rarely transferred to the recipient country.

The basic hypothesis about China's agency's staffing is correct, if 'agency' here means the ministry, which, to certain extent, can be described as an 'exclusive club'. But it is important to point out the fact that language skills and previous overseas experience is important in the selection of the personnel. Actually, most members of the 'club', by definition, must have these skills and experience. Yet, if we take into consideration the whole process of implementation of Chinese aid, we do find a lot of people who move in and out of the foreign aid business. This is again determined by the concrete form of the Chinese aid.

Another feature of China's foreign economic assistance was the role of 'ideological and political education' through which the decision of the central authorities would be turned into concrete action by all those involved in the process. Determined by the specific conditions, China's foreign aid was a much more complicated and arduous undertaking than that of the Western donors. Equipment and materials had to be shipped from China to the recipient country where construction, installation and testing would take place. It is also important to delegate operation and management in hand to local people. China has been unable to offer large sums of foreign exchange to recipient countries. However, China has enjoyed the advantage of technologies appropriate to developing countries and more abundant technical personnel of the right level. Therefore, China has sent an extremely large number of foreign aid personnel abroad. For agricultural assistance projects alone, more than 10 000 people have been dispatched to Tanzania at different times. Thanks to their ideological and political education, these Chinese foreign aid personnel were quite aware that their words and deeds represented the country. The abstract foreign aid principle of integrating patriotism with internationalism found concrete expression in their performance abroad. The 'political task' of economic assistance was accomplished with flying colours by overcoming various difficulties.

Relevant appraisal and feedback mechanisms have also been established in China's foreign economic aid system. Generally speaking, the colossal and complicated systems engineering of foreign aid is decomposed into concrete duties for every specific person through the principles of 'categorical administration' and 'staged responsibility'. Normally, a foreign aid project ends with the completion of construction, the attainment of designed capacity, the accomplishment of transfer or the fulfilment of the contract (for example, a two-year term for medical teams and expert teams for technical guidance). Therefore, in practice, the appraisal was also conducted in consideration of the concrete tasks for each particular unit or person. All those concerned are required to submit reports to competent superior departments regularly. The author read quite a number of such reports at the Chinese Economic Representative Office in Dar es Salaam which were submitted by the leading cadres of Chinese expert teams. The content of these reports ranged from progress of the project and existing problems to matters which needed the office's help to resolve and suggestions on the improvement in project management and even in China's foreign economic aid. The reforms of China's foreign aid and its management systems since the 1980s have, on the one hand, been promoted by the economic restructuring at home, and on the other, been gradually carried out by Chinese foreign aid personnel, including expert teams, officials in economic consulate (representative) offices and competent government departments, with inspiration from the solutions attempted of practical problems in the implementation of foreign aid. In order to do a good job in the foreign aid field and make explorations in the reform of foreign aid system, MOFERT has organized, in addition to regular meetings at the headquarters, on-the-spot discussions abroad with leading officials of missions (councillors or representatives) to exchange information, review problems and consider solutions.

Each and every modification concerning the five independent variables, small as it is, adds up to some necessary major revision of both the Chinese model and its position in the continuum. For example, it is difficult to say whether the Chinese agency has more or less autonomy compared with its Swedish and American counterparts, but it is certain that the Chinese agency is responsive to change. Adjustments have often begun at the agency level, leading to more formal decisions to reform at the political level.

The four-trap model set out in Chapter 1 provides one way to compare the foreign aid agencies in China, Sweden and the USA. After careful study of the Chinese foreign aid, we can see that certain modifications to the model are necessary. As the model rightly predicts, the accountability and coordination traps have not greatly affected the Chinese agency. The solidarity trap, though more relevant, seems to explain better the Swedish rather than the Chinese case. The insularity trap does depict one characteristic of the Chinese agency, yet this may not be the major cause of problems in Chinese foreign aid. To fully understand the lesson we can draw from the Chinese experience, we may need some other explanation.

Chinese foreign aid in general and that to Tanzania in particular, while not a total failure, has not been a complete success either. This is quite similar to China's experience in its own economic development back home. Even during its first three decades, the PRC witnessed significant economic progress, the start of industrialization being the most important. Yet the achievement was not compatible with the sacrifice made by the entire population. With a highly centralized system, big projects can be accomplished through concentration of the national resources. Yet stupendous disasters of the scale one finds in China's Great Leap Forward and Cultural Revolution are also possible. Here we have a hint as to where to find major traps that have prevented Chinese aid efforts from achieving much bigger success. We have to find traps 'with Chinese characteristics'. The author of this chapter would like to stretch the solidarity trap a bit by referring to the significant role of 'sovereignty' in Chinese foreign assistance.

Before explaining what these traps mean, it is perhaps necessary to say a few words about what the author has in mind when he talks about a 'trap'. As explained in Chapter 1, traps are those aspects of the foreign aid operations to which attention should be paid but, if the aid agency becomes too bogged down in them, they will prevent the efforts from achieving the targets. So, within certain limits, the trap may not be wrong or harmful. What is important is the extent. If one goes to the extreme, it turns into a real trap.

The sovereignty trap is an extension of that of sacrifice because it also involves relationships with recipients but with a much wider meaning. This trap, first of all, relates to the world outlook of the Chinese. Basically, the Chinese still regard the world as a collective of sovereign states, and feel that people from outside should not try to interfere in their internal affairs. Each country alone is responsible for the welfare of its citizens. To achieve this, every country, particularly the bigger ones, should rely mainly on their own efforts while seeking external assistance at a subsidiary level. During the pre-reform period, management of the enterprises was regarded as 'internal affairs' which should not be interfered with. It was not wrong to be sensitive to others' 'national feelings', but it was wrong to participate in the management. This respect for non-interference became a real trap in Chinese aid to Tanzania.

Sovereignty also has another aspect: China's foreign aid so far has been basically a bilateral effort. China, while enjoying some strong points (such as more appropriate technologies and experience in agricultural development), does have some serious shortcomings, the most important one being a shortage in funds, a low level of technology and inexperience in the market economy. Instead of seeking cooperation with other donors,

China has preferred to go it alone, thus limiting the impact of its aid (TAZARA, for example). When the railroad was being built, China was not capable of producing locomotives in an efficient way, but (considering the world situation at that time) China was not willing to introduce foreign elements into its assistance efforts. Neither did Chinese aid agencies in the beginning give enough thought to the viability of the productive projects. The projects were usually built at the recipients' request, and the Chinese believed that their job ended at completion of the project. We may conclude, therefore, that there was a genuine element of sacrifice in Chinese aid but that its rationale differed from that of Sweden. It included an aspect of insularity in that China operated on its own but, as a developing country, its aid was (and still is) a manifestation of South–South cooperation and thus a sacrifice of productive capacity that could have been installed in China.

CONCLUSIONS

In the 30 years from 1965 to 1995, China, while facing the heavy task of domestic economic construction, released large amounts of human, material and financial resources from other endeavours to provide economic assistance on a considerable scale to many Third World countries, including Tanzania. In whatever sense, this has bequeathed the country a fairly valuable legacy.

Analysing from the angle of international relations, one can say that the Chinese aid attained the expected objectives. There is no need for reticence about the fact that certain mistakes were made and lessons learnt in China's foreign assistance, the major one being the practice of not following the principle of 'acting according to the capability' for a period of time. However, on the whole, such assistance played a significant role in consolidating the recipients' national independence, enhancing the friendship between China and recipient countries, safeguarding regional and world peace and creating a conducive international environment for China's socialist modernization. Valuable lessons were learnt from the difficulties and problems that Chinese-aided projects encountered. China's economic aid enabled the setting-up of a number of projects in Tanzania. However, without necessary conditions such as proper macro- and microeconomic management systems, necessary management and technical personnel and a change in people's outlook, the productivity of these projects could not be brought into full play. In the final analysis, the problems Chinese-aided projects encountered were of the same nature as those in

Tanzania state-owned enterprises. The only difference (if any) between them might be the fact that the former survived owing to the vigorous rescuing efforts made by Chinese experts, foreign aid officials and the Chinese government. This intervention may, of course, have been a mixed blessing in that, if postponed, the evolution of these problems into a state of crisis would have demanded prompt solutions.

Proceeding from its own experience and realities, China made the construction of complete sets of 'turnkey' projects its major form of external assistance. Taking into account China's understanding of the objective laws of economic development at that time, one can hardly imagine that China would have adopted as its objective the establishment of independently managed commodity production units which assumed sole responsibility for profits and losses, exercised self-restraint and fostered self-development capacity under market economy conditions. By first and foremost transplanting its own experience from home, Chinese aid did not have much incentive to develop a full understanding of Africa's social formation and economic characteristics.

China did eventually learn from its mistakes and acquired a better understanding of African realities. In recent years, this has led to a series of breakthroughs in China's foreign economic assistance. The most important has been the modification of the non-interference principle as manifested in the shift towards greater mutuality on a commercial basis. Finally, China, although not a member of the donors' 'club', has begun in recent years to engage in cooperation with third parties, especially international organizations, in providing economic assistance to other countries. Such cooperation includes the utilization of funds from the UN system in training of relevant personnel with the entrustment of international organizations. The strengthening of international cooperation may be regarded as a new trail for China to be explored vigorously in the future so as to effectively overcome the restraint of fund shortage and to make more effective use of the foreign aid experience accumulated in the last three decades and of the advantage of the relatively low wages for technical personnel.

References

Chen Yulai and Xiaoke (198?) Zhongguo Feizhou Guanxi Dashiji *Chronicle of Sino–African Relations*, West Asian and African Research Institute.

Dangdai Zhongguo De Duiwai Jinji Hezuo (1989) *Contemporary China's Foreign Economic Cooperation*, China Social Sciences Press.

Dangdai Zhongguo Waijiao (1985) *Contemporary China's Foreign Affairs*, China Social Sciences Press.

Guanghui De Chengjiu (1984) *Brilliant Achievements – In Celebration of the 35 Anniversary of the Founding of the PRC.* Beijing: People's Press.
Lui Dexi (1995) 'Liangge Weiren He Lianggedaguo', *Two Great Personages and Their Relations with Two Great Powers.* Beijing: China Archive Press.
Maozedong Waijiao Wenxuan (1994) *Selected Works of Mao Zedong on Foreign Affairs*, Central Documentary Press.
Mofter: Guoji Jingji Hezuo, *International Economic Cooperation*, a publication of MOFTER.
Mofter: Zhongguo Duiwai Jinji Maoyi Nianjian, *Year Book of China's Foreign Economic Relations and Trade*, vol. 1–12, 1984–1995/96.
Pei Jianzhang (1989) Yanjiu Zhouenlai – Waijiao Sixiang Yu Shijian, *Study Zhou Enlai's Ideas and Practice in Foreign Affairs*, World Knowledge Press.
Wu Zhaoqi (ed.) Zhongguo He Feizhou Jingji Henzuo De Lilun Yu Shijian *Theory and Practice of Sino–African Economic Cooperation.*
Yafei Renmin Fandi Datuanjie Wansui (1964) *Long Live the Asian–African Peoples' Anti-Imperialist Solidarity*, People's Press.
Zhouenlai Waijiao Wenxuan (1990) *Selected Works of Zhou Enlai on Foreign Affairs*, Central Documentary Press.

6 Foreign Aid Agencies, 1965–95: A Comparative Assessment

Goran Hyden and Kenneth Mease

INTRODUCTION

This chapter draws together the findings of the case studies on foreign aid agencies and foreign aid to Tanzania during the period 1965–95, tracking the strategy and behaviour of three major donors: China, Sweden and the USA. It also examines the lessons that can be drawn from this study focusing on the common tendency among all three donors to fall into a trap that hampers their efforts. Finally, it discusses the need for a structural adjustment of foreign aid itself.

The individual case studies have employed a variety of time frames. In this conclusion we use three. Putting exact beginnings and endings on time periods which involve different countries, politics, personalities and economics is a problem. In several instances there is some overlapping or straddling of events and periods. What we have tried to do is pick points where significant events occurred for all three donors and Tanzania.

The first period is from 1965 to 1980. This period represents the birth and maturation of the Tanzanian republic from independence, through union with Zanzibar and the evolution of its political ideology of *Ujamaa*, the war with Uganda, the two oil shocks of 1973 and 1979, and the beginning of its confrontation with the IMF. This first period is characterized by high levels of aid from all three donors. Within this period there are several important changes. In 1973 the USA initiated its New Directions which solidified USAID's shift away from large infrastructure projects towards growing concerns with equity issues. This period was the 'golden era' of Swedish aid to Tanzania, and one during which the Swedes would not question anything the Tanzanian government proposed or did. It was also the period when China provided its most massive aid to Tanzania.

The second time period, one of transition, covers the years from 1981 to 1986. The period begins with the Reagan administration pressuring Tanzania to accept the IMF's SAPs. In this period, China's foreign aid was in a transitional period. China's domestic reforms, which were launched in 1978, began to find their way into China's foreign aid policies. Sweden began to question Tanzania's ability, if not sincerity, to achieve its socialist goals and increasingly felt pressure from fellow members of the OECD to join the IMF reforms. Swedish attitudes, however, were slow to change and Sweden soon found itself almost alone among OECD countries in resisting the demands for economic reforms in Tanzania. During the same period, the USA obligated no new spending. This was due to several factors, including the Tanzanians' reluctance to agree to the IMF's SAPs, and the Brooke Amendment (which was separate from the IMF policies) which forbade the USA giving aid to any country which was behind in its debt repayments. Therefore, USAID did very little in Tanzania during this period.

The third period began in 1987. By that time Nyerere had resigned and been succeeded by Mwinyi. Sweden had joined the other OECD countries and agreed to the IMF's economic reform package. In 1987 the USA resumed foreign aid to Tanzania. China, on the other hand, was beginning to argue that its foreign aid needed to benefit both China and Tanzania mutually. Much to the surprise of the Tanzanians, China suggested partnerships, rather than the turnkey gifts of the previous periods. China's position changed, and the third period became characterized by Tanzania's adoption of the IMF's structural adjustment policies.

DETERMINANTS OF STRATEGY AND BEHAVIOUR

In Chapter 1 Hyden and Mukandala defined the variables that influence strategy and behaviour: the source of aid projects, conditionality of aid, structure of the agency, staffing of the agency, and the use of feedback. In this section each variable is treated individually and discussed for each donor agency.

The 1965–80 Period

Sources of Projects

A simple way to conceive this variable is: who decides what is to be done – the donor or the recipient? In Chapter 1 we hypothesized that the USA would decide for itself, the Chinese would let the Tanzanians decide, and the Swedes would be in the middle. Our study indicates that the Swedes were the most attentive to the ideas coming out of Tanzania. They were drawn to the ideology of *Ujamaa* and Nyerere's non-aligned foreign policy. The Chinese were quite pragmatic. They tended to listen and then decide for themselves which projects to pursue. During the first period, the USA tried to accommodate the Tanzanian national development plans, but only to the extent that such plans coincided with US conditions.

Conditionality of Aid

Conditionality varies from a high level of conditionality where the donors impose rules or conditions on their aid, to low levels where the aid is given without conditions. We hypothesized that, in terms of level of conditionality, the USA would be high, Sweden in the middle, and China low. Sweden and China during this period imposed few or no conditions on their aid, while USAID provided assistance only on a conditional basis. There were essentially only two conditions for the Tanzanians to meet. First, from 1960 to 1973 the Nyerere government had only to maintain a form of neutrality that was not pro-Communist. Second, following the New Directions initiative from 1973 until 1980, Tanzania needed only to demonstrate sufficient poverty. In short, in terms of conditionality, our findings suggest that USAID conditionality was high, with China somewhat near the middle but closer to Sweden, which had low conditionality.

Structure of the Agency

The structure of the agency lies on a continuum from centralized to decentralized. In the first period Sida underwent the greatest structural changes of the three. From 1965 to 1970 Sida had no real field organization and was highly centralized. After 1970, Sida became more decentralized. It introduced the practice of country programming, which was distinctly different from USAID's country programming which began in 1963. The American approach was simple development planning on a country-specific basis, while retaining total control over the aid process. Sida's country programming, which was written at the field level, allowed the recipient country to have a voice in the design; Tanzania took an active role in shaping Swedish aid. During this period Sida also developed a sector-oriented approach. Aid was divided up into sectors which included social services, productive sectors (industry and agriculture), infrastructure, administration, management, and multisector (finance) and emergency relief.

The Chinese in the first period were very centralized in their approach to supplying aid. According to Ping, any changes in projects were impeded by centralized decision making. Policy issues moved slowly up the hierarchy. Organizational changes in the aid administration in the 1970s did not alter this centralized orientation.

According to Judith Tendler (1975), the uncertainty of the development task environment requires donors to be 'bottom-heavy' organizations, in which decisions are made at the level closest to the problem. However, USAID's political vulnerability has inhibited it from being bottom heavy. In the first period and beyond, the scrunity of USAID by Congress, and its unpopularity with the public, meant that USAID's attempts to decentralize and empower the field offices were met with Congressional pressure for more centralization. Field missions enjoyed substantial decision-making power, but limited the choices to a centrally-designed menu of options. There is thus no clear answer to the question of whether USAID is centralized or decentralized.

We hypothesized that the USA would be very decentralized, Sweden in the middle, and China highly centralized. Our findings suggest that China and Sida fit our hypotheses, while USAID is closer to Sweden than the original decentralized position.

Staffing

Our interest is the sources of personnel. Do they come from inside the agency and government, or do they come in from outside sources? Additionally, we are interested in changes in staffing, such as the use of outside contractors, consultants and NGOs.

In the early days of Sida, its staff was recruited from the prestigious Stockholm School of Economics. Overall, the staff was very qualified, professional and dedicated. There were two groups. According to Elgström, there were 'bankers' who were concerned with economic efficiency, and there were generalists who wanted Sida to be deeply involved in the day-to-day operations of their projects and who viewed aid-giving in moral terms. After 1970, Sida grew dramatically and the result was an agency where most officials were about the same age and shared the same political philosophy. During the 1970s Sida increased the use of contract employees, both in Sida projects and as officials inside the Tanzanian government. Of the three donors, only Sida placed aid employees in the Tanzanian government.

China's staffing was totally endogenous in this period. Ping describes the agency as having a club mentality. During the first period tens of thousands of Chinese worked on agricultural and railway projects. Because of the economic and social structure of China, no outside consultants or NGOs were used.

There were more direct hires among USAID's personnel in the early years of the first period. From project managers to secretaries, most were permanent US government employees. However, by 1967 USAID was replacing direct hires with contractors in an effort to reduce the overall size of the agency. Both USAID and Sida have also come to hire more programme management staff from the recipient or a third country.

We hypothesized that USAID staffing was exogenous, Sida a mix, and China endogenous. Our findings suggest these positions to be accurate.

Feedback

Feedback exists on a continuum, from low to high. It is information from the field. If there is feedback that is incorporated into the decision-making process, then the use of feedback is high. The use of feedback indicates learning. If there is little feedback from the field, or it is ignored, then feedback is low.

Sida, up till the early 1970s, had few people in the field. The lack of a strong field network certainly must have compromised the availability and use of feedback. This changed as Sida began to decentralize; it relied more heavily on feedback from its field offices. However, because of the strong ideological belief in Tanzanian socialism, Sida officials often put a positive spin on reports from the field, ignoring weaknesses on the recipient side.

It appears from the strategy of the Chinese that they must have received and acted on feedback from the field, but very little is known about this variable. The fact that the Chinese followed up on their turnkey projects by sending in technical assistance teams as early as the late 1970s suggests that they made use of feedback.

Starting in the late 1970s USAID began to develop people-level indicators. These indicators differed from earlier forms of feedback which were primarily output statistics, such as the number of students educated and the kilometres of roads built or improved. People-level indicators were designed to measure the effects of programmes at the level of the individual.

We hypothesized that the use of feedback would be high for USAID and low for China, with Sida in the middle. We found that USAID's use of feedback was high. However, the Chinese seem to have relied more extensively on feedback than anticipated, while Sida made much less use of it.

Period Two, 1981–86

Source of Projects

Sweden at this time was passing through its period of uncertainty and confusion, moving away from viewing Tanzania as an equal partner and its blind faith in *Ujamaa*. China, on the other hand, which realized that many of its projects were performing poorly under Tanzanian control, responded to Tanzanian requests for technical assistance. In this second period, new US obligations to Tanzania were reduced to zero. Therefore, the USA remained on the extreme agency-derived side of the continuum, while China moved to its original hypothesized position of country-derived aid projects, leaving Sweden in the middle.

Conditionality of Aid

The Chinese maintained their philosophy of respecting the sovereignty of the recipient country and imposed no conditions on its aid. Similarly, Swedes remained very unconditional in the second period. The USA, by contrast, hardened its position by insisting that Tanzania must accept IMF policy prescription and fulfil its debt repayment obligations.

Structure of the Donor Agency

Sida during the early 1980s continued to struggle with the sector organization which was established in the first period. The result was a series of turf wars among the sectors when cuts were proposed. In the second half of the 1980s there was a reorganization of the agency that made it more centralized in the sense of taking power from the country offices and giving it to Sida's three regional offices.

In post-reform China, aid agencies began to decentralize after 1979. According to Ping, field level personnel were given more authority. In 1982 existing aid administration agencies were merged into MOFERT. Aid was seen more as a contractual arrangement, rather than solely as a political venture. The structure of Chinese aid began to include contracting units, which assumed much of the responsibility of implementing new projects, and MOFERT decreased its direct involvement in projects.

USAID became more independent of the US State Department during the second period. It continued to implement its own efforts to decentralize, while Congress increased pressure by steadily augmenting the number of earmarks and mandates throughout the period. The most significant of these for the Tanzanian mission was the Brooke Amendment, which cut aid to countries that were in arrears on their debt repayment to the USA and that were not bound by an agreement with the IMF.

In the second period, USAID and Sida remained in the middle, with a combination of centralized and decentralized structures. China remained, as expected, highly centralized.

Staffing

Not much changed in the staffing of Sida in the early 1980s. The group that came on board during the expansion in the 1970s remained in place and, with them, the ideological approach to aid. The bankers had transferred to work in agencies other than Sida, thus posing no serious threat to the dominant organizational culture within the agency.

China continued to staff its agencies internally. During this period the Chinese cut back on sending large numbers of Chinese workers to Tanzania. Instead, most of the Chinese aid workers were part of the technical assistance programmes designed to help the Tanzanians maintain existing projects from the 1970. China remained a donor with very little hard cash. Therefore it was excluded from hiring outside consultants and NGOs to deliver its foreign aid.

USAID's internal staff was downsized and it increasingly relied on outside contractors, NGOs and private-sector initiatives. In Tanzania during this period, USAID staffing was at minimal levels due to the severe reduction in aid. USAID was becoming more a manager of sub-contractors than an agency running its own projects.

The positions of the donors changed very little from the first period. USAID became more exogenous, Sida remained a mix, and China remained completely endogenous.

Feedback

By the early 1980s, Sweden was moving away from total confidence in the Tanzanians' ability to chart their future. Whether this was the result of feedback from the field or a political decision based on agreements with the IMF is unclear; however, we are inclined to accept the latter. As Elgström found in his interviews, Sida officials felt that as Sida centralized and increasingly relied on consultants, the feedback from the field became less plentiful and useful.

China in the second period continued to act on feedback from the field, mostly as part of its technical assistance programmes. China used feedback wisely, shifting from building turnkey projects to salvaging projects from the 1970s.

USAID completed its conversion to people-level impact indicators by the mid-1980s in order to judge the success of its aid projects, although it took many missions and some time to understand how to develop useful indicators.

In the second period the positions of the donors did not change: USAID's use of feedback remained very high, China's use of feedback was unexpectedly high, and Sida's unexpectedly low.

The 1987–95 Period

Source of Projects

In the final period Sweden, which had now signed on with the IMF, began doing less listening and more dictating. China continued to support existing projects through technical assistance. Its primary policy change was to form partnerships tied to aid projects. The USA remained in the same position as before, dictating rather than listening. The source of USAID projects was agency-derived, while China and Sweden both moved closer to the US position, with Sida moving further than China.

Conditionality of Aid

After the Swedes decided to support IMF policies, their aid became more conditional, but not to the same extreme as the USA. China also, during this period, started to become more conditional in its foreign aid, but less so than Sida. Interestingly, China's change was not tied to IMF reforms, but instead was intended to foster partnerships with Tanzania. China became less interested in the turnkey projects of the earlier periods and more interested in projects which had the potential to provide some form of return to the Chinese. This was a reflection of ongoing domestic economic reforms making their way into China's foreign policy.

The Tanzanians resisted USAID conditionality. Sweden's signing on with the IMF was a set-back for Tanzania. When the Chinese decided to link their aid to partnerships, the Tanzanians raised the issue of national sovereignty, but to no avail. In this final period the USA remained consistent in its conditional approach to aid. Eventually, USAID went even farther than IMF guidelines and insisted that Tanzania abandon socialism and convert to multiparty democracy.

During the final period, USAID remained the most conditional. Sida and China both moved much closer to the US position than in the earlier periods. Therefore, USAID remained in the hypothesized position, while Sida made a considerable move towards a higher level of conditionality in its aid, particularly in the 1990s. China also took significant steps towards insisting on performance conditions and mutual benefits in its aid to

Tanzania. In short, by the mid-1990s all three donors had a markedly similar sharp tone in their aid negotiations with Tanzania.

Structure of the Donor Agency

We hypothesized that the USAID would be highly decentralized, Sida in the middle, and China very centralized.

In 1986 Sida underwent some major structural changes. Three regional departments were formed as the agency swung towards centralizing its operations. As Sida became more centralized, many officials complained that the agency did not learn as well as it had when it placed more of its own people in the field.

China's aid organization continued to become more decentralized. In 1993 a new aid management system was introduced. The goal of these changes was to take a more scientific approach to the projects and to standardize operations.

During this period USAID was fairly constant in its structure. By this point the US State Department no longer participated in the planning activities of the agency. In 1994 the Clinton administration launched a series of reforms which replaced project planning with results packages. As Snook explains, the agency, under siege for most of the time, was fighting for its very existence by 1995.

USAID ends up in the same position as the second period, in the middle. Sida is also in the middle and China is still the most centralized, but shows signs of some decentralization.

Staffing

After 1986, Sida was forced to reduce its own staff, and (as with USAID) more consultants were hired in their place. According to Elgström's interviews, these consultants were private contractors and NGOs who wished to maintain their new profitable relationships with Sida. The consultants quickly became very influential at the field level. Interviews suggest that it was not always clear whether Sida controlled the consultants, or vice versa.

China in the last period remained a donor with no outside consultants or NGOs in its foreign aid programme. It continued to use Chinese specialists to conduct foreign aid.

USAID, like Sida, saw its direct hire staff continue to be reduced. The use of consultants, NGOs, and emphasis on private sector initiatives continued to increase. NGOs became engaged in the management projects. As is the case with Sida, the increased reliance on non-governmental employees and organizations transferred effective control out of the agency.

USAID remains, as our original hypothesis suggested, with very exogenous staffing. Sweden is in the middle, as predicted, but during this period Sida moved closer to the US position. China continued to use government officials and specialists from universities and certain regions to staff its agency and projects. No true outside contractors were employed by the Chinese.

Feedback

Beginning in the late 1980s, Sida increased its use and appreciation of feedback as a valuable tool in aid policy. After a long history of ignoring bad news from the field, Sida became more accepting of information and quicker to respond. Starting in 1988, more attention was paid to the conditions of aid and to evaluations. For example, in 1994 Sida reacted to the Tanzanian tax exemption fraud by freezing balance of payments aid. This aid remained frozen for two years.

China continued to use and learn from field level feedback. In the late 1980s and 1990s the Chinese continued to provide their original projects with technical assistance, spare parts, and managers. The Chinese discovered in the earlier periods, from feedback, that their projects were in trouble. The Chinese not only stuck to making their projects work, but relied on feedback to adjust their strategies.

USAID continued its practice of seeking feedback on its projects. The transition to aid and politics being tied together increased the use of the people-level indicators. In this period indicators became a required part of all projects.

Our original hypothesis had USAID as a high user of feedback, Sida in the middle and China a low user. In the third and final period, USAID is, as we hypothesized, a high user of feedback. However, China is a close second to USAID and Sweden the lowest user, but much improved from the earlier periods.

AUTONOMY

Autonomy is the legal authority and ability to exercise discretion. In this book we are concerned with autonomy on two levels: (1) field level autonomy, where the field office has the freedom to act independently, and (2) home office autonomy, where the home office has freedom from too much interference from domestic political actors. We hypothesized that the level of autonomy influences responsiveness, and that autonomy influences strategy and behaviour.

USAID

Home Office Level Autonomy

The level of USAID's autonomy has always been mixed. In the early years of the agency, country missions were subordinate to the embassies, and USAID's autonomy from the Department of State was limited during this time. After the Vietnam War, USAID gradually gained independence from the State Department. While it gained this independence, it lost home office autonomy from the actions of the US Congress which passed mandates and earmarked its funds.

Different administrations have run the agency differently. The Kennedy administration took a shotgun approach to foreign aid which involved USAID in a great variety of projects. Nixon used foreign aid as an instrument of foreign policy. The Reagan administration broke the state-led approach of his predecessors and stressed more private-sector initiatives. Reagan also chose to select a smaller number of larger projects, rather than numerous small projects. The combination of low public support for foreign aid and an institutional tug-of-war over foreign policy between the executive and the Congress has kept USAID in the middle of a no-win situation. USAID's home office level autonomy is best described as mixed.

Field Level Autonomy

Snook found that at the mission level USAID has always been extremely aloof from the other donor organizations in Tanzania. USAID freed itself from its initial subordinance to the State Department, to the extent that the State Department was not consulted on the decision as to which countries to close down during the first years of the Clinton administration. The Tanzania Mission became increasingly more free from Embassy control, to the extent that, with rare exception, the ambassador's role is to simply endorse the plans of the mission.

Comparatively, the field offices of USAID have more autonomy than most donors. For instance, mission directors have the authority to obligate up to $5 million in spending without Washington's approval. This autonomous spending power is without equal among USAID's counterparts examined in this study. This does not necessarily mean that the field office does whatever it wants: for example, it must closely follow a variety of directives from Washington. All the same, Snook discovered that USAID staff take advantage of the huge number of directives that have built up over the years, and ignore directives to some extent if they believe it will help their projects succeed. Thus USAID's field level of autonomy is also hard to assess, and is at best mixed.

Sida

Home Office Level Autonomy

Sida has had high levels of autonomy from domestic political actors for most of the period examined. At the home office level, Sida has enjoyed strong support in the Riksdag and among the Swedish public. It also has significant autonomy under the Swedish constitution. No matter which party was in power, Sida enjoyed significant decision-making authority, free from Riksdag interference. Even when conservative governments were in power from 1976 to 1982, and again from 1991 to 1994, Sida enjoyed support from a majority of the Riksdag, and suffered little interference from the cabinet or individual ministers. Perhaps even more importantly, foreign aid has had the support of a large majority of the citizens. While the Riksdag technically controls the flow and amount of funds, in effect Sida was for most of the time able to do what it wanted until the end of the 1980s.

Field Office Autonomy

Sida's field level autonomy was greater in the first two periods; it has since been circumscribed. The financial autonomy of the heads of Sida's field offices was never very great and remained so throughout the period of study. What is more, the field offices were brought under the direct control of the ambassador in the early 1990s, thus subordinating them to a form of political control that is unique in the Swedish system. As it turns out, this integration of the Sida field office into the Embassy has proceeded without too many snags in most places and the ambassadors have typically allowed the Sida staff to do their professional work without interference. Given the growing significance of political conditionalities in Swedish aid, however, this integration has been regarded as appropriate and necessary so as to protect the Sida officials as civil servants from taking any political heat that may stem from the new, more conditional, approach to giving aid.

China

Unfortunately, in a study of this type sometimes there are gaps in the collection of information. In the Chinese case we were unable to get a concrete idea of the amount of autonomy present in their aid agencies. What we do know is that the Chinese moved towards decentralizing their aid agency structure after the reform period in the late 1970s. This led to the development of 'contractors', which suggests some degree of autonomy at the field office, or lower, level of the Chinese aid structure.

Summary of Autonomy

Over the entire period examined, Sida maintained the highest level of home office autonomy. USAID's autonomy was consistently mixed at both the home office and field levels. The case of China, with its many different agencies, ministries, and personnel that have been associated with foreign aid over the years, is hard to assess in terms of the degree of autonomy at either level. However, due to the strong centralized government we assume Chinese aid officials have had very little autonomy, although, in the post-reform era, Chinese foreign agencies have been granted more autonomy.

RESPONSIVENESS

Responsiveness is influenced by an agency's autonomy. Although it is not a given, greater autonomy fosters greater responsiveness. In this study, we expected responsiveness to manifest itself in agency relations with domestic political actors, recipient country policies or other members of the donor country.

China

While Ping admits that determining the amount of Chinese aid agency autonomy is very difficult, he suggests that the Chinese went through the most profound changes of all the donors. He argues that because of these changes, the Chinese agency had a fairly high degree of responsiveness. Based on our hypothesis – that autonomy and responsiveness are related to agency strategy and behaviour – we believe that at the very least we can say with a high level of confidence that the Chinese were responsive. Considering the centralized structure of the Chinese political system, this makes sense. We also feel comfortable saying that at the field level the agency was responsive, both to the recipient and to feedback coming from the field.

Sida

Elgström argues that Sida was in the 1970s extremely sensitive and responsive to recipient country demands. Sida was probably the donor agency which most wholeheartedly supported the idea of 'aid on the terms of the recipient'. The responsibility for strategy and orientation was largely put into the hands of the Tanzanians (even though they were wise enough to listen closely to their Swedish benefactors). In the 1980s and 1990s Sida has increased its responsiveness to the donor community. Since the end of the period of uncertainty in the mid-1980s, when Sweden signed on with the IMF structural adjustment programmes, Sida has also been more responsive to domestic influences and less likely to do unconditionally what the Tanzanians want them to do. While we feel that the degree of oversight in the US case is a trap, the weak political oversight and the resultant low demand of responsiveness to the Riksdag was also a problem. Because Swedish aid was very unconditional and the goals set by the government were very broad, the agency appears responsive, but not in a way that prevented it from staying the 'unconditional' course too long. Here the combination of relatively high autonomy, low accountability, and high responsiveness to the recipient was a recipe for frustration and failure for Sida.

USAID

USAID, as hypothesized, demonstrated a very high level of responsiveness to the legislature, while demonstrating the lowest level of responsiveness to the recipient. With USAID's volumes of rules and regulations it is no surprise that USAID is not very responsive. Moreover, as Snook points out, for the last 20 years USAID has been an agency under siege, leaving little room for independent thinking. In spite of the occasional move towards encouraging field offices to undertake more decision-making and planning, the agency's troubles prevented it from learning from mistakes.

Summary of Autonomy and Responsiveness

In Chapter 1, we hypothesized that the level of autonomy directly influences the degree of responsiveness, primarily in the form of laws and regulations. It also has a bearing on the relations that the agency has with organizations in the recipient country and other agencies in the donor community. Originally, we hypothesized the following relationships between autonomy, responsiveness and the three donors. On autonomy we had Sida enjoying the most autonomy, with China in the middle and USAID with the least. On responsiveness we hypothesized Sweden as being the most responsive to change, with China in the middle, and USAID the least responsive of the three.

We argue here that Sida had a high level of autonomy and that its responsiveness to the Riksdag was very different from that of USAID. Due to their philosophical bonding with the Tanzanians and broad policy goals set by Swedish policy-makers, Sida's position was quite unique. Certainly, in terms of responsiveness to the recipient, Sida had the highest level. We argue that this was only possible because it had a relatively high level of autonomy, or lack of direct control by the Riksdag. Lately, Sida's responsiveness to external actors has been driven by the IMF policies.

The US case is fairly straightforward. USAID scores low on autonomy and high on responsiveness to political actors. In terms of response to the recipient, and other external actors, the USA has always operated independently and therefore has low responsiveness on this dimension. Therefore, USAID's degree of responsiveness is mixed.

The Chinese case is not as clear as the other donors. We hypothesized that China would have low autonomy and responsiveness. Ping's research suggests that some combination of increased autonomy and relatively high levels of responsiveness has led to dramatic changes in how, why, and what kind of aid China engages in. While China is not a party to the IMF accords, China has moved towards a more market-oriented economy, and this is reflected in its desire to get some meaningful return from its foreign aid 'investments'. Therefore, while not formally responsive to external actors, the Chinese have changed greatly due to their desire to adopt more Western economic structures.

On autonomy we found that, indeed, Sida had the highest level of autonomy. The Chinese case is inconclusive, and USAID has a mix of low and moderate levels of autonomy. Concerning responsiveness, we found that China was the most responsive, with Sida and USAID about the same. Overall, we expected that Swedish strategy and behaviour in Tanzania would be more stable than USAID's over time but less stable than the Chinese. Our findings suggest that this hypothesis is true.

THE FOUR TRAPS OF FOREIGN AID

In Chapter 1 we hypothesized that donor organizations are vulnerable to four types of traps: accountability, solidarity, coordination and insularity, the point being that if one or more of these aspects of conducting foreign aid becomes overwhelming, its quality and effectiveness will suffer. These traps are all structurally determined in the sense that they follow from the system which is in place for conducting foreign aid. In the course of our study we encountered a broad range of evidence that aid agencies are very prone to falling into one of these traps. We also encountered a few aspects that could possibly be seen as additional traps. For example, we noticed the tendency among donors to alter programmes according to the latest development fads. Although such 'trendiness' might not be the result of formal coordination, we have decided to treat it as such, because it enhances precisely the phenomenon that we associate with this trap: corporatist conformity.

In Chapter 5, Ping noted that the problem China encountered in its aid to Tanzania was its excessive respect for the sovereignty of the recipient. The Chinese were reluctant for a long time to intervene, even though they witnessed the performance of their projects decline. We do not treat this as a separate trap here, but include it in the solidarity trap, again because it had the same effect as the latter: it left the recipient to decide what to do with the aid. Before proceeding to an analysis of how the three agencies performed with regard to the four traps, it may be helpful to first repeat what the traps stand for and then examine how the notion of traps can help our analysis.

Accountability

Accountability is responsiveness to the providers of resources. Because donor agencies are recipients of public funds, they have to a greater or lesser extent to account for their activities to their respective home government. What we call the accountability trap here is when this aspect is allowed to overshadow other considerations of foreign aid in such a way that it hinders the agency from being effective. Accountability for a donor becomes a problem when: (1) public opinion turns against foreign aid, or the recipient; (2) there is a lack of will to pay the taxes necessary to fund aid projects; (3) security or commercial interests overrule development considerations; and (4) domestic issues overshadow international ones.

Solidarity

By solidarity we mean here the idea that foreign aid should be given as an act of international solidarity where donor priorities give way to those of the recipient. Such aid is typically given without any strings or conditions attached. This approach, however, easily becomes a trap when: (1) ideological concerns override economic ones; (2) aid is given without any reciprocal requirements; (3) the recipient government's objectives tend to uncritically dictate foreign aid; and (4) feedback does not really serve as a corrective mechanism.

Insularity

Insularity refers to situations where organizations become so inward-looking that they allow autonomy to completely overshadow responsiveness considerations. It becomes a trap in the field of foreign aid when agencies, in an effort to protect their autonomy, try to fend off views of others whether they originate in the agency's own domestic political context, in the recipient country, or in the donor community at large. More specifically, insularity becomes a real trap when: (1) the agency believes it knows better than all others what needs to be done; (2) the political oversight is relatively weak; (3) the agency enjoys great autonomy because it is politically trusted; and (4) feedback is poor, non-existent, or simply ignored.

Coordination

A persistent call in the international donor community has been for greater coordination, the assumption being that if that happens, duplication and waste will be reduced. Coordination here refers more generally to the steps that individual donor agencies take to conform with a set of priorities or rules that they share with others. For an agency this means giving up a measure of its own autonomy. This tendency to coordinate becomes a trap when it generates a degree of corporatist conformity that limits both perspectives of aid and its implementation. More specifically, it becomes a trap when: (1) donors unite to impose conditions that take away responsibility and ownership for policy from the recipient; (2) donors perceive a need to be more effective in their own operations; (3) the consensus breeds a particular way or trend in how aid is conceived, which we refer to as trendiness; and (4) the capacity of a recipient's institutions is low.

It is possible to treat these four traps as lying at the extreme ends of two continua, one that refers to the question of where aid objectives, whether at the level of strategy or project, come from, and a second that refers to the question of how agencies operate. We call the first the *political* dimension, and the second the *managerial* dimension. Since we have no evidence to back up our claim that there is an ideal way of providing foreign aid, we are limiting ourselves here to the proposition that the more an agency is being pushed in the direction of any one of these traps, the less likely it is that its overall aid objectives will be reached. However, we do recognize that an agency may be pushed in one or more directions.

The four traps, then, constitute the furthest points of a conceptual territory within which donor agencies operate. This is illustrated in Figure 6.1

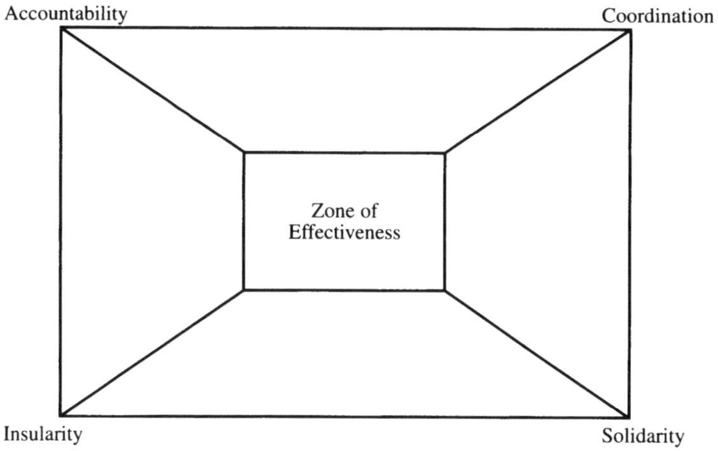

Figure 6.1 The location of the four traps in foreign aid

where the inner area represents a zone of effectiveness. Agencies operating in this zone, while they may have elements of one or more of the four traps, can (and most likely will) operate in a effective manner. Once outside the zone of effectiveness, we believe the agency's effectiveness is compromised.

We are interested in this study in examining where the three agencies included here are located on this map and how they may have moved position over time. We base our assessment on what, according to our findings, is the predominant feature of an agency's strategy and behaviour at any one time. We realize that some elements other than those we have identified as prevailing are present, but they do not form the core of an agency's behaviour or strategy. We will now turn to an analysis of each agency in relation to the four hypotheses we posed in the first chapter.

Sida

Our original assumptions with regard to the Swedish agency were that we would find it in two traps: those of solidarity and coordination. Our findings clearly confirm that Swedish aid to Tanzania has been driven largely by forces which have placed Sida in these two traps.

The agency was knee-deep in the solidarity trap for a period of almost 25 years. Ever since Swedish aid began in the early 1960s, it was assumed that it should be given without strings and on the premises set by the recipient. Because of the political affinity between the Social Democratic leadership in Sweden and President Nyerere and his government, this was pursued with particular vigour in the case of Tanzania. Few, if any, questions were being asked about Tanzanian decisions to use Swedish aid. In this respect, Tanzania may be an extreme case, as Swedish parliamentarians and others did raise questions about the aid to countries like Ethiopia and Kenya. Yet, because the principles which guided Swedish aid were the same for all countries, in the end the notion that Sweden had a moral obligation to provide aid without controlling its use came to apply even in the case of other countries. Sida fell particularly deeply into this trap during the 1970s when Nyerere's *Ujamaa* policies charmed many Swedes, including Sida officials, so much that good money was often thrown after bad even after it became clear that Nyerere's and Sida's policies were not very successful. Sida, and the Social Democratic leadership at the time, shut out any negative feedback that otherwise would have been a cause for revision of policy or even strategy.

Since Sida was so trapped, it also took long time, and a definite degree of pain, to climb out. During the first part of the 1980s, Tanzania struggled to find a way of restructuring its economy without giving in to IMF and World Bank demands. At the same time, Sida went through its own period of reassessment, the one that Elgström describes as that of 'uncertainty'. It was uncertain in the sense that it was not clear whether Sida could manage to get out of the trap. Although it was in the end the Swedes, together with representatives of the other Nordic governments (Denmark, Finland and Norway), who forced the Tanzanians to proceed with an accord with the IMF, it seems as if the decisive factor here had more to do with the conditions in Tanzania than political pressures from the Swedish Parliament. Sida and Swedish political leaders realized that Tanzania could not continue without financial assistance from the IMF and finally gave in when it was clear that its own attempt to support Tanzania's efforts to reform the economy had failed. To the extent that other factors played a role here, it seems that influences from the international donor community, notably the IMF and the World Bank, also contributed to getting Sida out of the solidarity trap.

Once able to move out, Sida, in the latter part of the 1980s, took a very decisive move in the direction of the coordination trap. During the 1960s and 1970s, Sida had seen itself as a trendsetter for other donors. Many European agencies accepted its lead on issues such as how to programme aid. Its own approach, however, had run its course by the mid-1980s and it now found itself outside the mainstream thinking, as represented by the international finance institutions. Sida had a long way to go, but decided that its future lay with the rest of the international donor community. It therefore decided to accept the neo-classical premises advocated by the IMF and the World Bank and coordinate its own aid with these institutions. By 1985, Sida was making its way out of the solidarity trap, but ended up falling into the coordination trap without too many questions being asked.

Those in Sida and others familiar with Swedish aid in the past ten years might consider it unfair if mention is not made here of the fact that the agency has been actively involved with the World Bank to include in its SAPs a greater focus on poverty. Although the Bank's move in that direction since 1989 no doubt has been determined also by other factors, Sida's influence cannot be denied. It is also important to note, however, that Sida's strategy and behaviour have taken place within the broader parameters of the policies set by the IMF and the World Bank. In other words, Sida has fallen into line with 'the Washington consensus'. In its relations with Tanzania in recent years, Sida has followed it quite strictly so as to add pressure on the Tanzanians to implement necessary reform measures.

Sida has never really run the risk of falling into the other two traps. Although it has always enjoyed a definite degree of autonomy, partly because of the administrative autonomy granted to all Swedish administrative agencies, and partly because of the political consensus in the Swedish Riksdag on the desirability of continued foreign aid, the agency has never become insular. Sida has allowed itself to be driven by exogenous factors, notably in the first two periods by what it interpreted as the priorities of the recipient, and in the third period by the signals from the donor community to conform and coordinate its actions with others.

Sida has also been able to avoid the accountability trap. Swedish politicians have by and large left the agency to do its job without interference. Parliament, through its auditors, has regularly recommended improvements in the system Sida uses for accounting and auditing, but none of these measures has really changed the overall operational mode of Sida. This is not to deny that Sida, particularly in recent years, has become more conscious of the need for accountability. The important thing about this new consciousness, however, is that it is being done from within and is not dictated by the Riksdag or its auditors. The latter have only drawn attention to the need for it.

Sida has, of course, become increasingly insistent on accountability principles in its interaction with Tanzanian institutions in recent years. This reflects in part its own new focus on greater accountability but is also driven by broader policy concerns about the need for better governance, an issue it shares with the other donors. For example, Sweden followed a Norwegian decision to freeze balance of payment support after an audit had revealed that the Minister of Finance in the early 1990s was illegally providing private businesspersons with duty exemptions on imported goods.

In concluding this assessment, one can say that the effects of Swedish aid in Tanzania fell far short of promise because Sida, during the 30 years covered by this study, was always caught in one trap or another. During the time its vision has hampered by being in the solidarity trap, the unintended effect of Swedish aid was to encourage corruption, as Mukandala points out in Chapter 2. With no conditions at all being applied and no attention being paid to evaluation or feedback, some Tanzanians were able to profit by taking advantage of Swedish generosity and solidarity.

It should be pointed out that during the first period (1965–79), misappropriation of the funds was less obvious because the money was largely used to provide political patronage rather than to enrich individuals outside the political sector (as was the case much more often after 1986). When Sida eventually fell into the coordination trap, Swedish aid suffered, partly because it was provided in the form of a generalized balance of payment support (that is, lump payments into the Tanzanian Treasury) over which it had no control, and partly because, by insisting on stronger conditionalities, it was difficult for Tanzanians to perceive Swedish aid as theirs. As a result, Tanzanians lacked motivation to act in a responsible and dedicated fashion. This issue remained very much on the minds of Swedish aid administration in the mid-1990s, although no solution had really been developed.

USAID

Our initial assumption was that USAID would most likely be found in the accountability trap with a slight possibility that it would also show up in the coordination trap. Our findings confirm that the agency has been caught squarely in the accountability trap for the whole period under study. We found little evidence that USAID appeared in any other trap.

USAID's predicament is largely the result of two phenomena peculiar to the American scene. The first is the system of government, based on the division of power between the executive, legislative and judicial branches of government. More specifically, USAID is an agency administered by the President, but authorized and funded by the Congress. While the agency enjoyed a brief initial honeymoon period during the Kennedy era, it soon became increasingly subject to control and intervention by the Congress. Various major and minor legislative instruments were approved by Congress which, in turn, demanded new administrative regulations.

By 1995 the USAID manual had grown to some 37 volumes and it is not surprising, therefore (as Snook notes in Chapter 3), that most agency staff found themselves doing things that were against official regulations. These had become so numerous and encroaching that positive action could only be taken by breaking them. The Mission in Tanzania, therefore, had good reason for complaining over the years that the Congressional mandates and earmarks had a negative effect on its ability to do its job. As a 1982 US government audit indicated, USAID was the most accountable to its legislature of the six largest donors in Tanzania. What was paid less attention in that report, as well as in other situations, was the fact that US aid was bound to be ineffective because of excessive demands for accountability back in Washington. While the Swedes bent too far in the direction of the recipient, American efforts were hampered by the regulatory imperatives of the Congress.

The second phenomenon that has given American aid its peculiar profile is the prevalence of a realist perspective in foreign policy. American foreign policy, including its foreign aid, is very heavily dictated by the notion that it must serve the national interest. What this translates into is that American considerations always come first. So self-evident is this to most Americans that they do not think of any alternative and typically regard those who act otherwise as naive, if not stupid. This ideological orientation in official US circles has had the effect of reinforcing USAID's position in the accountability trap. Even if individual agency staff often have a more charitable or altruistic outlook on foreign aid, the structures and official policy orientation of the agency have limited the extent to which they have been able to portray American aid as serving the recipient instead of the donor.

Tanzanians have had no difficulty in seeing that American aid is driven foremost by the Americans' own interests. They understandably label it as the most political and also most conditional of all foreign aid flowing into Tanzania. Although Tanzanians have typically not said no to American aid, it has never been particularly strategic to Tanzania with the possible exception of the TanZam highway, which the Americans built to compete with the Chinese who, at the same time, were constructing the TAZARA. As Mukandala notes in Chapter 2, US aid was never given to support the core MAC functions of the state. Tanzanians were by and large able to steer American aid into other sectors where, on more technical grounds, the Americans believed that they could make a difference. There was never much love lost between Tanzania and the USA – even during the Carter administration days when relations were quite close – and there was never any risk that USAID would fall into the solidarity trap.

The predominance of the realist perspective also meant that, in its relations with other donors, USAID never went out of its way to comply with policies or directives that were not its own. Its relationship with Congress would have been so complicated by any such move that it is understandable that the agency has always avoided coordination. USAID official records indicate that the agency has generally considered itself a trendsetter rather than a follower. Snook's chapter confirm that this perspective was widely held in the mid-1990s. If there was ever a tendency towards the coordination trap, it was in 1981 when President Reagan insisted on a new policy that reflected more directly the neo-classical economic agenda. Although this meant falling in line with the IMF, it was not difficult for the agency to do so because the initiative came from a domestic source: the President.

As expected, USAID never got near the insularity trap. The combination of Congressional oversight, with its rules and guidelines, and the unpopularity of foreign aid in political circles in Washington, kept USAID well away from this trap. As already indicated above, of the three donors examined here, USAID was the most scrutinized, both internally and externally.

We conclude this assessment of USAID with the observation that, having fallen deep into the accountability trap, the USA had little interest in conducting (let alone ability to conduct) foreign aid in ways that would render it productive or effective. Because American aid was driven more from home than from Tanzania, it was less stable and long-term than the aid provided by Sweden or China. Over the years USAID made many changes in its approach to aid in Tanzania which reinforced this *ad hoc* nature of its operations. For instance, at one time it built colleges and then stopped. At another it supported agricultural production and then stopped. At yet another, it improved rural roads, stopped this activity for some time, and then resumed it again. The fact that some of the aid was administered by contracting US institutions had some slight stabilizing effect, but not to the extent of removing the overall impression that US aid to Tanzania fell far short of expectations because the structural and operational conditions under which it was delivered were preventing any successes.

China

Ai Ping's chapter is the first systematic analysis of Chinese foreign aid published outside China. It demonstrates the peculiarity of Chinese aid, but also how in recent years it has become more similar to Western aid. All the same, China has arrived where it is today without the influence of OECD and other inter-governmental bodies that coordinate aid from Western countries.

We had hypothesized in Chapter 1 that China was the most likely to fall into the solidarity and insularity traps. Ping's account of the Chinese aid suggests that the solidarity trap proved to be the most serious. Although he prefers to refer to it as the sovereignty trap, we believe that what the Chinese did in its aid relations with Tanzania was an expression of international solidarity, especially in the period of proletarian internationalism. It manifested itself in ways that were different from the Swedish in that the Chinese were particularly anxious not to violate the political sovereignty of the host government. The latter was never explicit in the Swedish approach. Furthermore, the Chinese did follow up their projects and made sure that they functioned. This way of going about assisting Tanzania was necessitated by the fact that China had no foreign currency to give Tanzania. It could only provide aid in kind, in the form of labour and equipment. The presence of large numbers of Chinese aid workers served as somewhat of a guarantee that their projects would succeed. As long as the projects were managed and run by Chinese workers, they were also generally successful. The problem arose when these turnkey projects were handed over to Tanzania: this is when the Chinese act of solidarity became a trap. For a variety of reasons, stretching from lack of competent personnel to corruption, the Tanzanians who took over the Chinese projects messed them up. Out of respect for the sovereignty of the Tanzanian government, the Chinese felt too inhibited to do much about it even if they had their own personnel on the ground. The Friendship Textile Mill, the UFI and the Mbarali Rice Farm all suffered serious deterioration under Tanzanian management during the 1980s. By the 1990s they were almost beyond redemption. Chinese proposals to turn them into joint ventures, a way for the Chinese to gain more legitimate influence over the management of these enterprises, met with a cool reception from the Tanzanians. In 1995, in spite of a vigorous privatization programme in the parastatal sector, the Chinese had not been granted the right to buy part-ownership of their former aid projects.

There is no doubt that this is very much regretted by the Chinese but they have not approached the Tanzanians with any conditionalities. Instead, they have continued to be quite deferential to the principle that each government is sovereign in its own territory. What we find, therefore, is that although the Chinese would like to see greater accountability on the part of the Tanzanians, they have not insisted on this principle in recent years with the same degree of open pressure as have the Western donors, such as Sweden and the USA.

Ping's chapter indicates that the Chinese have gradually tried to move out of the solidarity trap by insisting on more commercial terms for their involvement in Tanzania. In so doing, however, they have not traversed the territory into the accountability trap. At the time of writing, the Chinese appear to be the one among our three donors that is least caught in a particular trap. Whether they will be able to retain this position is likely to depend on their ability to maintain a pragmatic approach to what they do in Tanzania.

We hypothesized that the Chinese would be the most insular. Our study does not confirm this. We found that the Chinese relied primarily on their own experts. They never engaged outside consultants or evaluators. All the same, they were continuously engaged with the Tanzanians in order to ensure the success of their projects. Even though they experienced their share of problems in engaging the Tanzanians, they continued to be involved with their counterparts. This would not sound particularly remarkable if it were not for the fact that many of the Chinese who came to Tanzania did not know much English or Swahili. Most of them, however, made a special effort to learn either of these two languages precisely with a view to avoiding the insularity trap.

The Chinese always operated on their own and were never even close to falling into the coordination trap. They never followed the trendiness that was apparent in Western aid although, by the 1990s, their approach to foreign aid resembled that of both Sweden and the USA. In recent years, the Chinese have become interested in working with other aid agencies, notably the specialized organs of the UN, but such ventures still constitute the exception rather than the rule.

What legacy has Chinese aid left behind in Tanzania after some 30 years of active involvement? Our interviews with Tanzanian officials indicated a considerable respect for what China, itself a developing country, has achieved. At the same time, there is evidence that other Tanzanians have been ready to take advantage of the Chinese approach which presupposes non-intervention in Tanzanian affairs. The TAZARA, the Friendship Textile Mill and the UFI were all very strategic investments in the Tanzanian economy. They all constituted vital elements in an economic take-off process. Unfortunately, the Tanzanians were either unwilling or unable to take advantage of these investments. Instead, because of poor management, they eventually became liabilities rather than assets to the state. What were extremely promising starts eventually collapsed. This means that the Chinese have never received any repayment on their loans to Tanzania. Their aid has by default been turned into grants since the Tanzanians are unlikely to get the funds to pay their loans back and the

Chinese, on their side, are unlikely to press for such repayment. In short, this is evidence that the Chinese, even if they are not really trapped much any more, are guided by solidarity considerations.

Summary

This comparative assessment leads to the following concluding observations. The three donors studied here have followed quite separate routes to where they are today. To plot the evolutionary trajectories of our three donors over the 30 or so years that we have followed them, it may be helpful to return to our original map (see Figure 6.2) on which we located the four traps. We can see that USAID has remained most stable; that is, it has moved only a relatively short distance, and largely within the confines of the accountability trap. Sida, in contrast, manifests the longest, and most radical, move: from deep in the solidarity trap to a position way inside the coordination trap. China, finally, has moved but much less dramatically than the Swedes. Its own trajectory is confined to the solidarity side of the political continuum, although it is clear that in recent years Chinese aid has become much more concerned with the principles of accountability.

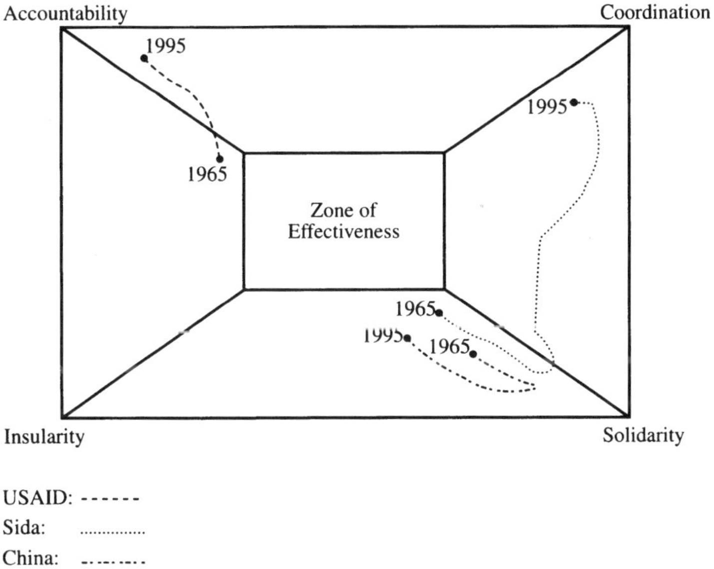

Figure 6.2 Evolutionary trajectories of donor strategy and behaviour: USAID, Sida and China 1965–95

LESSONS LEARNT

We have studied the aid agencies because we believe that they constitute a forgotten variable in the study of foreign aid. Our project has provided ample evidence of their influence, not only in the context of implementing policies, but also in serving as front-line organizations in shaping the image of foreign aid in recipient countries. Furthermore, our study has also demonstrated that, in spite of considerable differences in strategy and behaviour among the three donors over time, they have all experienced great difficulties in achieving the objectives of foreign aid. None of the agencies can really use their experience in Tanzania as evidence of success of their efforts.

The conventional explanation of these failures is that the problem lies with lack of commitment and/or capacity on the recipient side. To be sure, that is part of the explanation. Tanzania, like other African countries, failed to make productive use of foreign aid. With a different approach or set-up, it is possible that Tanzania could have been much closer to where countries like Thailand and Indonesia are today. While there is no doubt that Tanzania has wasted an enormous number of opportunities to move ahead in the past 30 years, it would be wrong to absolve the donors from responsibility for its current predicament. The donors have proved to be part not so much of the solution as the problem. By focusing on the aid agencies themselves, we have moved inside foreign aid in search of explanations. We have come out of this exercise with the conclusion that the way foreign aid has been administered to date has not fostered public confidence in the enterprise. The donors have tended to accentuate strategies or behaviour that have landed them in one of the four traps we have identified. The result has been that recipient governments have ended up in serious debt and/or in extensive dependency on foreign aid. As Mukundala's account of the recipient's tale illustrates, Tanzania has become a virtual beggar, unable to finance even its core state functions. Tanzania may be unique in some respects, but our findings are likely to apply to many other places, particularly in sub-Saharan Africa.

Given the poor reputation that foreign aid enjoys in both donor and recipient countries, there are many who will argue that we have reached the end of the era of foreign aid. This perspective, which is particularly pronounced in the USA, is understandable, especially in a country where foreign aid is rationalized in the context of a perceived national security interest. Because the motives for giving aid are more diverse in other countries, there is no reason to assume that we would necessarily see foreign aid disappear altogether from the international scene. Nonetheless, even its advocates can no longer continue providing foreign aid in a business-as-usual manner. Donor governments need to radically examine the premises on which development assistance should be given in the future. That is the only way to eliminate the risks of future trap-prone behaviour. The final question that we would like to address here, therefore, is what are the specific recommendations that may be derived from this study? We see at least four lessons that should be guiding the principles of future development assistance.

1. Donor Control of Aid Does Not Enhance its Effectiveness

This is an obvious point but it is remarkable to see how donors continue to insist on control on the assumption that without it their aid will be misused, and certainly not achieve the expected objective. USAID has been particularly prone to operating on this premise but so have other donors as well, particularly those for whom aid projects in developing countries are perceived as symbols of national prestige. The more donors exercise control, direct or remote, the less likely recipients are to get involved in doing a good job. The aid administrators are being asked to do an impossible job. Although the project may succeed under donor-controlled management, it is very unlikely that it will continue to do well once that involvement comes to an end. Much of Africa has become a graveyard of abandoned aid projects precisely because the donors were too anxious to be involved themselves. They pre-empted the chances for locals to get involved by using the wrong approach in trying to help build local capacity.

2. Giving Aid on Recipients' Terms Does Not Promote More Effective Aid

The Swedish, but also the Chinese, experience of giving aid to Tanzania on terms where the recipients have almost full sovereignty proved to be a recipe for disaster. The Chinese respected the sovereignty of the recipients by allowing their needs and priorities to prevail. The implementation of these projects, however, lay in the hands of Chinese experts and workers. They carried out their responsibilities with the utmost efficiency but, once they began to withdraw, their projects could no longer be maintained at the same level of performance because the Chinese had not succeeded in motivating their Tanzanian counterparts to acquire the same high level of motivation and skills. The Chinese, therefore, have been obliged to return to salvege their old projects, initially with technical assistance but more recently by acquiring joint ownership.

The Swedes, by contrast, experienced problems with their aid quite early on, because they had far fewer people on the ground; hence Tanzanians had ultimate responsibility for both policy formation and implementation from the very beginning. Swedish experts were assigned to Tanzanian institutions, but they typically had very little influence on the overall management. Even if many of them were well liked by their Tanzanian counterparts and most of them did a good job, the conditions under which the Swedish operations were set up were not congenial to promoting an effective use of the support provided. One project placed Swedish experts to work under Tanzanian administrators and managers in the ministry responsible for cooperative development. This project was sponsored by all four Nordic governments to support the development of cooperative unions and societies. It was continued for more than 20 years, even though it was clear early on that is was not going to yield the expected benefits. Because the cooperative philosophy appealed to the Swedes, there existed a strong cooperative lobby in Stockholm, and because the Tanzanians continued requesting funds for this project, it was allowed to go on with little attention being paid to the critical feedback that had piled up as a result of bi-annual evaluations. If the Americans tended to be too sceptical of the ability of the Tanzanians, the Chinese and the Swedes tended to have too much confidence in the ability of public institutions to do the job that they funded.

3. Donor Coordination Does Not Promote More Effective Aid

The idea that the results of foreign aid will improve if donors coordinate their activities better has become part of the lore of the international development community, particularly in the past ten years. Their argument is based on two principal premises. The first is that by coordinating their aid, donors can avoid duplication and thus become more efficient as a corporate community. The second is that through coordination donors can reduce the opportunities for recipient governments to play off one donor against another and thus become more effective in putting pressure on a particular government to act in accordance with the will of the donor community. This has become particularly important since the 1980s when economic, and later political, conditionalities were being imposed on recipients of aid by SAPs, supported by the USA and Sweden.

The problem with this approach, however, is that coordination takes place at a level at which the recipients are not allowed to participate. Because they are, after all, the ultimate users of the aid, their behaviour tends to try to avoid the donor conditions at any cost. The aid relation becomes a zero-sum game rather than a positive-sum one from which both parties stand to gain. Because it is the consultations that go on in donor corridors that determine a particular aid package, it is understandable that recipients feel no commitment to its underlying rationale. The end result is that foreign aid fails.

4. Foreign Aid has Reinforced rather than Reduced Existing Weaknesses in Recipient Institutions

The accumulated experience of American, Chinese and Swedish aid to Tanzania indicates that the very institutions in that country which could have catalysed its development effort have considerably weakened rather than strengthened since independence. As Mukandala notes in Chapter 2, Tanzania initially took a very sceptical view of foreign aid but eventually succumbed to its lure and power, only to find in the 1990s that foreign aid has become as much a curse as a blessing. Tanzania is not only one of the poorest countries in the world, it is also one of the most aid-dependent. It is not surprising that some critics both in the West and in Tanzania are arguing that aid has become a means of exploitation rather than development.

It would be a mistake to blame this turn of events on foreign aid only, but it would be naive to ignore its contribution to the creation of Tanzania's present predicament. The massive flow of outside funds into recipient institutions (initially only governmental ones but more recently also NGOs), has had the effect of diverting priorities in both strategy and behaviour among Tanzanians. Because of the fungible nature of these funds, it has been possible for these institutions to do other things that their leaders consider important either for themselves as individuals of as managers of public trust. There has been no pressure on them to ensure that there is a positive and constructive relationship between received revenue and expended funds.

Aid has also had a negative influence on local accountability. Because the donors have been so massive in their transfer of resources, recipients have found it more important to nurture their relationship with donors than with their own local constituents. Through their governance and democracy programmes the donors have more recently tried to foster greater local accountability, but much of this work has become stranded because of the overwhelming presence of the donors themselves. The donors have tripped themselves up when it comes to promoting more transparency and accountability in recipient country institutions.

In Tanzania in the pre-structural adjustment era, Nyerere's government was one of the least corrupt in Africa. Despite the obvious failings of

Ujamaa, the bureaucracy of the Tanzanian government had low levels of corruption. However, after structural adjustment was imposed as a condition of aid in 1986, the situation worsened. As devaluation and inflation led to higher costs of living, government officials, like other Tanzanians, were forced to find additional sources of income. Their salary lasted for only a week instead of the whole month as before. These circumstances led to the disintegration of public morality and an ensuing rise in corrupt behaviour among government officials. This is the downside of the SAPs in Tanzania, as elsewhere in Africa. These programmes have had the effect of reducing citizen dependence on the government. Much of this has resulted in promising private and voluntary initiatives by local Tanzanians. The SAPs, however, have also reinforced another form of dependency; that of the government on donors. As suggested above, the Tanzanian government has become more concerned about meeting the accountability criteria of the outside agencies than those of the country's own citizens. Although the new government of President Benjamin Mkapa wishes to deal with this anomaly, its ability to move on its own is limited. Based on the findings of this study, we believe that the donors themselves must take greater responsibility for reforming foreign aid in partnership or collaboration with recipient country governments.

RETHINKING FOREIGN AID

Foreign aid has for fewer supporters today than in the past. This is true not only in the USA but also in other countries, including Sweden. It has become a tainted enterprise. The question is whether foreign aid should be salvaged and, if so, how can that be done?

The moral argument for foreign aid is no weaker today that it was 35 years ago. In fact, if anything, the need for the richer countries to support the developments of their poorer counterparts is stronger today given that the rift between them has increased rather than declined. Thus the moral argument, examined by Riddell (1987), amongst others that we have a commitment to assist fellow human beings in need, is one that applies not only to our immediate relatives or friends but to everyone in today's world. Certain groups take this for granted and act accordingly. There are numerous examples of private and voluntary groups in both the USA and Europe which do a wonderful job in working with underprivileged people in poor countries. The moral argument alone, however, is not enough to convince more hard-nosed analysts why foreign aid should be continued.

It is clear that an insular approach to the poorer countries of the world is extremely shortsighted. It may appear to those who look at the world only through the narrow realist lens that the poor countries of Africa are of little concern to the richer countries today. The problem with this approach is that it is confined to making assessments of only contemporary, or even immediate, factors. There is no attempt to adopt the big picture or the long view. This may be particularly disadvantageous in analysing countries such as Tanzania. To be sure, it is a poor country today, but it has natural resources that make it a potentially rich one. The challenge is still how to develop the institutional and human resource base in ways that enable both Tanzanians and others to take advantage of this resource base. Furthermore, by abandoning the poor countries, their resources will be harnessed by others. For example, in Tanzania both East Asian and Middle East countries are getting involved. In addition to the tenacious Chinese, Koreans, Japanese and Malaysians are involved, as are investors and charitable organizations from Oman. In a realist perspective, foreign aid is a means of maintaining a sphere of influence. Once that sphere has been weakened and others have entered, it will always be harder to come back. Foreign aid, therefore, should have its role even in a cold-hearted realist perspective.

The moralist and realist perspectives apart, however, the true challenge that this study has laid bare is how foreign aid can be handled better. Our main conclusion is that the operational dimension of foreign aid is really the critical one, particularly today when its future is at stake. But is there scope for improvement at the operational level?

We believe there is. Some donors will find reform easier than others but, with a few taking the lead, others are likely to follow. Because donors are so desperately looking for things that work, they will soon join ranks in pursuing the same approach. Such has been the story to date and there is no reason to assume that it will be radically different in the future.

The bottom line must be to put an end to the high level of aid dependency in which countries such as Tanzania are caught today. This is embarrassing to donors and recipients alike. Donors are currently more involved in the central affairs of these recipient countries than they really want to be; they would like to disengage. For the recipient, the situation is, if anything, even more embarrassing. As Mukandala stresses in Chapter 2, the key functions of government are directly or indirectly funded with the help of donors. The ability of a recipient country to behave as a sovereign state is severely circumscribed. The spectre of recolonization is viewed by many Africans as real, although we believe that the threat of withdrawal but the donors is a more likely scenario should foreign aid continue to falter.

To find a middle ground between recolonization and withdrawal – and thus seek a new lease on life for foreign aid – it is important that money earmarked for development projects or programmes is not channelled directly to governments and NGOs. Recipient governments must be compelled to find revenue for their own MACs from within the country. Governments must be encouraged to collect revenue from within so as to cover the costs of their own recurrent expenses. NGOs must be required to do the same, because otherwise they will continue to be just the extended arm of a donor agency with little or no support from members. In short, the organizations that receive foreign aid must be better grounded in the socio-economic realities of the recipient country. Funds for development should be made available on a competitive basis through public institutions that are independent of the executive and thus not liable to become just another instrument of patronage politics. Governments and non-governmental organizations would compete for development funds by being required to submit feasible and professionally competent proposals for assessment by qualified staff and a board of trustees of these autonomous public funds. They would be somewhat like banks or research councils that provide complementary finances for institutions which meet their core requirements from other sources. This model has already been examined by a group of experts from both donor and recipient countries (African Association for Public Administration and Management and Dag Hammarskjold Foundation 1995). A first such specimen (a cultural development trust fund) was established in Tanzania in 1998. It constitutes perhaps the most promising new initiative in rethinking foreign aid by addressing many of the aforementioned weaknesses, particularly as they have manifested themselves in countries with weak governments and high levels of aid dependency.

This model implies a structural adjustment of foreign aid that is long overdue. We have demonstrated in this study that none of the approaches adopted by such a diverse range of donors as China, Sweden and the USA has worked. No other donor country as of now has produced a workable alternative. We realize that conducting aid operations involves complex decisions and intricate relationships. Reforming foreign aid is not easy.

We believe, however, that a major reason why attempts at reforming foreign aid in the past have not worked is that they have not gone for enough. They have always assumed that those reforms do not involve major changes by the donors themselves. To the extent that donors have engaged in reforms it has been exclusively in terms of agency administration: for example, more decentralization, more focus on regional than sectoral concerns, and more contracting of outside consultants.

The autonomous fund model is so far the most radical but also the most practical way of restoring the credibility of foreign aid as an instrument of development. It operates on the assumption that was espoused in the early years of foreign aid: that it is only complementary to domestic efforts. It goes beyond being merely a rhetorical device by insisting that local actors take ultimate responsibility, with donors assuming a secondary, yet important, role as accountable partners. It stimulates local initiatives and has the potential to strengthen both state and civil society by encouraging competition among respective organizations, not over patronage but over such issues as who can come up with the most feasible and sustainable project in a given sector. Finally, it is a model that will help reduce aid dependency and encourage African states to be more inclined to collect their own domestic revenues to pay for their recurrent expenditures.

CONCLUSIONS

This study has tried to do many things in one in order to provide a new interpretation of foreign aid. It has tried to link the micro- with the macro-perspective on foreign aid by examining how aid agencies as actors in the foreign aid process influence the outcome. In this respect we have moved beyond those many studies which treat foreign aid foremost as an instrument of foreign policy. We have used a comparative approach, including here not only one donor country but three. This has provided us with a broader set of insights and lessons than would have been the case had we followed the path of many others (both consultants and academics) who look at only one agency at the time. Third, we have included a longitudinal dimension. We believe that, in order to fully appreciate the current predicament of foreign aid, it is necessary to track its history since its inception. We have done so particularly with a view to seeing how these agencies have shifted position over time and for what reasons. This has provided us with a sense of the dynamics that drive the behaviour and strategies of these agencies, and thus shape the overall impression left behind of foreign aid. Fourth, we have incorporated what is essentially a case study approach. We wanted to provide as thorough a picture as possible of the three agencies included here.

We recognize that what we have achieved with this study is not perfect. We found that information was easier to gather for some variables than others. Moreover, the data available for scrutiny, particularly in China, was limited. All the same, we conclude that the way this study was designed did help us gather information that sheds new light on a topic that is important but not very well studied. We also believe that our decision to include China, in spite of anticipated problems, was right since it allowed us to present data here that cannot be found anywhere else outside China.

Finally, therefore, we see this study as a valuable complement to other books that have focused on foreign aid in recent years, for example, that by Steven Hook (1996) and the various studies that have been conducted by the Norwegian political scientist, Olav Stokke, under the auspices of the European Association of Development Research and Training Institutes. As Stokke (1996:16) notes in his most recent volume, foreign aid finds itself at a crossroads in the latter part of the 1990s. This means that a better understanding of this system is needed and new approaches to gathering knowledge are worth exploring. We have taken one step in that direction here and believe that the material presented above forms a valuable ground for further explorations.

References

African Association for Public Administration and Management (AAPAM) and Dag Hammarskjold Foundation (1995) *Autonomous Development Funds in Africa: Report from an Expert Consultation in Kampala, Uganda, 4–6*. Uppsala: Dag Hammarskjold Centre.

Hook, Steven W. (ed.) (1996) *Foreign Aid Toward the Millennium*. Boulder, CO, and London: Lynne Rienner.

Riddell, Roger (1987) *Foreign Aid Reconsidered*. London: James Currey; and Baltimore, MD: Johns Hopkins University Press.

Stokke, Olav (ed.) (1996) *Foreign Aid Towards the Year 2000: Experiences and Challenges*. London: Frank Cass.

Tendler, Judith (1975) *Inside Foreign Aid*. Baltimore, MD: Johns Hopkins University Press.

Index

Made in the USA
Las Vegas, NV
28 October 2024

10599744R00144